The Tibetan Government-in-Exile

This book provides a detailed account of the structure and political strategies of the Tibetan government-in-exile, the Central Tibetan Administration (CTA), in northern India. Since its founding in 1959, it has been led by the 14th Dalai Lama who struggles to regain the Tibetan homeland. Based on a theoretical approach on exile organizations—and extensive empirical studies in Asia—this book discusses the CTA's political strategies to gain national loyalty and international support in order to secure its own organizational survival and the ultimate goal: the return to Tibet.

The book is organized around two fundamental questions: first, how the CTA fosters its claims to be the sole representative of all Tibetans over the last decades in exile; and, second, which policies have been carried out in order to regain the homeland. The book is divided into four substantial chapters:

- The historical background, providing a review of pre-1959 political Tibet

- A theoretical section which covers the critical position of exile organizations

- An examination of the exile Tibetan community and government from the early years

- An analysis of crucial CTA policies.

Innovative and unique, this book combines a political science approach with Tibetan studies to analyze exile Tibetan politics in particular, and exile governments in general.

Stephanie Roemer received her PhD from the Free University Berlin, Germany. Her research interests are political developments in contemporary South Asia, with a special emphasis on migration and refugee studies.

Routledge advances in South Asian studies
Edited by Subrata K. Mitra
South Asia Institute, University of Heidelberg, Germany

South Asia, with its burgeoning, ethnically diverse population, soaring economies and nuclear weapons, is an increasingly important region in the global context. This series, which builds on this complex, dynamic and volatile area, features innovative and original research on the region as a whole or on the countries. Its scope extends to scholarly works drawing on history, politics, development studies, sociology and economics of individual countries from the region as well as those that take an inter-disciplinary and comparative approach to the area as a whole or to a comparison of two or more countries from this region. In terms of theory and method, rather than basing itself on any one orthodoxy, the series draws broadly on the insights germane to area studies, as well as the tool kit of the social sciences in general, emphasizing comparison, the analysis of the structure and processes, and the application of quali-tative and quantitative methods. The series welcomes submissions from established authors in the field as well as from young authors who have recently completed their doctoral dissertations.

The Tibetan Government-in-Exile

Politics at large

Stephanie Roemer

Routledge
Taylor & Francis Group

LONDON AND NEW YORK

First published 2008
by Routledge
2 Park Square, Milton Park, Abingdon, Oxon, OX14 4RN

Simultaneously published in the USA and Canada
by Routledge
270 Madison Ave, New York NY 10016

*Routledge is an imprint of the Taylor & Francis Group,
an informa business*

Transferred to Digital Printing 2010

© 2008 Stephanie Roemer

Typeset in Times New Roman by
Swales & Willis Ltd, Exeter, Devon

British Library Cataloguing in Publication Data
A catalogue record for this book is available from the British Library

Library of Congress Cataloging in Publication Data
A catalog record for this book has been requested

ISBN 10: 0–415–45171–X (hbk)
ISBN 10: 0–415–58612–7 (pbk)
ISBN 10: 0–203–92814–8 (ebk)

ISBN 13: 978–0–415–45171–0 (hbk)
ISBN 13: 978–0–415–58612–2 (pbk)
ISBN 13: 978–0–203–92814–1 (ebk)

Contents

Illustrations

Abbreviations

ATPD	Assembly of Tibetan People's Deputies
CIHTS	Central Institute for Higher Tibetan Studies
CRCT	Central Relief Committee for Tibetans
CTA	Central Tibetan Administration of His Holiness the Dalai Lama
CTE	Council for Tibetan Education
CTPD	Committee of Tibetan People's Deputies
CTSA	Central Tibetan Schools Administration
DIIR	Department of Information and International Relations
EU	European Union
FCRA	Indian Foreign Contribution Regulations Act
GOI	Government of India, New Delhi
IC	Identity Certificate
Indian Rs.	Indian Rupees
LTWA	Library of Tibetan Works and Archives
NDPT	National Democratic Party of Tibet
NGOs	Non-Governmental Organizations
PLA	People's Liberation Army
PLO	Palestine Liberation Organization
PWA	Lhasa Patriotic Women's Association
RC	Registration Certificate
RFA	Radio Free Asia
SARD	Social and Resource Development Fund
SFF	Special Frontier Force
SHSC	Second High Scholarship Committee
TAR	Tibet Autonomous Region
TCHRD	Tibetan Centre for Human Rights and Democracy
TCV	Tibetan Children's Village
THF	Tibetan Homes Foundation
TIPA	Tibetan Institute of Performing Arts
TIRS	Tibetan Industrial Rehabilitation Society
TMAI	Tibetan Medical and Astrological Institute
TPFM	Tibetan Freedom Movement

TPPRC	Tibetan Parliamentary and Policy Research Centre
TSGs	Tibet Support Groups
TUA	Tibetan United Association
TWA	Tibetan Welfare Association/Tibetan Women's Association
TYC	Tibetan Youth Congress
UN	United Nations
UNHCR	United Nations High Commissioner for Refugees
USA	United States of America
VOA	Voice of America
VOT	Voice of Tibet
WWF	World Wide Fund for Nature

Acknowledgements

Many people have helped in making this book possible. While naming all would be impossible at this point, a few stand out. Those who are not mentioned by name remain in my thoughts nonetheless. My interest in Tibet was supported first by Dieter Weiss of the Department of Economy at the Free University in Berlin, who encouraged me from the beginning to carry out research in the exile Tibetan community. Without his guidance and helpful suggestions my general interest in the exile Tibetan community probably would not have led me to write a book on that subject at all—many thanks to him. Most importantly, during the final years, my first supervisor, Eberhard Sandschneider, working at the Department of Political Sciences at the Free University in Berlin and the German Council on Foreign Relations, lifted my spirits, especially during critical stages of this work, with indispensable suggestions and inspiring conversations. Many thanks also to the scholars and students of the Department of Tibetan Studies of the Humboldt University in Berlin and my second supervisor Toni Huber, David and Xaver in particular, who all motivated me through their own interest and knowledge. I also want to thank Tsewang Norbu of the Böll Foundation and Kunchok Tsering for their detailed information on the exile Tibetan community before and after my fieldwork in Asia.

I am grateful to the Berlin Scholarship Program (Nafög) and the German Academic Exchange Service (DAAD), which supported me financially during two years of my research. Without this funding, this book would not have speedily come to fruition.

I am also grateful to the exile Tibetans, Indians and western scholars who were equally helpful and important for my work. Especially, I want to thank those who I met during my travels to India, Nepal, Great Britain and Taiwan and who contributed to this work with insightful and invaluable information, while drinking many cups of tea!

I would like to thank my friends Wangdup, Tenzin, Tsering, Tashi, Suresh and his family, Irene, Georgios, Trine and Tina. Special thanks also go to all my interview partners, of whom a considerable number asked not to be listed by name. Thank you to Tashi Tsering, Director of the Amnye Machen

Institute in Dharamsala, for his friendship and the provision of abundant information on Tibetan history and the exile community.

Furthermore, I want to thank the officials of the Tibetan government-in-exile, Tenzin Woeser and Ugyen Chaksam in particular, for their time and efforts in answering my questions since 1999! There are the employees and scholars of the Library of Tibetan Works and Archives in Dharamsala, especially Pema Yeshi and Lobsang Shastri, to whom I am very obliged as they provided me with interesting reading material. I am also very grateful to my friend Frances for the inspiring time we spent together and her energy in editing the first draft of this book and Paddy for making it publishable.

Finally, though, my thanks go to my family, and my partner, Ruprecht, who has always supported and encouraged my research. Without their help, understanding and love, this work would not have been possible.

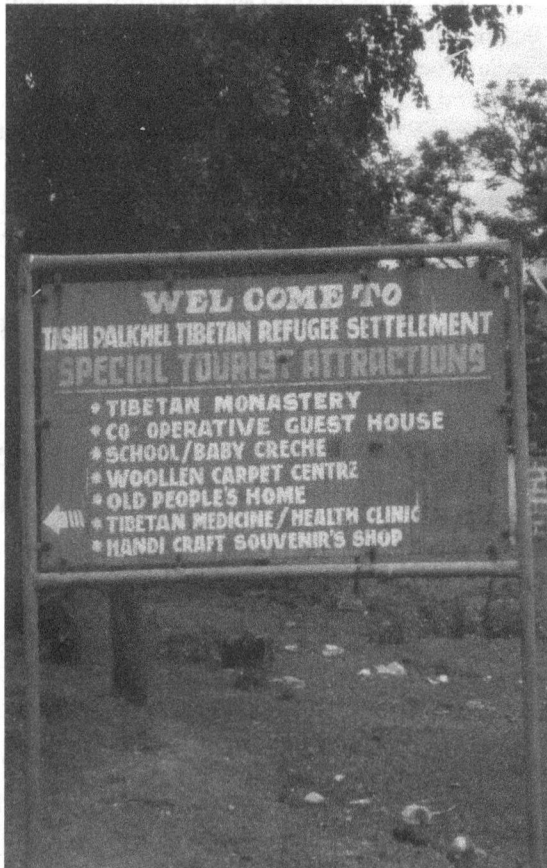

Plate 1 Welcome sign of the exile Tibetan settlement, Tashi Palkhel, Nepal, 2003.

1   Introduction

The early morning sunrays shine through my window and encourage me to go for a small walk before breakfast. I am in north India in a town called Dharamsala, which in Hindi means 'resting place for travelers' (Bhattacharjea 1995: 9). This former British hill station on the southern edge of the Himalayan mountain range is the exile headquarters of the Tibetan government-in-exile, the Central Tibetan Administration of His Holiness the Dalai Lama (CTA). On my walk through the already busy streets, I see Tibetans at the side of the pathways. They wait for Yeshi Norbu, the 'Precious Jewel', better known in the Western world[1] as the 14th Dalai Lama who is, at present, the Tibetan religious and political leader. The Tibetans have already been waiting for some time and I see them still standing at the same spot, accompanied by some Western tourists, when I return from my early walk. While they burn incense and quietly murmur mantras, the Westerners exchange information on Buddhist philosophy classes, which they have attended during previous days. The majority has not been to Tibet yet, but they are happy to visit 'Little Lhasa' to get to know Tibetan culture and religion. I decide to accompany the crowd, waiting in the last row. After some time, the 14th Dalai Lama passes by, escorted by Indian and Tibetan bodyguards, some even armed. The 'Precious Jewel' is smiling while the tourists look at him with great appreciation, and the Tibetans devotedly bow their heads. He enters a nearby building, the so-called Tibetan Reception Centre of Dharamsala. Inside, he blesses those Tibetans who have recently arrived in exile, most of them are children. The Tibetan leader leaves the place after an hour, heading downhill towards his private complex that is surrounded by barbed wire fence.

As I sat in the Berlin U-Bahn, I watched the Embassy of the People's Republic of China and caught a glimpse of a small demonstration in front of the glass facades of the impressive new building. The demonstrators carried colorful flags and posters demanding 'Free Tibet' or 'Release the 11th Panchen Lama'.[2] The group of approximately 20 people of both German and Tibetan heritage was patiently waiting for any reaction from the Chinese diplomats. Most of the Tibetans who migrated to Germany a few years ago still find themselves in a pitiful situation regarding their social integration and employment opportunities. In contrast, the German demonstrators are well-off and part of a growing community that tries to change the political situation of the people in the entire Tibetan-populated area through the communication of human rights violations or ecological and economic disasters. Only a few of them have been to Tibet or experienced life in the Tibetan exile settlements in India and Nepal. The majority, rather, lives on second-hand information distributed by the exile government or various international non-governmental organizations, which exemplifies contact with the exiled Tibetan community. They can be endlessly listed, starting with numerous political demonstrations and discussions on Tibetan topics, such as eco, human and women's rights—events that are organized by more than 400 Tibet Support Groups worldwide—religious ceremonies, traveling activities of the 14th Dalai Lama to TV programs, articles in newspapers and lifestyle magazines that focus on Tibet. All that publicity contributes to a shimmering picture of Tibet that has increasingly fascinated uncounted ordinary people in the Western world.

From an academic point of view, numerous studies have proved that 'Tibet' is not a clear-cut term that can be easily characterized. In everyday promotion by the mass media, Tibet emotionally refers to a nation; to a country; to a religion; to a way of life or to a plight. It polarizes people into being either pro-Tibetan or pro-Chinese, either interested in spiritual and mental development or in material wealth and consumption, into peaceful or aggressive characters, into eco-friendly or careless people.

A military invasion of Tibet by the Chinese People's Liberation Army in 1950 finally led to the Chinese takeover and the flight of the young 14th Dalai Lama to India in 1959. He was followed (at time of writing) by more than 120,000 Tibetans who left their homes and now live scattered all over the world. The events in 1959 caused the formation of two different Tibetan communities: the majority of Tibetans who still live within the borders of the PRC and the exile community, which is located to a large extent in India and Nepal. Both Tibetan communities have undergone considerable changes during the last decades: in China, by a large-scale political and economic transformation; in exile, by dealing with new political, social and climatic conditions. At present, two authorities claim to be the sole and legal representative of Tibet regarding territory and people, both in the homeland and in exile: the Chinese government in Beijing and the Tibetan government-in-exile in India. Both administrations carry out different political strategies to emphasize their claims. While the government in Beijing enjoys diplomatic recognition by the main players in world politics, the Central Tibetan Administration ekes out an internationally unrecognized but well-known existence.

Leaving the Chinese position to one side, this book will deal with the phenomenon of governments-in-exile. The Tibetan cause serves here as an example on the basis of which I portray a procedure of analyzing an 'exile organizational structure'. Due to the fact that political activities in exile are highly complex, the purposes of this book are, first, to analyze the Tibetan government-in-exile to make Tibetan exile politics more transparent, and, second, to develop further the existing understanding of governments-in-exile. Consequently, this book should not be understood purely as a Tibetan-related research. It is rather an empirical study that focuses on the expansion of the present academic stand on the topic of governments-in-exile, which can be used to understand exile activities in general. As a consequence, the results of the book may contribute to optimize Tibetan political activities in exile and international support.

The theoretical research on political structures in exile has been neglected so far, surprisingly since the phenomenon of refugees and migrations has become a major topic in the arena of global politics. Even if not communicated directly, the growing number of people who are either forced to, or voluntarily migrate has increasingly been determining economic transfers and political actions. Especially political organizations of exiled people have become a topic of internal politics and security matters. Furthermore, formerly exiled people play a crucial role in reshaping collapsed political systems. In the empirical part of this book, I focus on exile Tibetan politics, which have no international political relevance yet, but are rather well known due to the traveling activities of the 14th Dalai Lama.

Scholars who conducted research on the exile Tibetan community encountered a complex administrative structure and frequently changing political strategies. The embedding of these political structures, both in terms of administration and politics, in a theory of governments-in-exile, eases the dealing with the CTA in making its movements transparent and, moreover, also transferable to other governments-in-exile. In this regard the book does not claim to be a complete account of exile Tibetan activities since 1959 but rather an unveiling of political patterns to understand the previously sketched examples.

The literature

The phenomenon of 'exile organizations' has been the topic of numerous case studies, which portray different facets of the structure and nature of certain 'exile communities'. But there are only limited works that have attempted to develop an integrated theoretical approach to the nature of organizations in exile. This lack of academic attention can be attributed to the structure of political sciences and jurisprudence, which distinguish between national and international politics and national and international law respectively. Political structures in exile are fringe areas of both fields.

Due to the political events during and after the Second World War, when several European governments left their countries because of the Fascist invasion, governments-in-exile became a topic among jurists. In this context fall the works of Meyer and Torczyner (1943), Lourie and Meyer (1943), and Oppenheimer (1942). A systematic and overall approach on governments-in-exile was first presented in 1953 by Mattern, who analyzed the status of European exile governments (1953). Another noteworthy piece of research is Talmon's theory of governments-in-exile in international law (1998).

In political science, Yossi Shain, a scholar at the Universities of Georgetown and Tel-Aviv, conducted systematic and far-reaching research on numerous former and still existing exile organizations to find overall characteristics of exile organizations in general and governments-in-exile in particular (1989, 1991). His theoretical approach is at present the only existing theory of governments-in-exile in political science. Because of such limited academic attention towards exile organizations, I give high credence to his research and take his findings on governments-in-exile as a basis for further theoretical developments and the portrayal of exile Tibetan politics. Furthermore, I want to mention the work of Alicja Iwańska, who specifically looked at the Spanish and Polish exile governments and developed theoretical categories to compare the two cases of exile (1981).

Compared with the little research on governments-in-exile, the studies on Tibet are abundant. I only want to mention the research works that provided me with an overall and lasting introduction to the topic of the exiled Tibetan community in general and the Tibetan government-in-exile in particular. While anthropologists have undertaken extensive research, works on Tibetan exile from other disciplines are somewhat limited. These works concentrate on subjects like education, health or political events of the entire period between 1959 and the present. The most important for my own research were written by Goldstein (1975a,b, 1993), Klieger (1992, 2002), Nowak (1984) and Frechette (2004). Furthermore, I used the works of Ardley (2002), Hoppe (1997), Schmitz (1998) and Sautman (2000). The accounts on the Tibetan pre-exile times of Shakabpa (1967), Richardson (1984), Carrasco (1959) and Michael (1982) provided me with an overview of society, politics and religious life in central Tibet in the early twentieth century.

Additionally, I want to give importance to the numerous publications of the CTA that illustrate the official view on exile Tibetan life in the communities and the Tibetans' political struggle and history.[3] But these accounts are not sufficient for a scientific analysis, as they serve the exile Tibetan political objectives, rather than show the conditions in a neutral way. With regard to the theory on exile governments, most of the materials are produced to elicit a response from potential donors and international supporters of the exile struggle. In addition, the data are partly exaggerated to fit the anticipated schemata to represent the CTA itself in a most critical and support-worthy manner.

I read most of the references on Tibet and exile Tibetan life during my field studies in India and Nepal between 1999 and 2006, while the theoretical background was the major concern of my work in German libraries. The center of the empirical analysis is the exile Tibetan community in India because India serves as host country for the majority of the exile Tibetans and the Tibetan government-in-exile itself.

The basic empirical research methods were participant-observations of Tibetan exile life and interviews. Most of the interviews I conducted in English. In cases where my interview partner had no knowledge of the English language, mostly elder Tibetans, I used the help of Tibetan friends to translate. The interviews are not recorded because the majority of my Tibetan interview partners became insecure when they spotted a tape recorder, or they even refused to answer. Consequently, I came to rely on my notes and memory to transcribe the interview immediately afterwards. Many interview partners did not want to be mentioned in the context of politics and wanted to remain anonymous. The reason for such reluctance could not be exactly verified; one interview partner said that these Tibetans probably did not wish to be involved in 'for Tibetans very emotional and sensitive topics' (anonymous interview, 2006).

In general, the Tibetans in exile were willing to support me with the details and data for which I was looking. For instance, I was given the chance to take part in the exile Tibetan parliamentary sessions, to study daily with the support of the librarians in the Library of Tibetan Works and Archives in Dharamsala, which contains a large collection of Tibetan and foreign language references on Tibet related topics, or to get without significant problems an appointment for interviews. But I also encountered certain difficulties during the fieldwork. To a large extent that was because of the perception of many exile Tibetans, who assumed that I was just another western Buddhist, volunteer, sponsor or traveler in town who could be helpful in terms of financial and material aid or to get a passport to the Western world. It was not always easy to convince my opposite that I was just interested in the Tibetan exile context and had nothing to offer or promise. Furthermore, I met very few other scholars so the opportunities to exchange views and opinions with others who worked on similar topics were strongly limited.[4]

Research and content

This book is divided into four chapters: historical background, theoretical considerations, a portrayal of the exile Tibetan community and the Tibetan government-in-exile followed, by an analysis of the CTA policies according to the outlined theory, then summary and conclusions. The main research questions are:

1 How did the CTA foster its claims to be the sole representative of all Tibetans over the decades in exile?
2 Which policies have been carried out to regain the homeland and how can they be explained and characterized?

Taking these two questions as a starting point, the following hypotheses are presented:

1   The representative claims of the CTA are to a large extent based on Tibetan history and on international support, which has been granted to the exile Tibetan community since 1959.
2   The functioning and political legitimation of the CTA as Tibetan government-in-exile, is determined by the institution of the Dalai Lama.
3   The structure and policies of the CTA can be explained with Yossi Shain's political theory (1989, 1991) of exile organizations. According to his theory, the political survival of any exile organization depends to a large extent on the degree of granted national loyalty and international support and recognition.
4   Both foci of a government-in-exile, to gain national loyalty and international support, are interdependent. The striving for national loyalty and international acknowledgement leads to policy effects that support each other but also create discrepancies. Consequently, the amended theory of governments-in exile provides a model to categorize CTA policies and to explain discrepancies caused by the struggle for national loyalty and international support.

Chapter 2 gives an overview of traditional Tibetan society, economy and political life. It serves as a basis to understand the exile Tibetan context. Since the initial years in exile, the CTA has represented itself as the *de-facto* government of Tibet, which derives its legitimation out of a direct succession of the central Tibetan government in Lhasa. Based on the general overview I examine the political events that finally led to the Chinese military takeover in 1959, which in turn caused the departure of thousands of Tibetans from their homes to India, Nepal and Bhutan.

Chapter 3 provides a theoretical framework from which to analyze Tibetan exile politics. The center describes Yossi Shain's approach towards a theory of exile organizations. Shain examines an exile organization's difficult position within national and international politics. In this context, he stresses the importance of securing national loyalty and international support for any exile organization to maintain its political structure and to achieve the set goal: the return home. Furthermore, James Wilson's organization theory (1973) is presented, which looks particularly at organizations with voluntary membership. Wilson assumes that an organization needs to invest certain incentives to motivate its present and potential members to perform certain requested tasks that contribute to the organization's survival and the achieving of set goals. Such an assumption is important in the context of exile governments as it provides an analytical approach to look at the efforts of such administrative structure to cultivate any kind of support. In the next step, I combine Shain's and Wilson's research findings and herewith provide a new theoretical focus that can be taken as the basis for an analysis of my empirical data. In this regard, the theoretical focus is to examine the efforts of an exile government to overcome their critical political position.

Chapter 4 provides an overview of the organizational structure of the exile

Tibetan community, which, according to Shain's theory, is most important in terms of an exile government's claims and goals. In the middle, are the main social, economic and political developments in the exile Tibetan community from the beginning to the early twenty-first century. First, the initial years in Indian exile and the efforts that were made by the CTA, assisted by international aid organizations, to rehabilitate and resettle the numerous Tibetans are drawn up. Main questions relating to this are: Why did India serve as host country for the thousands of Tibetans and the newly founded CTA? What role did the CTA play in the process of resettling and rehabilitation? The answers show that the initial years in exile were an important period for the CTA to establish a powerful position, which was to be expanded in the following years. Second, details of the main policies of the CTA's struggle against the Chinese invaders are given, followed by an examination of the Role of the 14th Dalai Lama within the CTA and the legislative, executive and judicial powers. Next, an account of the three major exile Tibetan NGOs and their roles in exile Tibetan politics is given. Finally, the chapter looks at the annual budget of the CTA, to find patterns and the priorities of its work.

Chapter 5 exemplarily analyzes the CTA policies that are implemented to induce loyalty among all Tibetans and to secure international support and recognition. This analysis is based on the amended theoretical approach on governments-in-exile. In the center are the investments of the CTA to motivate members of the Tibetan nation and potential supporters of the international community to take an active part in the exile Tibetan struggle. The findings of the empirical data support the theoretical considerations but at the same time open up new perspectives that have not yet been considered. Consequently, the theoretical implications are further developed.

At the end of this Introduction, it is prudent to point out that Tibetan terms are written according to the phonetic transcription. Their transliteration is examined in Appendix 1, according to Turell Wylie's spelling standard (1959).

2 Modern Tibet: A historical account

This chapter summarizes the situation in Tibet in the first half of the twentieth century. While at certain stages I look back to more ancient times, my main focus is the period between 1900 and 1959. It describes an important time as the exile Tibetan community refers to it in the current political discussion on the present and future status of Tibet. Traditions and values of the 'old times' significantly determine the exile Tibetan's perspective of their homeland and the political claims of the Central Tibetan Administration of His Holiness the Dalai Lama (CTA).

First in this chapter, the boundaries of Tibet will be defined before giving a brief account of the social and economic situation in Tibet. Then I will illustrate the political situation in Tibet, which was characterized by an interconnection between religion and politics—a relationship that is still in use in the exile context. The last part of this chapter sketches the political circumstances on the eve of the breakdown of the Tibetan political system, which finally led to the Chinese takeover, causing the departure of thousands of Tibetans from their homeland. As the data on Tibetan history covers to a large extent the central Tibetan part only, the eastern and north-eastern areas will not be a particular subject of this chapter.

Definition of the area of Tibet

The questions: 'What is Tibet?' and 'Who are the Tibetans?' can be answered in many ways. The area of Tibet can be defined from a geographical, ethnic or political point of view: Geographical Tibet is known as the world's largest plateau—the 'roof of the world'—which is enclosed by giant mountain ranges: the Kunlun, the Himalayas and the Karakoram. The definition of ethnic Tibet goes beyond these natural frontiers. It represents all those regions that were once entirely, or at least by a majority, of people of Tibetan origin, i.e. geographical Tibet, Bhutan, the eastern and western territories of Nepal and the present northern Indian regions of Ladakh, Lahul, Spitti and Kinnaur, parts of Arunachal Pradesh and Sikkim (Clarke 1997: 7–9; Dhondup 1977; Shakya 1982; Samuel 1993: 100–12). The boundaries of political Tibet have changed over time due to wars waged with Tibet's neighbors:

China, Bhutan and Nepal. The later examined political circumstances in the early twentieth century provide different alternatives to define the Tibetan area, from the proclamation of Tibetan independence in 1913 by the 13th Dalai Lama (1876–1933) until the invasion of the People's Liberation Army (PLA) in 1950, the area of political Tibet was determined by two armistice negotiations (1932 and 1933) which described an area that was almost identical with the boundaries of the present Tibet Autonomous Region (TAR). This Tibet comprises the western region of Ngari and the central Tibetan Ü and Tsang regions with the Tibetan capital Lhasa. At the Simla conference in 1914, with Tibet, Britain and China, Tibet's political boundaries were intended to be fixed resembling almost the area of geographical Tibet, which included the eastern provinces of Kham and Amdo, although it was decided to divide political Tibet into an inner and outer region, following the example of Mongolia. But the agreement was only signed by the British and Tibetan plenipotentiaries and therefore was not valid in China (Schmitz 1998: 8–10).

Central Tibet was to a large extent under the control of the government in Lhasa. The town was the capital and political and religious center. Since its founding in the seventh century by the first Tibetan King, Songtsen Gampo (605–49),[1] Lhasa had developed into the cultural and commercial center by the reign of the 5th Dalai Lama (1617–82), and had become the biggest town in the territory of the present TAR by 1950 with approximately 30,000 inhabitants (Bronger 2001). But the eastern provinces, Kham and Amdo, mostly remained independent from the central government in Lhasa, in spite of its continued attempts to incorporate them. In fact, by 1959, only less than half of Kham, parts of central Tibet (Nagchu and Chamdo) and the whole area of Amdo were not under the control of the Lhasa administration. These regions rather were ruled by local chieftains and religious dignitaries (Samuel 1993: 64–98). After the Chinese military takeover in 1959 and the departure of the 14th Dalai Lama, the area of political Tibet changed again in 1965. The central and western regions became the TAR while Amdo and the eastern parts of Kham were incorporated into the Chinese provinces of Qinghai, Gansu, Sichuan and Yunnan.

Defining the area of Tibet has been an important issue prevailing in the political negotiations on the status of Tibet between Beijing and Dharamsala. While the Chinese authorities talk about Tibet meaning the TAR only, the CTA defines Tibet as the entire area of the TAR and the eastern regions. This so-called ethnographic definition,[2] also known as Bö Cholka Sum (Tibet of the three regions/provinces), focuses on the unification of the three main Tibetan regions of Ü-Tsang, Amdo and Kham (Schwartz 1996: 9–10). It is based on common ethnic, cultural and emotional grounds of its inhabitants to belong to one nation.[3] But despite such similarities, the inhabitants of the different Tibetan regions vary to a certain extent in their language, customs and lifestyle. The area of ethnographic Tibet is twice as big as the present TAR, which represents one-quarter of the present People's Republic of China (PRC) territory. So one can summarize there is a wide gap between the

Chinese definition of the Tibetan area and the Tibetan viewpoint of a unified Tibetan area of the three regions/provinces. This book will refer to the Dharamsala definition of the Tibetan area because of the main research topics: the exile Tibetans in general and the Tibetan government-in-exile in particular—while keeping in mind that the Chinese definition and that of international law are different.[4] Map 1 illustrates the different borderlines of Tibet and its neighbors.

There are no reliable population figures in absolute terms for the different Tibetan areas before the Chinese invasion.[5] Thomas Wiley notes that the area of ethnic Tibet comprised around 6 million people, while approximately 2–3 million people populated political Tibet (International Commission of Jurists 1960: 290). This population figure is equivalent to the estimated numbers presently published by the CTA.

Society and economy

One can only talk of Tibetan societies in the plural for the entire period since there was very great social and economic variation to be found across the geographical region of Tibet. The following section gives an insight in the social and economic conditions of central Tibet. Due to Tibet's policy of isolation before the mid-twentieth century, research on Tibetan traditional society and economy is sparse and only limited references cover the period between 1900 and 1959. As seen in the following, Tibetan society can be divided into monastic and lay people but also into the social status of the people.

Monastic population

Religion was, and still is, the fundamental driving power in Tibetan social and political life—nothing worked without the religious institutions. Par Bataille (1992: 36) notes: 'Everything revolves around them [the monks]. If someone, against the likelihood, were to turn away from religion, he would still derive his meaning and his possibility of expression from the monks'. Tibetan religion is based to a large extent on the teachings of the historical Buddha, the Indian saint who lived around 500BC. Buddhism posits a constant cycle of birth, death and rebirth of all sentient beings, better known as karma, which offers an explanation of present existence as it is based on the actions of previous lives and the actions of this life determine the next one. As seen later, this religious concept provided a basis for a stable social order in Tibet and legitimized the power of the ruling strata. It reduced frustration and anger in social relations because a Buddhist's social status, as the person believes it, represents the amount of merit that has been collected during previous lives (Norbu 1991b).

When Buddhism was brought to Tibet in the seventh century, it did not immediately achieve mass popularity and rather remained a religion of the Tibetan elite. That time was characterized by a dominance of a pre-Buddhist

Map 1 Tibet and its neighbors (Norbu 2001b: xv). From *China's Tibet Policy*, Dawa Norbu, Copyright © 2001, Routledge, Taylor and Francis Ltd. Reproduced by permission of Taylor and Francis Books UK.

religion, Bön, which has a faceted pantheon of different spirits as well as demon-gods that inhabit all parts of the Tibetan landscape. The first successful but still limited spreading of Buddhism took place one century later but collapsed due to the political assassination of the anti-Buddhist king Langdarma in 842. The second attempt to spread Buddhism began about 100 years after that incident. From the eleventh century onwards, the impact of Buddhism in Tibet grew constantly and four major sects of Tibetan Buddhism formed: Nyingmapa, Sakyapa, Kadampa that was reformed by the scholar Tsongkhapa (1357–1419) and has been known since then as Gelugpa sect, and Kagüpa. All four sects were widely subdivided and founded powerful monastic complexes with numerous branch monasteries all over the country. The monastic communities enjoyed relative independence as they held control over their own internal discipline. By 1950, the number of Tibetan monasteries had risen to over 6,000 and the monastic population, monks and nuns,[6] counted around 600,000.[7] These figures indicate that monasticism was a mass phenomenon in Tibet.[8]

By the seventeenth century, the Gelugpa had developed into the most powerful sect and it has been the dominant religious and political power in Tibet ever since (Richardson 1976: 18–23). This growing influence and prestige of the Gelugpa in comparison with the other three Tibetan Buddhist sects was mainly due to the following circumstances: first, the Gelugpas did not face any organized opposition from the other sects and second, they allied themselves with the, at the time, powerful Mongols and the Lhasa government. Third, the sect was predominantly represented by the three monastic universities around Lhasa: Sera, Ganden and Drepung—monasteries with superior religious and political power compared to others. Such power was based on their economic strength and their enormous number of monks. These monastic complexes maintained their own monastic forces, which had access to guns and ammunition and appeared as a competing armed power by dwarfing the Tibetan army.

Tibetan Buddhist monasteries were spread all over Tibet forming networks of overlapping allegiances, which was an important factor in giving an integrative and unifying structure to a naturally segmented country (Carrasco 1959: 21). Over time, the development of a close-knit group of numerous satellite monasteries played a dominant role in the growth of the monastic population because the conscription of young men and women all over the country was eased. Traditionally, there were three different ways for a Tibetan to enter a monastery: One alternative was that a Tibetan family sent one of its sons to a monastery. This far-reaching decision was made by the family based on religious motivations or economic constraints, such as shortages of material and financial resources. Another possibility occurred when a child was found to be a reincarnated tulku. Then the boy was brought to a particular monastery to be trained and educated as a religious dignitary. As compensation, the family received diverse economic and social benefits from the monastery. The last alternative for entering a monastery was based on the decision of the young man himself who wanted to dedicate his life to religion (Goldstein 1993: 21–2). In that context, it is interesting to mention that the monkhood of the young man provided him with the opportunity to raise his social status through intensive studying and serious dedication to religion. In this regard, the monasteries softened the strongly developed stratification of Tibetan society.

Tibetan monasteries were first and foremost religious institutions, i.e. centers of studying and practice. Different levels of ordination determined the involvement in the religious, intellectual and practical activities of each monk. Only one-third of the entire monk population took full ordination and subsequently fully dedicated their lives to the study and practice of religion. But Tibetan monasteries were more than centers of esthetic religious practice as the remaining two-thirds of the monks lived as novices—without full ordination—and were specialized in arts, crafts, politics or business. Some of them even lived in Tibetan communities instead of in monastic complexes where they carried out religious as well as educational and social work. They were involved in the management of large monastic estates and acted as traders and practitioners of Tibetan medicine (Michael 1982: 132–6). In this regard, monasteries also served as places for social interaction during religious festivals for the local and nomadic population, centers of education, and important sites of commerce and trade. Their enormous economic power was also seen by Sir Charles Bell who stated that the annual budget of the clergy in 1917 was twice as large as that of the government and eight times larger than that of the Tibetan army.[9]

Lay people

People in Tibetan traditional society were to a large extent involved in the pastoral and farming sector, which secured the national demand for food. The central government owned all fertile land and theoretically reallocated it to the aristocracy and the monasteries including the incarnated Lama's associated estates (labrang). But the practice showed that in most cases, the land was for long periods either in the hands of monasteries (between 37 and 50 per cent of the arable land), the Lhasa government (around 25 per cent) or aristocratic families (around 25 per cent), passed on a hereditary basis from generation to generation (Redwood French 2002: 118–20; Goldstein 1998: 19).

The fields were partly lent to Tibetan peasants, the so-called miser, who cultivated small plots of land along rivers in the southern and eastern regions of the country with high altitude barley, wheat, peas, mustard, radish and potatoes. The misers were subdivided into three strata: the trälpa who were taxpayers and landholders; the düchung who had no permanent landholdings and were rather known as small householders; and the so-called serfs, who worked on demesne fields and in return, received food and shelter.[10] Nomadism also played a dominant role in Tibetan economics. Nomads (drogpa) held large herds of yaks, sheep and goats and produced animal products that were used both for their own subsistence as well as for trading for barley, tea, cloth, sugar and other products. Nomads were subject to taxation by the authority under whose jurisdiction they lived, the central government, the district administration or a local chief. In relative terms, the tax obligations of the nomads were less compared with those of the taxpaying peasants (Wiley 1986: 9–10). The tsongpa, the traders and private entrepreneurs, also described a large social group who were involved in long-distance trade between Tibet and the adjacent countries. The lowest stratum in Tibetan society—outcasts and people who carried out professions which were seen as 'unclean'—comprised 10 per cent of the population. This stratum had various functions in society, e.g. they were sometimes used as messengers by Lhasa officials or pursued professions such as metal work or tanning; they also worked as butchers, smiths, ferrymen, fishermen, shoe-makers, scavengers, musicians or beggars (Aziz 1978: 56–7; French 2003: 184–91; Richardson and Skorupski 1986: 89; Fjeld 2005: 28–9).

By 1950, the Tibetan aristocracy consisted of between 150 and 200 families.[11] Membership was automatically given by birth, thus the ennoblement of outstanding individuals was rare. Apart from a few exceptions (Tsarong 2000), only those families in which a new Dalai Lama was born were ennobled. Each aristocratic family possessed at least one manorial estate that was granted by the Lhasa government. These properties represented the main base of their wealth and were, in general, immune from confiscation. In central Tibet, the number of aristocratic landed property rights was higher than in Kham and Amdo, where monasteries played a more dominant role. The estates were rarely sold by the aristocratic families and traditionally required compensation; each aristocratic family was obliged to send at least one male family member to serve in the Lhasa government, but there were also estates which did not depend on such service. According to Melvyn Goldstein, there were differences within the aristocracy depending on status and prestige, which he identified due to a correlation between the position of the aristocrat in the administrative structure in Lhasa and the size and number of his landed property (Goldstein 1968: 145; Clarke 1997: 112–26; Fjeld 2005).

Apart from the distinction between monk and lay people, the Tibetan population can be also divided into five social strata. Heidi Fjeld points out that there seem to be two norm systems defining these social categories: on economic and political factors and on purity, morality and religion (2005: 25, 33–4). Figure 1 portrays such social distinction.

The peak of the population pyramid was reserved for the ruler, a Dalai Lama or Regent. The following social stratum was formed of incarnate religious dignitaries (Lamas or Tulkus) and the Tibetan noble families, acting mostly in the role of landlords and wealthy businessmen. Together they constituted the political and economic elite of traditional Tibet. The majority of the Tibetans, around 90 per cent of the entire population, were members of the following two social strata that comprised different kinds of peasants,

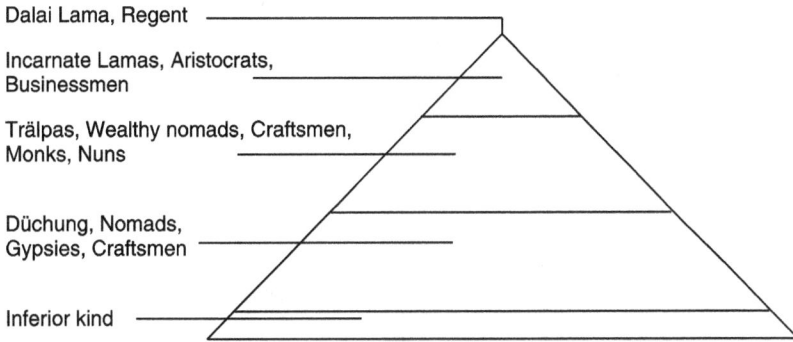

Figure 1 Stratification of the Tibetan Society, 1900–1959 (*Source*: Bronger 2001: 48;
Fjeld 2005: 2).

nomads, craftsmen and simple monks and nuns. The last stratum represented
the people who earned their livelihood with 'unclean professions', and the
outcasts.

The Tibetan social system is often compared with the feudal structures
of the European Middle Ages, a view that is still controversially discussed
among Tibetologists.[12] The Chinese government has often used the argument
of a feudal Tibetan state, where serfs had to work for the well-being of the
high mundane and religious strata of the society, to legitimize the PLA's
invasion of Tibet. But, apart from that discourse, it can be stated that the
Tibetan social structure was characterized by a strongly developed and sustainable hierarchy. Social mobility within the different sub-strata of Tibetan
society was possible but rarely did it lead upwards to a higher stratum, as in
the aforementioned monkhood (Goldstein 1968: 46).

Central and local administration

This section portrays the central and local administrative structure at the
beginning of the twentieth century, which describes the basis of the present
claims of succession of leadership by the CTA. The Tibetan government in
Lhasa was established by the 5th Dalai Lama and named after his residence
in Drepung monastery, Ganden Phodrang. This government assumed political dominance over central Tibet and partly over the eastern regions during
the regency of the 'Great Fifth'. This territorial control was limited again in
1727 by an invasion of the Chinese in the eastern Tibetan regions.

The Ganden Phodrang government was divided into two civil services: a
monastic wing—tsekhor—and a lay wing—drungkhor. The total number of
officials was fixed at 350,[13] half monk, half lay. Furthermore, the entire structure was characterized by a clear-cut hierarchy accompanied by a ranking
system. The head of the government, a Dalai Lama or, in his absence, a
Regent (gyeltsab) had theoretically ultimate authority over all government

decisions because all action needed to be approved by him. While a Dalai Lama could be born into every social stratum, the Regent was chosen from the Gelug monasteries Sera or Drepung. Through this choice, these monasteries were able to influence political affairs to their own advantage.[14] The Regent could be expelled from office and was answerable to the national assemblies, tsongdu, which met only occasionally and therefore were not permanent bodies. According to Goldstein, there were three different kinds of assemblies (standing committee, full national assembly, and abbreviated national assembly) which acted mainly as consultative bodies that represented primarily the monks of the three powerful monasteries around Lhasa but were not in the position to initiate and determine governmental action (Goldstein 1993: 19–20). Next beneath the ruler came a Prime Minister (silön or lönchen), an office that was not permanent. The Prime Minister was directly appointed by the ruler and was to act as a link between him and a lay cabinet, the kashag. This executive body consisted of a council of ministers: three of the four ministers, kalons, were secular officials, while one was a monk.[15] The cabinet held control over all secular matters, represented in 32 departments, such as finances, foreign affairs, military affairs or grain collection. The different responsibilities were split among the ministers who handled domestic affairs like the supervising and appointing of both the lay officials working directly under the kashag and the state and district commissioners, the issuing of postal stamps, the printing of money or the granting of tax exemptions. The cabinet's authority was limited as it had no authority over religious affairs, a sphere that was handled by the lord chamberlain or chikyab khenpo, under whom worked four secretaries, the drungyik chemos in the peak secretariat, the yigtsang. These secretaries looked after all ecclesiastic affairs, i.e. everything concerning the monk officials and the judicial affairs of all civil cases appearing between and within the numerous Tibetan monasteries. The chikyab khenpo, in addition to his post, also headed the clerical staff belonging to the Dalai Lama and thus was responsible for the forest department, the Dalai Lama's private treasury, and the public parks around Lhasa (Richardson 1984: 18–25; Goldstein 1993: 10–20; Petech 1973: 7–12). Figure 2 summarizes the structure of the Tibetan government in Lhasa.

The government officials were either recruited from the Tibetan noble families or from the Gelugpa monasteries. As mentioned before, every aristocratic family had to send at least one male family member to serve in government. Only in exceptional cases could a member of a non-aristocratic family enter into the civil service. The official career of a young aristocrat started at the age of 14 when he entered the finance department, after successfully passing a selection process, whereafter he could be nominated for a post after years of studying. In this context it is important to note that the ruler had no effective control over the selection and training of lay officials—the entire process lay in the hands of the finance department (Michael 1982: 53; Goldstein 1968: 157–60).

The monk officials were chosen to a large extent out of the monastic

```
                        ┌─────────┐
                        │  Ruler  │
                        └─────────┘
                             │
                        ┌─────────┐
                        │  Prime  │
                        │ Minister│
                        └─────────┘
                             │
┌──────────────┐      ┌─────────────┐      ┌──────────────┐
│     Lord     │──────│   Cabinet   │──────│   National   │
│  Chamberlain │      │             │      │  Assemblies  │
└──────────────┘      └─────────────┘      └──────────────┘
       │               │ │ │ │ │
┌──────────────┐      ┌┐ ┌┐ ┌┐ ┌┐ ┌┐
│     Peak     │      ││ ││ ││ ││ ││
│  Secretariat │      ││ ││ ││ ││ ││
└──────────────┘      └┘ └┘ └┘ └┘ └┘
                      Departments and Offices
```

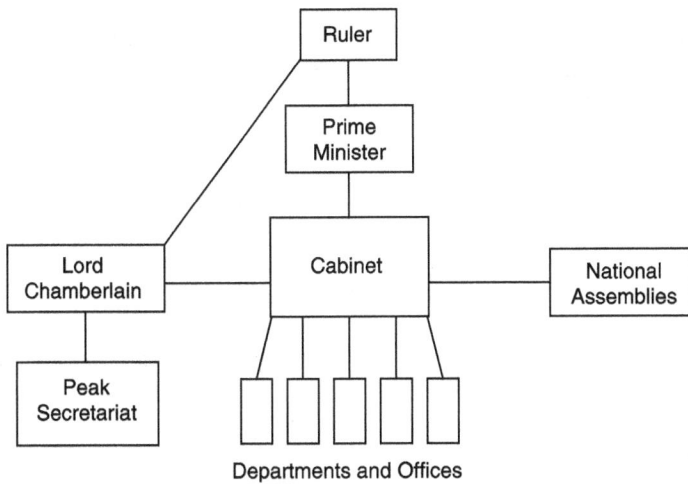

Figure 2 Structure of the Tibetan government in Lhasa (Michael 1982: 54–5; Goldstein 1993: 11).

population of the powerful Gelugpa monasteries Ganden, Drepung and Sera. The selection process was exclusively carried out by the monastic society; hence a small ecclesiastic circle recruited itself again and again. According to Goldstein, the officials of the religious governmental wing were subdivided into three different types: the better officials, drungdrag, coming from aristocratic families; the middle officials, drungdring; and the large group of the common ones, the drungkyü. The first two groups provided only 10–15 per cent of all monk officials but acted exclusively in high positions. It is interesting that those who descended from aristocratic families were working in such positions. They sometimes had no allegiance to any monastery and therefore served the interests of the state and their lay aristocratic members. Consequently, to a certain extent, the aristocracy also controlled the religious wing of the government. Goldstein (1968) stated:

> Almost all aristocrats who became monk officials procured high positions. This penetration of the monk officials segment by the aristocrats at the high levels acted to offset a clear-cut divergence of orientation between these two segments of the bureaucracy, and to afford the aristocracy, as an interest group, some influence over the policies and goals of the monk officials.
>
> (Goldstein 1968: 155–6)

In addition to the government officials, around 150 clerks (nangzen) served in the administration—posts were passed from father to son on a hereditary basis. They were neither counted in the category of officials nor had any political power (Goldstein 1968: 160).

The governmental activities were financed by various kinds of taxes, including money, goods, animals and labor, paid by estate holders (noble families, monasteries), farmers and nomads. The amount was determined by the Lhasa government but numerous estate holders revered to special conditions written down in ancient documents. The total government revenues were relatively low and mostly spent on religious affairs and festivals but also ended up in the pockets of local governors (Fjeld 2005: 24–5).

Tibet's administration at the regional level was divided into seven major units.[16] These regional units were subdivided into more than 240 districts. Both the governors of the regional units, called chikyab or garpön, and the district commissioners, dzongpön, were appointed by the central government for a three-year term. The governor's responsibilities lay mainly in maintaining law and order, safeguarding the frontiers and collecting revenues. The district administration was in charge of the collection and the transfer of taxes to Lhasa and the handling of minor judicial cases (Petech 1973: 12–13).

The lowest administrative level represented around 20,000 villages and hamlets where Tibetan life took place without major involvement of the government. At the village level local leaders were responsible for the functioning of daily life and the fulfillment of obligations to the lords. The headmen were either elected or they inherited the post (Michael 1982: 120–2). They generally enjoyed great political influence at the regional level and were particularly important for the dzongpöns because without close cooperation with them, the Lhasa officials were *de-facto* powerless.

According to Goldstein, the government in Lhasa carried out centralizing functions, which can be attributed to its responsibilities in the following fields: it commanded the Tibetan army, which was, compared with other countries at the time, ill-equipped and mainly responsible for securing the eastern borders, but was also stationed in bigger towns like Lhasa and Shigatse (Richardson 1984: 17). The Tibetan government controlled the existing communication and transportation network and was additionally in charge for issuing Tibetan coins and stamps. It regulated the export and import flows of essential goods, such as salt, wool and tea, and it took charge of court appeals (Goldstein 1971: 176–7). But despite these tasks, the Lhasa administration faced certain difficulties that restricted its effective control. First, while the majority of Tibetans were peasants and herders, they had none or only limited contact with the officials and with the politics that took place in the capital. As mentioned previously, tribal headmen were responsible for daily life and even acted as tax collectors. Second, the enforcement of Lhasa law was restricted because both local headmen and monasteries enforced, to a large extent, their own regulations according to regional traditions. Nevertheless, '[t]he fact that the central government did not exercise day-to-day control over the whole population did not mean that it did not exercise superordinate political authority and rule, for it clearly did' (Goldstein 1971: 176).

It can be summarized that the Tibetan government in Lhasa was highly stratified at the central and regional level. It consisted of hundreds of officials who can be roughly divided into ecclesiastic and lay servants. The ruler, either a Dalai Lama or a Regent, held ultimate power over governmental affairs, while the monastic and lay wings acted subordinately. The Ganden Phodrang government carried out centralizing functions but encountered limitations in effective control at the regional level. Without the interaction of Lhasa officials and local headman and monasteries, the implementation of any central regulation was almost impossible.

Lama state: the union of politics and religion

Tibetan Buddhism has been a unifying factor among all Tibetans. But according to Goldstein, religion also had a fragmenting and conflicting influence on Tibetan society, which was portrayed in prevailing rivalries between the lay ruling elite, the monk officials and the monasteries. Hence, rival interests define modern Tibetan history (Goldstein 1993: 36–7). Most of the political quarrels took place in Lhasa inside the Potala palace, the residence of the Dalai Lamas, and within the numerous monasteries. These conflicts were characterized by intrigues, discretion and constantly changing coalitions. Brück summarized Tibetan history as a permanent struggle to centralize separated tribes and regions, to create powerful religious and cultural units and to enhance the economic, political and religious power of particular groups in Tibetan society (1999: 31). As religion had such an immense impact on the political circumstances of the pre-1959 Tibetan system, I examine here the basic religious and political approaches that determined life.

The major concept of Tibetan politics can be described as a union of religious and secular power (chösi nyiden). It became characteristic for Tibetan politics in the process of unifying the disparate forces within the Tibetan political sphere, as it '. . . demonstrates the commitment to a religious state made by this government, and also represents the essence of Tibetan national identity' (Ardley 2002: 11). It was introduced in the administrative structure of the Tibetan government by the 5th Dalai Lama and was represented in the shared responsibilities of clerics and aristocratic layman in the administration. Furthermore, it became obvious in the attachment of political action to divinations by mediums or oracles (Nebesky-Wojkowitz 1995: 444–54; Rahul 1992: 45).

Based on the link between religion and politics, the monasteries derived their claims to power within Tibetan state and society. But they had no meaningful representation or direct involvement in the running of the Ganden Phodrang government, which was the cause for major tensions between the two parties from time to time. This, as seen later, led to periodic instability in central Tibetan society and politics. But any possible interventions in the monasteries' position as religious institutions were made in their interests to maintain and expand their power in the political, economic and religious spheres (Goldstein 1993: 21–4). As a result, conflicts between the religious and the secular governmental wings appeared; rivalries occurred and politicians were preoccupied mainly with themselves, which meant that by the early twentieth century, Tibet was, as discussed later, vulnerable to the interests of foreign powers and remained a politically backward country (Ardley 2002: 16–17).

The tulku-concept of reincarnation

The union of politics and religion is also reflected in the succession of leadership: the concept of reincarnation, or the so-called tulku-concept. It illustrates a unique peculiarity of the Tibetan political system. Based on the Buddhist cycle of rebirth, the present ruler succeeds when recognized as the rebirth of the previous holder of power. While most people and beings are victims of birth, death and rebirth, tulkus have the choice to manifest themselves in a human form—hence, the rebirth of a tulku is strictly voluntary. This makes them different to the rest of all beings and underlines their claims to devotion, power and authority. Once introduced in the fourteenth century, the tulku-system operated parallel to the hereditary succession of rulers and created a series of rebirths where each ruler became the rebirth of the previous one and linked all parts of the lineage.

The concept of reincarnation was introduced at a time when the politico–religious situation in Tibet made it necessary. According to Wylie, three fundamental reasons led to the creation of this concept. First, there was a need for a leader who was able to secure administrative continuity. Such a charismatic hierarch was to hold political power invested as an 'anthropomorphic god': 'The metaphysical transmission of governmental authority from one to another in perpetuity would eliminate the sibling rivalry inherent in a biological lineage' (Wylie 1978: 584). Second, such an incarnated leader theoretically followed monastic vows and therefore was not expected to have any, or at least limited, intentions of accumulating political or economic power to foment a rebellion—an assumption that also emphasizes the stability of the political system. Third, the portrayal of the reincarnated person as a 'god' over generations was important in transferring the personal charisma of the reincarnated ruler to the charisma of office—a change that Wylie interpreted as '. . . essential to the establishment of a hierocratic form of government that could survive as an institution regardless of the charisma of any individual hierarch' (1978: 584).

The concept of reincarnation first emerged in the lineage of the Tibetan Kagüpa sect and was taken over by the Gelugpa sect in the seventeenth century at the event of its seizure of power. In a system of 'rule by incarnation' the suzerain (head of state) was in a position that was never questioned and all decisions he made were never criticized. Such superior leadership provided the political sphere, but also Tibetan society, with structure and order. The political system showed its weakness at times when a reincarnation was absent, either when the new incarnation of the ruler was not yet found or too young to assume power, a 'worldly' human (a Regent) ruled who, at worst, used his position for his own aspirations to power (Wylie 1978: 580).

The institution of the Dalai Lama

The tulku-concept characterizes the succession of the Dalai Lamas. When looking at the institution of the Dalai Lama, history inevitably leads again to the times of the 5th Dalai Lama. He turned it into the core symbol of Tibet and strengthened its significance and potential. Nevertheless, for several centuries the Dalai Lamas played virtually no important political role, they were solely theoretical heads of the Tibetan government (Goldstein 1993: 17). The 5th incumbent also identified links between a Dalai Lama who is seen as the reincarnation of the Buddha of compassion (the Indian avaloketishvara or Tibetan chenrezig) and the first Tibetan king, Songtsen Gampo. According to Tibetan mythology, chenrezig is the founding father of the Tibetan people. Embodied as a monkey he coupled with an ogress who gave birth to the first six Tibetans, from whom sprang all Tibetan ethnic groups. Hence all Tibetans have a sacred link to the Dalai Lama, which underscores the unity among all Tibetans and the strong convictions in the power of the institution in ruling over the whole of ethnic Tibetan territory (Huitzi 1993: 24–5; Rahul 1995: 29).

The institution of the Dalai Lama had its beginnings in 1578 when the Tibetan Buddhist scholar, Sonam Gyatso (1543–88), visited the chief of a Mongol tribe, Altan Khan (1507–79). Sonam Gyatso worked successfully to convert the Mongols to Buddhism, a duty for which he received as appreciation from the Khan, the title 'Dalai Lama'. This title is a mixture of the Mongolian word 'Dalai', meaning ocean, and 'Lama', the Tibetan equivalent to the Indian word 'guru', which denotes teacher. Literally translated, the title means 'ocean teacher/guru', a term that refers, in the eyes of the 14th incarnation, to the office he holds (Dalai Lama 1996: 1). The title was applied by the Gelugpa sect and bestowed posthumously, based on the tulku-concept, to Sonam Gyatso's two predecessors. Consequently, Sonam Gyatso goes down in history as the 3rd Dalai Lama. The 5th Dalai Lama was finally offered the governance of Tibet by the Mongol, Gushi Khan, after defeating the Mongol's rival, who supported the powerful Kagüpa sect. When the 5th Dalai Lama acquired temporal and spiritual authority over Tibet, the supremacy of the Gelugpa sect in Tibetan political life was established, which has since prevailed.

Once a Dalai Lama died the next incarnation could be found from within every stratum of Tibetan society, which prevented an excessive growing of power of the already ruling strata, the aristocracy and clergy. To find the new Dalai Lama the state oracle interpreted the comments that the previous Dalai Lama had left regarding the new incarnation and high dignitaries were consulted:

Given the Tibetans cultural acceptance of the incarnation of Lamas, all that was required for the institutionalized charisma to function properly was some adequate mechanism to insure widespread belief that the incumbent was selected for the position. Here again, the mode was not new, but it was elaborated on and enhanced in grandeur. Mere humans could not by themselves properly determine the incarnation, and the institutionalization depended on supplying the selection process with supernatural supports. The speeches and comments of all late Dalai Lamas would be examined for any possible clues as to where he would be reborn.

(Goldstein 1968: 161–2)

When a likely candidate was found, the boy, usually between the age of three and four years, had to pass certain tests that would show him to resemble (in mannerisms, choice of certain personal objects and recognition of key members of his entourage) the deceased Dalai Lama. After passing the tests successfully, he was confirmed by the state oracle and brought to Lhasa where he was ordained as a novice monk, a ceremony that was followed by religious teachings. At the age of 18 years, the Dalai Lama usually assumed full spiritual and temporal power, which he held for life. The families of the Dalai Lamas were also brought to Lhasa, where they were admitted into aristocracy and received sizeable financial and material resources.[17]

Traditionally, many different functions were attached to the institution of the Dalai Lama. For instance, as religious leader, a Dalai Lama would spend considerable time in meditation, studying, teaching and giving blessings. Furthermore, he would meet with other religious dignitaries. With the seizure of power of the Gelugpa, the Dalai Lamas increasingly acted as politicians, too. In this role, which was especially dominant during the leadership of the 5th, 13th and the most recent 14th Dalai Lamas, they handled all kinds of worldly matters, reaching from the granting of land to the sanction of state property leases to negotiations in the international sphere. Such political tasks stood in contrast to the Dalai Lama's upbringing, who spent his childhood years in total protection and isolation. From an early age he would be separated from the regular life of the Tibetan people and instead instructed by religious teachers in religious philosophy and political matters. Goldstein stated that '[t]his is very important for his political role since it meant that he could not obtain first hand knowledge ... He could not go and find out anything for himself' (Goldstein 1968: 164). The 14th Dalai Lama added:

Everywhere I went, I was accompanied by a retinue of servants. I was surrounded by government ministers and advisors clad in sumptuous silk robes, men drawn from the most exalted and aristocratic families in the land. My daily companions were brilliant scholars and highly religious adepts. And every time I left the Potala ... I was escorted by a procession of hundreds of people.

(14th Dalai Lama 1996: 2)

While a Dalai Lama was technically both head of state and religion, his rule was limited in certain aspects. First, the Dalai Lama's traditional polity comprised only a certain section of the Tibetan area. Large territories outside the central Tibetan part (like Kham, Amdo, Ladakh or Zangskar) and swathes within this area (like the area under the rule of the Panchen Lama around the powerful Tashilhunpo monastery or that of the three monastic universities around Lhasa: Sera, Ganden and Drepung) seriously challenged the authority of the Dalai Lama in particular and that of the Lhasa government in general. Second, the tulku-concept of reincarnation produced, as mentioned before, long periods (usually around 20 years) of inter-regnum, during which the territory was ruled by a system of Regents. In this regard, the authority of the Dalai Lama's incarnation lineage derived more out of a symbolic presence than political power (Mills 2003: 332–3).

One of the most crucial attributes for the institution of the Dalai Lama is charisma. According to Weber, such an extraordinary personal characteristic is one need among others to achieve legitimate political domination. Charisma is described as '. . . a certain quality of an individual personality by virtue of which he is considered extraordinary and treated as endowed with supernatural, superhuman, or at least specifically exceptional powers or qualities' (cited in Ardley 2002: 86). In the Tibetan context, such charisma is 'routinized' through the combination of the Dalai Lama's mythological authority as patron of the Tibetan people and his traditional authority, linking him to chenrezig, the first king of Tibet and the previous Dalai Lamas. That routine provided a base of stability of leadership, which has lasted up to the present.

Additionally, in the Tibetan cultural context, there is a deep respect towards elders, where the judging of an ancestor is unacceptable. To do so would risk a person's national affiliation because the person would be setting himself above the head Lama. For Tibetan people, regardless of their belonging to a social strata, geographical heritage or religious affinity, the Dalai Lama is the divine leader of their nation. Whatever he says will not be criticized by anyone—a tradition that has become ingrained for all Tibetans since the institution came into existence.

The priest–patron relationship

In external Tibetan affairs, the combination of religion and politics was also dominant. Tibet's powerful position in Central Asia came to an end in 842 when King Langdarma was assassinated, and for the time being, the spread of Buddhism in Tibet was limited. For the next four centuries political rule in Tibet was characterized by intrigues between different fragmented authorities. In the early thirteenth century, the Mongols became dominant in the central Asian region and strived to conquer China. This made the Tibetans afraid of becoming yet other victims of the Mongols' hegemonic plans. To avoid such an occupation, the ruling Sakyapa sect sent a delegation to

Genghiz Khan (1162[?]–1227), the Mongolian leader, with an offer of submission (gifts and religious blessings). The Mongol accepted the offerings and guaranteed Tibetan autonomy by letting them nominally surrender to a foreign suzerain. This event was the beginning of the priest–patron relationship (chö yön) between Tibetans and Mongols. The ruler of Tibet was in the position of a head Lama, who was regarded as religious advisor and priest of the Mongol Khan, who in return acted as patron and mundane protector (Snellgrove and Richardson 1995: 144–8).

The priest–patron relationship had a revival four centuries after the Chinese repulsion of the Mongol conquerors in the fourteenth century; an event that ended the Mongol patronage of Tibet. During the following centuries, the Mongols constantly tried to regain power over China and also in Tibet after the death of the 5th Dalai Lama. In the early eighteenth century, they even tried to capture the young 7th Dalai Lama (1708–57), an attempt that was thwarted by the Tibetans with the help of the Chinese. To escort the young boy to the lion's throne, the Manchu Emperor, Kang Xi, sent troops to northeastern Tibet. In the same year, the young Dalai Lama and the Chinese Emperor made a contract and renewed the priest–patron relationship, which from then on existed between the two rulers. Initially, the Tibetan–Chinese chö yön relationship had a pragmatic dimension, because both sides had tried to defeat the Mongol tribes, but also a political dimension. As an expression of the Chinese role as Tibet's patron, the Emperor Yong Zheng stationed two representatives (amban) and a contingent of Chinese soldiers in Lhasa (Snellgrove and Richardson 1995: 148–55; Nowak 1984: 13–15; Goldstein 1993: 44).

In addition to the external measurements of the priest–patron relationship, it can also be interpreted as a basic unit of social order and culture, portraying the son/father relationship in patrilineal societies. It describes an obligation to show respect and support towards elders during their life—a system that is also characteristic for the Tibetan monasteries and their relations with the lay population—while the laymen ensured the survival of the monks in the role of patrons of their work, the latter contributed to Tibetan society through their religious practice and accompanying functions (Carrasco 1959: 120–1).

In summary, it can be stated that the combination of religion and politics fundamentally shaped Tibet's internal and external political position. Tibet maintained—with powerful neighbors like the Mongolians and Chinese—the concept of the priest–patron relationship that determined the country's outer security. In the domestic area, religious concepts significantly influenced the political structures. The devotion towards a Dalai Lama by all Tibetan people is understandable considering that this institution is linked to the Buddha of compassion and the first Tibetan King. Based on the close relation between politics and religion, the succession of Tibetan leadership was determined by the tulku-concept of reincarnation, which provided a frame to ensure stability. Only in times when such a leader was missing did the Tibetan political system tend to instability and showed certain characteristics of weakness, which will be topic of the following section.

Tibetan politics: 1900–1959

This section will give an overview on the external and internal political factors that finally led to the flight of thousands of Tibetans from their homeland. This historical account is predominantly based on the research works of Melvyn Goldstein, Tsepon Shakabpa and Hugh Richardson.

Foreign policy

By the end of the nineteenth and beginning of the twentieth century, Tibet had become the bone of contention of British, Russian and Chinese politics. During the time of the Great Game[18] all three empires tried to have influence in Tibet. For the British, Tibetan territory was important in geostrategic and economic matters. Russia, a newcomer in international politics at this time, tried to make up time and headed eastwards towards the Pacific and south to the British frontiers. Until that period, Russian–Tibetan relations had been for almost 300 years exclusively based on Buddhism.[19] China faced at the time a political change as the ruling Manchu dynasty was declining. Nevertheless, the Chinese rulers were unwilling to lose political ground in Tibet, which was under their protection before the 1880s in the context of the aforementioned chö yön relationship.

When the British General Curzon became Viceroy of British-India in 1898, an already existing Russo-phobia among the British was revealed. Because of the Chinese political weakness, the British suspected that a power vacuum would emerge, which could give the Russians a chance to gain ground in the Tibetan sphere. They also saw Tibet as being very beneficial from an economic point of view, as a promising market for the British–Indian tea industry and for establishing trade routes. After a Sino–Russian treaty was signed in 1902, which fostered the Chinese territorial claims in Tibet in exchange for Russian freedom for maneuvering in Central Asia, Curzon proposed a tri-party conference between the three powers to defeat the Russian influence. London reacted reluctantly by sending a small delegation to central Asia under the command of Colonel Younghusband, to negotiate on trade relations, grazing rights and the course of the borders.[20] The delegation, which was accompanied by a military escort, was not allowed by the Lhasa government to go further than Kamba dzong in south Tibet. But it continued its journey in the direction of the capital. As a consequence, the British encountered Tibetan resistance forces, but which were poorly armed and easy to defeat. When Younghusband reached Lhasa he regretted the circumstances and number of deaths by which he arrived (Richardson 1984: 85). By this time, the 13th Dalai Lama had left the capital for Mongolia, so the British met only the powerless Chinese ambans. Before leaving Lhasa in 1904, Younghusband signed an agreement with an ad-hoc gathering of the remaining Tibetan officials. It provided the British with the rights to open trade markets in the Tibetan towns Gyantse, Yatung and Gartok, defined the border between Sikkim and Tibet and made Tibet a British protectorate. The latter fact in turn restricted Tibet's ability to negotiate with any foreign power and therefore torpedoed an agreement between China and Britain, signed in the 1890s, that had empowered China to handle Tibet's foreign affairs. But without the Chinese signature on the new agreement, it only showed a *de-jure* change of Tibet's political status. The new link between Britain and Tibet gave the Tibetans a chance to participate in European technical improvements that were slowly introduced in Tibet in the following years.

In 1905, Russian and British politics faced a turning point. Russia lost its political strength when defeated by the Japanese. In Britain, a new and more liberal government came to power, which focused on the improvement of Anglo–Chinese relations. In April 1906, a new agreement between the two powers was signed, which undermined the Anglo–Tibetan agreement of 1904. Tibet was now under Chinese suzerainty, while the British were still able to follow their own interests. This agreement was backed up by another pact between Russia and Britain in 1907. Despite the different agreements, the Tibetans did not follow any of the negotiations because they had been neither taking part in the 1906–7 meetings nor were they officially informed about the results. Consequently, Tibetan politics were not directly affected.

In the following years the Chinese ambition to gain control over Tibet grew. Already in 1910, Chinese troops marched into Lhasa after achieving considerable military control in eastern Tibet. The 13th Dalai Lama fled and sought political shelter in British–India. He stayed until 1912 and became close friends with the British envoys. In 1911, the revolution in the Chinese mainland led to the foundation of the Chinese Republic under leadership of the Kuomintang. This event also had an impact on the Chinese soldiers stationed in Lhasa, who rebelled against their officers and returned to their homes by 1913. Between that year and 1959, there was no official Chinese representative stationed in Lhasa. Meanwhile, the newly founded Chinese government tried to gain power in Tibet by sending in a military mission in 1912–13, which retook some of the eastern Tibetan areas of Kham (Goldstein 1993: 65–6).

Between 1913 and 1914 a tripartite conference between Britain, China and Tibet took place in Simla, a town in northern India. In the present political discourse in Dharamsala, much creditation is put on this conference because it determined at the time the borders between China and Tibet, as well as the nature of Chinese suzerainty over Tibet. But according to Kolmas:

> it is considerably difficult to assess and evaluate the Simla Conference (1913–1914) and its outcome in all theoretical and practical aspects, and considering the permanent unavailability of some sources related directly or indirectly to the course and conclusions of Simla proceedings, it is also impossible, as a matter of fact.
>
> (1993: 12)

The conference was initiated by the British to resolve the unclear and unstable situation—to secure the northern frontiers of British-India. All plenipotentiaries[21] came together with divergent ideas and ambitions. The Tibetan and Chinese delegation especially differed widely concerning the status of Tibet and the Sino–Tibetan frontiers. Britain mediated between the two parties trying to find a common ground based on its own interests in installing a politically stable and reliable Tibetan government, free from outside influence but which would have a much closer relationship with the British Empire than before. The negotiations lasted for six months and ended in a draft form of a tripartite agreement that was only signed by Tibet and Britain; China disagreed with the outcome and therefore refused to sign. The main outcomes of the agreement can be summarized as follows: First, Britain and China acknowledged Chinese suzerainty over Tibet with the addition that Tibet was divided into an inner and an outer region. The outer region covered the central area, was intended to be politically controlled by the Dalai Lama administration and was to have an autonomous status. Second, while the Chinese had considerable influence in inner Tibet, their representation in the outer Tibetan region was limited to one Chinese representative with an escort of 300 men. Third, the British expanded their privileges in Tibet; they were able to station a representative in Lhasa and expand their trading activities. Fourth, a clear frontier between Tibet and India was determined, the so-called McMahon line (Goldstein 1993: 71–7; Richardson 1984: 107–20).

A crucial point of that conference was that a delegation from Tibet's central government signed a pact with a sovereign power. This fact is interpreted controversially. Some see it as a sign of Tibetan independence, while others criticize the Tibetan's qualification due to their incomplete sovereignty (Sinha 1987: 5–12; Kolmas 1993: 12–16; Shakabpa 1967: 251–8). The 'winners' of the Simla Convention were the British as they expanded their influence in Tibet. Tibet itself lost its unity, as it was from then on divided into two regions and still needed to fear Chinese military intervention because of the Chinese's refusal to sign the agreement and the resulting non-acceptance of the outcome.

Soon after the Simla conference, the First World War broke out and drew British attention from Asia to Europe. As expected, the situation between China and Tibet continued unresolved and the period after the conference until the Second World War was characterized by sporadic fighting and rumors of a forthcoming Chinese intervention. The Tibetan government resisted negotiating directly with the Chinese and tried to persuade them to sign the Simla Convention. Finally, the 13th Dalai Lama asked the British for help, which was answered half-heartedly by sending a small supply of arms to Tibet, providing some rudimentary military training in Gyantse and the allowance of four Tibetan boys to be educated in Britain. Still, there was neither a permanent British nor Chinese representative in Lhasa.

The Second World War had only marginal effects on Tibet as the country remained neutral rather than being actively involved in the act of war. At the end of 1941, Sino–Tibetan relations reached another peak with the Chinese government's intention to build a road through Tibet. The Tibetan government refused the implementation of the project. China was politically too weak to push it through as:

> Chiang Kai-shek was unable to impose his will on Tibet militarily because of British diplomatic pressure, the war, and lack of control over his border governors, and he feared that if Tibet were included in a postwar peace conference Britain and the United States would present the truth about Tibet's current de facto independent status and perhaps even bestow upon it jural independence.
>
> (Goldstein 1993: 522–3)

Instead Chiang Kai-shek altered his initial approach and focused on Sino–Tibetan friendship to solve the Tibet question peacefully. In 1944 a Chinese mission entered Tibet to discuss the Tibetan status and invite the Tibetans to take part in a meeting in Nanjing in the year 1946. The Tibetans refused the invitation but sent a goodwill mission to prevent the host's anger. As the Tibetan delegates arrived in China, the meeting was postponed. Waiting for a reception, they were continually urged to take part in a meeting of the Chinese National Constitutional Assembly. Finally, the Tibetans attended as observers but were treated by the Chinese as members of the assembly. Even though the Tibetans did not sign the final resolutions their participation in the meeting alone gave the Chinese leadership cause to see Tibet as part of China (Goldstein 1993: 550–9).

The year 1947 offered the Tibetans two opportunities to foster their *de-facto* independent status and make them visible in the international sphere. First, Tibetan delegates took part in a semi-official Asian Relations Conference in India. They demonstrated their political independence by attending under their own flag and independently from the Chinese delegation. Furthermore, the Tibetans were treated equally, just like the other delegates, and, most importantly, like the Chinese (Goldstein 1993: 563). Second, at the end of that year, the Tibetan government dispatched its first international trade mission to India, Europe, North America and China to discuss trade regulations and check on international perceptions of Tibet. While the Tibetans were accepted in Europe and North America by carrying their Tibetan passports, the welcome in India and China was far from the expected recognition because a discussion started over the validity of their traveling documents (Goldstein 1993: 561–606; Shakabpa 1967: 294–7). The Indian reluctance to welcome the Tibetans and discuss political issues was partly because India, at the time already independent from the British Empire, downgraded the importance of Tibet in its politics instead of continuing the British focus on the maintenance of Tibet as a buffer in Asia. The new Indian leadership tended more to the idea of a pan-Asian order, where India and China would act as leading forces in a close partnership.

In summary, these external factors caused a relative vulnerability of Tibet after the end of the Second World War. This political situation was partly rooted in Tibet's inability to make reliable allies during the years of the Great Game as well as during and after the Second World War. The circumstances challenged Tibet's *de-facto* independence and were once more supported by the internal problems during that time.

Domestic policy

The 13th Dalai Lama, also known as a great reformer, was influenced in his longing for modernization by the British officer in Sikkim Sir Charles Bell.[22] Anticipating Chinese attacks on Tibet, Bell suggested, among other things, the expansion of the Tibetan army from the existing 5,000 to 15,000 men. Also during that time new technologies were introduced in Tibet such as a telegraph line and a hydroelectric plant. But Tibet's slow progress towards modernization and reform was interrupted by a serious internal dispute that appeared in Tibet in 1922 between the 13th Dalai Lama and the 9th Panchen Lama.[23]

Among Tibetans, the Panchen Lama has a similar reputation to the Dalai Lama, and is regarded to be the incarnation of the Buddha of wisdom.[24] While many Tibetans looked up to the Panchen Lama as a spiritual leader, the Dalai Lama was, without question, the leader in the practical and worldly sphere. Both Lamas acted in a teacher–disciple relationship, depending on the age of the individual reincarnation. The Panchen Lama resided in his monastery, Tashilhunpo, and was the most powerful religious dignitary outside Lhasa. Tashilhunpo was effectively a state within the Dalai Lama ruled Ganden Phodrang state with a high degree of autonomy in all of its affairs, vast landholdings as basis for taxation and great wealth due to centuries of Chinese financial support. With the 3rd and 4th incarnations of the Panchen Lama, the prestige and influence of Tashilhunpo grew because of the relative weakness of the institution of the Dalai Lama between the end of the seventeenth and the nineteenth century.[25] The differences between the 9th Panchen Lama and the 13th Dalai Lama[26] started out of the Dalai Lama's demand that the Panchen Lama should make a payment to the Lhasa government to cover the costs of expanding the Tibetan military. Meeting that demand would have diminished the status of the Tashilhunpo monastery and so instead of fulfilling the payment, the Panchen Lama fled to Mongolia and later to China (Goldstein 1993: 110–15)—an incident that caused great sorrow all over Tibet:

> Even the firmest supporters of the Dalai Lama were shaken; and a whole train of portents and oracles, which are wont to appear in Tibet at times of crises, were reported from all parts of the country. The less well-disposed hinted darkly that this was one of the results of introducing modern ideas.
>
> (Richardson 1984: 127)

The situation of an exiled Panchen Lama influenced the already existing latent tension between Tibet and China. Moreover, the conservative and powerful Tibetan monasteries used the flight as an advantage in their opposition to the British influence in Tibet. Already angry about new technologies and improvements that were brought to Tibet, the monkhood widened the gap between Tibet and Britain. Due to unmistakable pressure from the monasteries, the 13th Dalai Lama had to decelerate his reforms of the Tibetan society and political system. Thus, he proved to the monastic community that Tibet was still able to act independently from the British.

In addition to these problems, people from Kham fought around 400–500 major battles both against the Chinese but also the Lhasa government, between 1911 and 1935. These armed guerrilla forces increasingly occupied the central Tibetan military. The fighting intensified after the death of the 13th Dalai Lama in 1933 and the eastern Tibetans, moreover, sought a separate state, independent from any Han and central Tibetan control.

After the death of the 13th Dalai Lama the search for the reincarnation started. The Panchen Lama, who was traditionally responsible for the candidate, recommended three children from his exile basis in China. The new Dalai Lama, one of the Panchen's candidates, was finally found in 1934 in a peasant family in northeastern Tibet, an area that was ruled at that time by a Muslim leader. Many negotiations and payments were needed until the boy could be brought to Lhasa,[27] which exemplarily shows the limits of the central government to enforce its rule. The 14th Dalai Lama was installed in Lhasa at the beginning of 1940; a ceremony that was attended by British and Chinese representatives.

Meanwhile, an interim ruler of the Tibetan government was needed. The choice was given to a young and inexperienced monk, Reting, who became Regent in 1934 and in the following years, gradually gained control over the Tibetan administration. In the meantime, the domestic struggles for power between reformers and conservatives continued (Goldstein 1993: 146–212). A Chinese mission reached Lhasa to offer their condolences for the dead ruler and check on the political situation in Tibet. From that visit onwards, a *de facto* Chinese representative lived in the Tibetan capital. According to Hugh Richardson (1984: 224–51), regular monetary payments were made to the new Regent, Reting, and his officials to secure their loyalty. The contributions from the Chinese also caused suspicion among the Tibetan people that the Chinese government was trying to enlarge its influence in Tibet. This mistrust was accompanied by rumors about the Regent's private life, which was unacceptable for the monastic community because he was viewed as too much of a money-making ruler rather than a statesman. As a result of growing internal pressure, Reting resigned from his post in 1941. He was followed by Taktra, an elder and more learned incarnate Lama who restored the high level of moral discipline and ethical standards that had characterised the reign of the 13th Dalai Lama. Taktra ruled until 1950 when the 14th Dalai Lama was old enough to assume the official duties. Taktra's inter-regnum was interrupted by another internal dispute on a high political level—the so-called Reting conspiracy. By 1947, the political elite of Tibet was divided into pro-Reting and pro-Taktra forces. After Taktra had survived an attempted assassination that was suspected to be organized by Reting and his followers, Reting was immediately imprisoned. This judgment caused a three-week rebellion between the Tibetan army and armed monks of Sera monastery who supported Reting. The whole Reting conspiracy was evidence of domestic dissent and was proof of the continuing Chinese intentions (Richardson 1984: 172).

To sum up, one can say that Tibet's relative weakness was to a large extent rooted in its inability to be modernized, first, because of a powerful monastic opposition to the government and second, because of continuing internal quarrels between different factions of the Tibetan elite. Especially the death of the 13th Dalai Lama's dispute with the 9th Panchen Lama and the Dalai Lama's death in 1933 exposed Tibet to political objectives of others. The events accelerated and finally led to the fall of Tibet.

Chinese takeover and Lhasa Uprising

After the surrender of Japan in 1945 and the end of the Sino–Japanese War (1937–45) the communists tried to expand their influence in China and a civil war began. They gradually gained territory and Chiang Kai-shek resigned his post and fled with more than two million Kuomintang followers to Formosa/Taiwan. In 1949, the communists occupied Beijing and Mao Tse-tung proclaimed the People's Republic of China (PRC). By that time, the Tibetans had successfully urged all Chinese to leave Tibet. This brought Tibet back to the time of Sino–Tibetan relations between 1913 and 1934.

In the course of a general transformation of China under the new leadership, Tibet became a prime target of the communist ideology of reunification with the Chinese 'motherland'. The liberation of Tibet was already proclaimed in 1949 and started to be implemented a year later when around 40,000 Chinese soldiers of the PLA crossed the borders in the east and the west. The Chinese troops made easy progress in occupying the border areas because the Tibetans were neither politically prepared nor militarily equipped to defeat them. Additionally, the Lhasa government was not even informed about the struggling at the borders. Only with the arrival of thousands of Tibetans in Lhasa who had fled from their homes, the inhabitants of the capital finally became suspicious.

In the foreign sphere, independent India still rallied to the Simla position willing to grant Tibet only limited diplomatic and military support. Despite sending ammunition, the Indians were reluctant to intervene directly in the anticipated upcoming confrontation between Tibet and China fearing a Chinese attack on their own territory. Solely in 1950, India protested against the use of force by the PRC in Tibet. The Chinese leadership replied that the Chinese takeover of Tibet was solely an internal political matter and therefore not a basis of discussion with any foreign power (Goldstein 1993: 719–29). As Indian–Tibetan relations had been strained since 1947 and therefore no substantial assistance was to be expected, the Tibetan government appealed at the end of 1950 to the United Nations (UN) for help. At the time, the UN was pre-occupied by the Korean War and hoped that China and Tibet would find a peaceful solution. Only El Salvador took the Tibetan appeal seriously and supported its position morally by raising the Tibetan question officially in front of the UN General Secretary.

In contrast, the USA became more and more interested in the situation. Relations between Tibet and the USA had begun in 1908[28] and were refreshed during the Second World War, when the USA was interested in an overland alternative to the existing Burma Road. At this time, the USA was closely allied to Chiang Kai-shek in pursuing the war against Japan. With the end of this war, Tibet was no longer considered a strategically important area—a position that changed with the proclamation of the PRC a few years later. With the fall of Chiang Kai-shek the Tibetans slipped now into the role of an anti-communist force that fitted perfectly with US foreign policy. The interest of the USA in Central Asia to fight communism was never officially communicated but found its expression in military support of the eastern Tibetan guerrilla forces that attacked the Chinese invaders.[29]

To summarize, the international situation at the end of 1950 for Tibet was difficult. The USA, Great Britain and India refused any official diplomatic and military assistance to fight the PRC, the UN was unwilling to consider the invasion of the PLA in Tibet, and the Chinese were on their way to Lhasa. Worried about the increasing tension in the country, the Tibetan government and national assembly empowered the 15-year-old 14th Dalai Lama with full political and religious power. After consulting the state oracle, the young ruler was urged by the kashag to flee Lhasa. Following this advice, the 14th Dalai Lama lived for almost a year in the border areas in southern Tibet, close to Sikkim and Bhutan, where as a last resort, he could easily escape and not fall prisoner to the Chinese.

During his absence, a high-ranking delegation left Lhasa for Beijing in 1951 to discuss the question of Tibet. There, the Tibetans signed the so-called 'Seventeen Point Agreement', where they officially acknowledged the Chinese intentions to liberate Tibet, which meant the end of Tibet's *de-facto* independence. The question about the Tibetan delegation's authority to sign the agreement and, moreover, use the seal of the absent Dalai Lama has been controversially discussed between Chinese and Tibetans since then. In the eyes of the exiled 14th Dalai Lama and numerous scholars, the 'Seventeen Point Agreement' was invalid because the Tibetan delegates signed the document under Chinese pressure (Goldstein 1993: 763–72; Grunfeld 1987: 108–10; Dalai Lama 1996: 68–70; Shakabpa 1967: 304; Schmitz 1998: 139–40). The Chinese in contrast insisted on the document's validity because of which they derived their authorization of the later invasion and the dispatching of thousands of soldiers to Tibet (Ran 1991; Wei 1989: 29–33). It is suspected that because the agreement secured the supreme role of the Dalai Lama, the political positions of the Lhasa officials and also determined the preservation of Tibetan religion and culture, the Tibetan political elite was probably reluctant to question it right after the signing. On the verge of the negotiations about the 'Seventeen Point Agreement', the Tibetan delegates were urged to recognize the new incarnation of the 9th Panchen Lama, who had died in 1937 in Chinese exile. Both the Tibetan government and the PRC favored different candidates. Because of the unwillingness of the Lhasa government in earlier years to take up a definite position for one of the candidates, finally the PRC favorite from northeastern Tibet was recognized as the 10th Panchen Lama.

Shortly after the return of the 14th Dalai Lama to Lhasa in July 1951, the Chinese military also reached the capital. In the beginning, the Chinese soldiers acted peacefully and reserved and even brought gifts for the Tibetan people. Moreover, they improved the infrastructure, e.g. construction of new roads, which was interpreted by the British as planned action that '. . . had at least two objectives—to win popularity and to win minds' (Richardson 1984: 194). Between 1954 and 1956, the conditions in central Tibet remained relatively peaceful. But later, the Chinese occupation increasingly developed into a farce for the majority of the Tibetans. The initial welcoming atmosphere shown towards the Chinese changed after their first ideological involvement and confiscation of land. Additionally, more and more soldiers poured into Tibet dominating the local population and causing a shortage in the national food supplies. Increasing numbers of eastern Tibetans fled their homes to central Tibet also because a US-supported guerrilla war developed.

In August 1954, the 19-year-old 14th Dalai Lama and 16-year-old 10th Panchen Lama went on an official visit to Beijing to celebrate the Five Year Anniversary of the Proclamation of the PRC. There they attended meetings of the Chinese People's National Assembly and met with the Chinese leadership, the soviet leaders Khrushchev and Bulganin and the Indian president Jawaharlal Nehru (1889–1964). As mentioned before, India was at that time interested in friendly contacts with the PRC and signed with China in 1954 a bilateral 'Agreement on Trade and Intercourse between the Tibet Region of China and India' (Shakabpa 1967: 306–9; Arpi 2004).

In the spring of 1955, the Tibetan delegation returned to Tibet without any success regarding Tibet's *de-facto* independence. A year later, a high ranking official delegation went from Beijing to Lhasa to set-up the Preparatory Committee for the Autonomous Region of Tibet. Even though the 14th Dalai Lama was appointed chairman and the 10th Panchen Lama vice-chairman, they did not bring forward any new proposals. This was because the committee functioned only along the lines of already-made preliminary decisions by the Chinese leadership. In 1956, the Dalai Lama and Panchen Lama traveled to India to join the celebrations of the 2,500th Anniversary of Buddha's birth. There they enjoyed much sympathy from the Indian masses and met again with Nehru, who advised them to work together with the Chinese leadership.

By the autumn of 1958, the Tibetan guerrilla forces had grown strong and controlled most of eastern and southern Tibet. In response to this strength, the Chinese urged the 14th Dalai Lama to intervene on their behalf, which he refused to do. The atmosphere in the relationship between the Chinese army and the Tibetan population was swelling and became more tense during the winter months. The situation exploded after the Tibetan New Year in spring 1959, when the Dalai Lama was invited to watch a theatre show at the Chinese military camp in Lhasa. The Chinese request that the 14th Dalai Lama was welcomed without bodyguards fed the rumors in the streets of Lhasa that he was going to be kidnapped. By that time, the Tibetan capital was filled with thousands of Tibetans from all over the country who had fled the PLA, but also with crowds of monks who annually came at that time into town for pilgrimage. On March 10th, a mob of around 30,000 armed Tibetans gathered in front of the Norbulingka palace where the Dalai Lama was residing. His attempts to control the situation and reduce the mounting tension failed and instead, confusion and uncertainty grew hourly among the people in Lhasa. On the night of March 17th, the Tibetan ruler, his family and a few close officials and consultants escaped from Lhasa and fled towards the Indian border. The Chinese found out about the escape much later and reacted with an assault on the people. The three-day long rebellion across the whole country ended with the death of thousands of Tibetans (Norbu 1982: 7–17).

Meanwhile, the 14th Dalai Lama was guarded by Kham guerrilla fighters on the Indian border. On the tenth day of his flight, the 14th Dalai Lama proclaimed a new provisory government and cancelled unilaterally the 'Seventeen Point Agreement' at a small border town in southern Tibet (Dalai Lama 1996: 155). With that act, the Dalai Lama denied the acknowledgment of the Chinese military 'liberation of Tibet'. At the end of March, the small group crossed the border to India, where they were welcomed by the Indian president Nehru, some Tibetans who had already left their homes in the early and mid-1950s and a crowd of journalists from all over the world.

In Tibet, people remained confused about the entire political situation and hoped that the Dalai Lama would soon return, with the help of India and the UN. But instead, the PLA gradually took over the whole country. China legitimized the invasion with the need to end the Tibetan traditional autocratic and feudal system that was not tolerable. As a consequence, the Tibetans faced enormous restrictions regarding their way of life which came to its height during the years of the Chinese Cultural Revolution (1966–76) when Tibetans, like many other people in the PRC, suffered from starvation, persecution and the destruction of their culture.

But the focus of this book is not the Tibetan community inside the borders of the PRC, but rather those Tibetans who followed the example of the 14th Dalai Lama and left their homeland. Looking at the Tibetans in exile, several questions arise, e.g. Which problems did the Tibetans encounter in the new surrounding? How could they build up an organizational structure in exile? What efforts did they make to free their homeland? Before examining the exile Tibetan life in general and the function of the Tibetan government-in-exile in particular, I look at the situation of a government-in-exile from a theoretical perspective.

3   An approach towards a theory of governments-in-exile

This chapter focuses on Yossi Shain's theoretical approach on governments-in-exile. Such a step becomes necessary because, first, a theoretical background serves as a frame to draw a clear picture of the Tibetan exile politics. Second, with the help of a theory problematic and at first sight incomprehensible political strategies of the Central Tibetan Administration (CTA) can be explained. Moreover, the example of the CTA can extend Shain's theory and critical aspects of the status of exile governments in general become clearer.

The first section classifies the terms 'refugee' and 'exile' while the next step characterizes the nature of any exile government according to Shain's theory. Special emphasis is given to a government-in-exile striving for national loyalty and international recognition and support. The last part of the chapter provides additions to Shain's theory, which finally leads to a modified theoretical model to analyze exile Tibetan politics.

The struggle from abroad to free the homeland

The nature of an exile struggle is portrayed by the definition of the people who participate in it. There is a main distinction between the terms 'refugee' and 'exile'. The term 'refugee' relies on the criteria of the United Nations High Commissioner for Refugees (UNHCR), which gives a clear definition and is codified through the 'UN Convention on Refugees' in Geneva in 1951, the international law on refugees. According to this convention, a political refugee is a person:

> who is outside the country of his nationality, or if he has no nationality, the country of his former habitual residence because he has or had well-founded fear of his persecution by reason of his race, religion, nationality or political opinion and is unable or, because of such fear, is unwilling to avail himself of the protection of the government of the country of his nationality, or, if he has no nationality, to return to the country of his former habitual residence.

(Kimminich and Hobbe 2000: 366)

These UN criteria have no universal application and even if a country has ratified the Geneva Convention, it still has the option either to recognize certain people as refugees or to withdraw this status. Such a decision is mostly linked to the granting of asylum, which is also a function of national criteria rather than international regulations. Consequently, no country is obliged to grant asylum to people regardless if they fall within international standards of being refugees or not. Furthermore, the Geneva Convention says that internationally recognized refugees cannot be forced to return home as long as there is an anticipated fear that the person will suffer from persecution—a non-refoulement regulation that represents the Magna Carta of the international law on refugees (Verdross and Simma 1984: 800–1).

Following the UN criteria, refugees are defined according to their need for protection, which clearly applies to the factors that led to migration[1] and not to the activities abroad. But such differentiation is crucial in a discussion of an exile situation because activities that are specially designed to end a people's stay abroad refer to the term 'exile'.

According to Shain, exiles are persons who are engaged '. . .in political activity directed against the policies of a home regime, against the home regime itself, or against the political system as a whole, so as to create circumstances favourable to their return' (1989: 15). This definition implies that political exiles are involved in a struggle to return home from a base abroad; a political involvement that ranges from full commitment to marginal activities. Iwańska attributed to exiles the characteristic of political activists who aim to replace or overthrow the present ruler at home (1981: 3). Exiles organize themselves into organizations to return home. With regard to the Tibetan case, I refer to the term 'exile' because of the emphasis on political activism.

Shain outlined four factors that determine the nature of any exile organization: its history, its political claims, the origin of its members and the degree of national and international support. Exile organizations vary between informal and fragmented forms to highly organized non-governmental or even governmental structures. While non-governmental and less organized exile groups only represent a segment of a nation, see themselves as one alternative among others to represent the entire nation or have only a short history of existence, governmental and semi-governmental structures claim to be either the sole or at least the best alternative in terms of organizational stability and political commitment to the present political structures at home. Among all exile organizational structures, governments-in-exile represent the most sophisticated form regarding their organizational level, origin, degree of claims and the granted outside support. Three aspects characterize the political activities of a government-in-exile. It presents itself as a lawfully elected organization that enjoys a legitimate status to rule a nation (people and territory); claims a traditional representation, an argument that emphasizes the legitimacy of its political aims; and acts as authentic spokesman of one nation and therefore for the national interest, which is mostly done with the help of a 'charismatic' leader in the forefront (1989: 27–8).

A government-in-exile's claim to represent the entire nation as the legally chosen organization is important inasmuch as there is potentially more than one organizational structure, either in exile or within the home territory that claims similar power and status (Shain 1991: 5). In this context, an exile government is in a disadvantageous position as it lacks effective power over the claimed territory and people. Only through the nature of its administrative set-up and implemented policies is it able to unify all members of the nation and foster its claimed position of power—which is in any case a difficult task. It can only be successfully handled through the promotion of unifying ideas and goals that represent the entire nation or at least make the countrymen accept certain compromises.

Based on these theoretical considerations, Shain classified governments-in-exile into three dynamic groups according to their background and goals:

1   There are governments-in-exile which aim to overthrow and replace the native ruling system at home. These organizations neither ask for changed borderlines nor question the existence of the state itself. They rather claim to be the legitimate representative of their nation by portraying themselves as lawfully elected bodies, as traditional or authentic groups with charismatic leaders. Examples of such exile governments are the Spanish republican government-in-exile (Iwańska 1981), the Bourbons and the Romanovs, or the authentic Iranian anti-Shah campaign under an exile leadership.

2   There are governments-in-exile that focus on the creation of a new and internationally recognized state. They operate from outside their claimed territory and can be considered as 'pre-state self-determination-oriented or decolonization-orientated governments-in-exile' (Shain 1991: 3). Examples are the Angolan struggle against colonial Portugal, the anti-colonial efforts of the Algerian government-in-exile, and the struggle of the Palestine Liberation Organization (PLO) (Said 1980).

3   There are governments-in-exile that struggle for political independence to regain power over a territory that they had lost during wartime. In that category of deposed exile governments fall several European governments-in-exile caused by the Fascist's invasions in the Second World War, such as Yugoslavia, the Netherlands and Poland (Oppenheimer 1942; Iwańska 1981; Mattern 1953).

Furthermore, there are governments-in-exile that are unclassifiable because they fall into more than one category or pass through different categories during time. Examples of such multi-goal orientated governments-in-exile are the Baltic states of Latvia, Lithuania and Estonia, or the Tibetan case. They strive for the independence of their home countries (category three) and the right to self-determination (category two) (Shain 1991: 2–5).

In summary, Shain defined exile governments as:

opposition groups that struggle from outside their home territory to overthrow and replace the regime in their independent, occupied or claimed home country. These groups refer to themselves as governments-in-exile, national committees, provisional governments, national revolutionary councils, national liberation movements, and in other ways that reflect their claim to be the sole or at least the most viable alternative to the existing home regime.

(Shain 1991: 2)

Iwańska called them the '. . . purest bureaucratic structure currently in existence' (1981: 4) as governments-in-exile are both formal organizations and social movements.

The political success of an exile government's struggle in terms of replacing or overthrowing the present ruler in its independent, occupied or claimed home country is dependent on two crucial factors: its ability to secure loyalty within its own national community and to gain international support and recognition. Shain stated that there is a '. . . competition among contestants for power in the state [that can be described] as a struggle for loyalty and recognition, for national and international support of their claims to power' (1989: 17). The importance of national loyalty and international support derives from the little room for political maneuvering of a government-in-exile compared with sovereign governments. The ability for political activism is determined by the host country, which offers the people who left their homeland a base for organized political activities from abroad, by international political developments, by the present leadership at home and by the people a government-in-exile claims to represent. In this regard, exile governments operate on shaky political ground because they depend on the politics of the home and host countries and shifting allies in the global political arena. Because of the importance of national and international actors, the following sections will focus on a government-in-exile's strive for loyalty and support.

Governments-in-exile and national loyalty

Exile activities have played a significant role in shaping the character of the term 'national loyalty'. Despite the fact that political exiles have always challenged the ruling forces at home, nationalistic thoughts have been kept alive. Until the seventeenth century, loyalty was characterized by the allegiance to the ruling faction, as it was in the time of the ancient Greek polis, in the system of the feudal admission to the lord or in the sixteenth-century political posting that carried specific responsibilities according to wealth, rank, status and religious power. At these times, the state was seen as a unit of which the people were an inevitable part and not expected to act in their own interests. The idea of this tight relationship between state and person was embodied in King Louis XIV (1643–1715) who promulgated: '*L'état c'est moi.*' But with upcoming progressive ideas and a consolidation of territorial states, sovereign leaders succeeded as objects of political loyalty—a new concept that was first highlighted in the French Revolution of 1789, which gave the final blow to the *ancien régime*. The change in France forced numerous aristocrats to migrate to German and Austrian territories and later also to Britain and Russia where they formed exile communities that aimed to get support among other Europeans to restore the old power of the Bourbons. They finally succeeded and returned in 1815 but by the 1820s, the traditional concept of loyalty had lost its popularity and instead, French people had adopted the idea of competition for loyalty among all strata. Today it is still the dominant concept for succession of power in Western societies (Shain 1991: 3). As mentioned before, the claimed status of a government-in-exile to be the legitimate representative of a nation depends to a high degree on the loyalty of the members of its national community. According to Shain, loyalty is demonstrated by a general acceptance to the present political circumstances. Ann Frechette defines loyalty as '. . . a feeling of allegiance of commitment to a person, institution, ideal, product, or cause' (2004: 17). In contrast, support refers more to an active assistance in operational, financial or diplomatic form.

National Diaspora

The national Diaspora represents one source to award its loyalty towards a government-in-exile. Extensive research has been done on national Diasporas in different academic fields, which results in different theoretical approaches.[2] According to Shain, Diaspora:

> can be understood as a people with a common national origin who regard themselves, or are regarded by others, as members or potential members of the national community of their home nation, a status held regardless of their geographical location and their citizenship status outside their national soil.
>
> (Shain 1989: 51–2)

As with Shain, I differ between those who live in the same host country as the exile government and those who stay in a different host country—a distinction that becomes important later in the analysis of the Tibetan case: 'Abroad' living members of the Tibetan exile community are those who live for instance in North America or Europe.

   The process of mobilizing all members of the national Diaspora to be loyal to a government-in-exile is on the one hand determined by the exile government's political goals and expectations about the Diaspora's extent of engagement for the national struggle. On the other hand, it is a function of the Diaspora's material and spiritual situation and its composition. While those who live in the same country where the exile government is established are important in terms of contributing labor, capital, time, information and intellectual means, the members of the national Diaspora abroad often have better access to material and financial resources. They are in a position to secure an exile government's financial survival and help to reduce its daily hardships through substantial monetary transfers. Due to better access to the international community, e.g. through local closeness or language abilities, they are able to mobilize international support. In this regard, abroad-living members of the national Diaspora are called upon periodically by an exile government to express their loyalty to a particular case, which in turn is interpreted as their loyalty to the nation in general (Shain 1989: 50, 57).

Regarding the Diaspora's composition, Iwańska and Shain emphasized that Diaspora communities are not homogeneous. An exile government faces certain difficulties to categorize its national Diasporas regarding size, origin, faith and political involvement. The Diaspora's scope and scale is predominantly a measure of the home government's politics, e.g. poor socio-economic or political conditions or an active migration policy in the homeland influence the number and composition of a Diaspora (Shain 1989: 52; Iwańska 1981: 44, 47). Iwańska classified a national Diaspora according to its members' level of political involvement. First, there are so-called core members: political activists who are organizationally and spiritually integrated in a government-in-exile. In the exile Tibetan context, they are for instance officials who work in the CTA, in its institutions or in exile Tibetan NGOs. Second, there is the group of rear guard members: persons who are loyal to an exile government but temporarily passive because of lacking time, energy or access to a specific ideological milieu. Shain added that the most promising sub-group are recently arrived exiles who were politically active and considered as troublemakers by the present home government. They are at most internationally recognized political refugees as they were forced to leave the homeland due to political threat and persecution (1989: 55). Third, there is the large group of those who share some latent patriotism and cultural solidarity rooted in a common national heritage. They are not actively involved in politics but still emotionally linked to the national cause. The most important segments within this stratum are students and the well educated. An education abroad has enabled them to develop and deploy their skills to exploit new financial, material and intellectual resources. Their activism is in most cases interpreted as loyalty to the exile government (Shain 1989: 53; Iwańska 1981: 44).

In the context of an exile government's loyalty, one question is naturally posed: Are members of the national Diaspora, despite their regional heritage, citizenship and language, nationalists, or traitors of their own nation? To answer this question one needs to look at the relation between exiles and their national compatriots who are still living in the homeland.

Insider–outsider dilemma

In the first years after departure from home, exiles are mostly preoccupied with their orientation in the new political, social and economic environment. Upcoming conflicts and psychological problems of these 'rootless' people who are geographically separated from home and psychologically dispersed create certain strains and difficulties. After some time has passed it becomes obvious that these experiences have shaped views and expectations in exile which are not likely to be similar to those at home. To bridge these differences on a common ground is the task of the exile government (Shain 1989: 23–4).

In this context, Shain mentioned the so-called insider–outsider dilemma. There are two national opposition groups to the present ruler at home, which struggle at worst in a competing situation for the position to be the legitimate representative of the same nation. On the one hand, there are those who stay back in the homeland (called insiders) and on the other, those who fled to exile (outsiders) and built up an exile government. According to Shain, the outsiders' geographical distance to the home territory, their absence from important happenings and limited ability to retain a foothold at home, may result in break between the two parties (1989: 77). This gap is widened by different social, political and economical living conditions, ideological bases and goals and views on how the present political system at home should be changed or overthrown. In the worst case scenario, both groups may fight each other instead of concentrating their energies to fight the home government. These rivalries have considerable weakening effects on the national struggle and may even strengthen and stabilize the position of the present leadership at home. Then a government-in-exile even becomes a target of the home government's politics focusing on the deepening of already existing factional structures and intrigues through the spreading of rumors, the withdrawal of citizenship and the use of worldwide spies and secret services. In short, splits are intended to be deepened and made more substantial (Shain 1989: 146–7, 154–5).

Insiders and outsiders generally agree that the ability to replace the present rulers at home from an exile basis is limited and an almost impossible mission. As a result, the flight is looked at by insiders with skepticism, as it is interpreted as a personal decision to escape from impending repression rather than a necessity to free the home country. This tendency is emphasized by the present ruler at home while portraying the exile forces as disloyal and puppets of foreign interests, accompanied by propaganda campaigns, confiscation of exile's private property, persecution of friends, families and relatives, etc. Consequently, exiles encounter an increasing isolation and find themselves in a position of disloyalty. Additionally, they face gradual changes in the insiders' attitude towards them who question the outsiders' representational claims. Such distrust may even be accelerated by the appearance of an exile government that gives reason to the assumption that it is unable to create international support, to respond to the insiders' needs, or that its leadership is hopelessly divided and estranged (Shain 1989: 80, 146). Iwańska said that the inability of an exile government to '... ease the economic and political hardships experienced by the home population ... [is] often attributed to indifference, incompetence, and sometimes even to the selfish preoccupation of the exile elites with the pursuits of the good life in the free world' (1981: 54). Additionally, exiles on their side often feel constant worries about those they left behind.

To avoid a problematic relationship between insiders and outsiders, both need to acquire sophisticated skills to build up and maintain open or clandestine communication systems. Exiles need to be informed about daily developments and perform manifold tasks to perpetuate pre-exile loyalties and to maintain their political supremacy at home. In this regard, an exile government needs to portray itself as serious representative of and fighting force for the nation's cause, for instance through acts of violence, which are carried out at least in the same scope and scale as the ones of their compatriots at home, to show the exiles' will to sacrifice for the national struggle. The creation of sophisticated communication systems at home are more likely in a less hegemonic political environment, e.g. the contact between insiders and outsiders can be intensified through phone calls, written messages and steady visits (Shain 1989: 84–8). The contact with insiders enjoys the highest priority in the political activities of a government-in-exile. As long as there is an internal opposition, an exile government will try to aid and abet it because only with internal compliance, members of an exile community can be mobilized to take an active part in an exile government's struggle in a long-term perspective (Shain 1989: 45). Cooperation with insiders is also important to secure a government-in-exile's political future after the desired breakdown of the ruling system at home.

To define the relationship between insiders and outsiders, Shain found the following factors: first, the home government's tolerance of an internal opposition is crucial in the process of developing a fruitful insider–outsider relationship. Thus the contacts between insiders and outsiders are usually interrelated to the political circumstances at home (Shain 1989: 146). Second, importance is also given to the pre-exile relationship between insiders and outsiders. Organizational structures, ideological bonds, cohesive leaderships, existing national sensibility, discipline and experiences with clandestine operations become essential for the exile context. According to Shain, the pre-exile political stratification and elite's ranks continue in exile—a phenomenon that is understood as the routine of charisma (1989: 30–1, 77–9). Third, the complexity of the relationship between insiders and outsiders is compounded by domestic developments in the social and political sphere over time. Extreme cases of instability at home (civil wars, a slow process of alteration in the structural bases of the society, assassinations or the natural death of the leadership) or the turnover of generations have a considerable impact on the relationship between insiders and outsiders (Shain 1989: 92).

Citizenship

In the insider–outsider relationship the concept of citizenship becomes important. Citizenship implies a source of an individual's national pride and is a symbol of a cultural and political identity that is shared with others. Consequently, the loss of citizenship is often interpreted as a loss of identity (Barbalet 1988: 2). Citizenship is portrayed in holding a passport and usually acquired by birth or after some time of naturalization. It gives evidence of the loyalty of a people to a government in interaction with members of other citizenships. The concept contains an obligation for a government to grant security to its citizens at home and abroad. In this regard, a government decides who deserves to be protected and hence who gets citizenship and when it will be withdrawn. In return, a government expects gratitude from its citizens, i.e. loyalty to its politics regardless of their place of residence.

Home governments discern the importance of citizenship and the damage they can do to the exile struggle by withdrawing it from the activists. According to Shain, they tend to '. . . manipulate citizenship as a stick-and-carrot mechanism' (1989: 150). Such twofold policy of granting and withdrawing citizenship is principally employed for propaganda purposes. On the one hand, home governments tend to instrumentalize citizenship to put pressure on the exiles to return. It is especially effective among those who already have second thoughts about the exile struggle and tend to return home. The withdrawal of citizenship may convince them to return to struggle for their nation's cause under the leadership of the home government instead of a government-in-exile (Shain 1989: 150). On the other hand, home governments will deprive citizenship from the exiles, while calling them national traitors. Such strategy may influence the exiles psychologically; their self-confidence may be lowered and feelings of displacement possibly will occur. Moreover, the initial revolutionary energy may be increasingly diminished while the bitterness about their situation could increase. In general, the retraction of citizenship is often accompanied by massive propaganda campaigns by the home government to destroy, officially, the national affiliation with the exile organization and break the contacts between insiders and outsiders. Once citizenship is withdrawn, the return to the homeland becomes problematic due to the statelessness of the exiles. They go back as strangers and their claims for power are questionable in the process of rebuilding a new political system. Examples are the Italian Fascists who considered the opposing forces abroad as 'self-interested outlaws' (Shain 1989: 149) or the Caribbean dictators during the 1950s who withdrew citizenship to discredit their exile opponents.

The practice of granting and withdrawing citizenship becomes especially important for exiles when a host country offers or even forces them to take the host's citizenship. Despite a positive short-term vision of living in exile by enjoying the privileges of full citizens in the host country, the dream of a quick return disappears all of a sudden. Many exiles avoid taking a new citizenship because old values and traditions are anticipated to vanish, contacts with families, friends and compatriots back home may lose intensity and questions of nationalism will appear anew. Taking another country's citizenship becomes for most exiles a 'kiss of death' (Shain 1989: 153), lowering their credibility among other exiles and their compatriots at home. On the one hand, such decision may be interpreted as a confession to the home government's charges of national betrayal. On the other, the degree of the exile's condemnation by the home government and its opposition depends in Shain's opinion also on how the new citizenship of the exiles is perceived by both sides: either as problematic or not. In this regard, exiles with a new citizenship try to minimize the perception of it as a renunciation of their former national commitment and rather portray their decision as an important step in the national struggle to overthrow the present ruler in the homeland (1989: 153).

Regarding the problems that accompany the exiles' change of citizenship, the question remains: How does an exile government react to the granting and withdrawing of citizenship both by the home and host governments? It can be anticipated that an exile government may either discourage exiles to take a new citizenship or at least portray the change of citizenship as a necessity to contribute to the national struggle in order to foster its own political position as the leading force. The Tibetan government-in-exile even found a third way, by creating an 'exile Tibetan citizenship' (see Ch. 5).

Governments-in-exile and international support and recognition

The second main focus of an exile government represents the international community, including nation-states, NGOs, transnational organizations and individuals. Governments-in-exile rely heavily on international support, either in material or diplomatic means, because it helps considerably to continue the exile struggle and secures the political survival of the organizational structures in exile.

> Many exile organizations ascribe vital importance to foreign support for their struggle, and strive to make their case international. They endeavor to generate and cultivate international enmity toward the home regime and to earn recognition for themselves at the regime's expense, so as to undermine and eventually overthrow and replace it.
>
> (Shain 1989: 110)

A government-in-exile needs to consider that international actors operate according to their own goals and political, economic and social objectives. In general, humanitarian interests play only a subordinate role for a potential supporter. Consequently, an exile government needs to convince them that the exile struggle is related to the potential ally's own political objectives (Shain 1989: 124). The crucial question then arises: How can exiles encourage potential international patrons to act on their behalf without denying critical aspects of the exile struggle?

The highest diplomatic acknowledgement that an exile organization can obtain is international recognition, which demonstrates a general acceptance to be a nation's representative. Such status provides an administration with diplomatic immunity, access to control material and immaterial resources, and jurisdiction over fellow nationals (Balekjian 1970: 3–5). According to Talmon, recognition is determined by the will of the recognizing authority to establish official relations with another authority assuming that it fulfills certain criteria (1998: 21–33). Generally, international law is arbitrarily interpretable regarding recognition and does not contain any coercive meanings that would oblige a government to recognize another one. Instead, governments are free to adopt, change and interpret the various concepts and doctrines of recognition in international law according to their own political objectives, ideology[3] and principles (Talmon 1998: 33). Recognition is even granted, regardless of an aspirant's degree of effective control inside a nation-state and hence does not forcibly need to be in line with a political ability to represent and implement a national will. Theoretically, recognition cannot be granted simultaneously to different opposing authorities that claim to represent the same nation, i.e. recognition of one political agent automatically implicates the non-recognition of the opposing force. But the practice shows that recognition is solely motivated by the political objectives of the recognizing power. This may lead to a situation where two or more authorities with the same representational claims are recognized in such position. Shain stated that the practical implementation of international law makes its conventions meaningless and is a result of an increasing tendency in world politics to use non-recognition as a political tool to de-legitimize political opponents (Shain 1989: 113). In this context, exile governments may become important for opponent governments or bargaining chips in international conflicts, as was the case during the Cold War when, for instance, African countries found themselves in such a position. Pro-exile arguments are the direct result of a sponsoring government's animosity towards the home government and its will to win the favor of a government-in-exile. Consequently, under the guise of international support, a third country may try to exploit exiles for its own interests (Shain 1989: 118–19).

Only a few exile governments are internationally recognized. The majority only receive unofficial diplomatic and operational support. Unofficial diplomatic support ranges from minor declarations to an exile government's favor and symbolic gestures to continuation of diplomatic relations. The higher the degree of diplomatic support, the more likely it will be accompanied by operational help, either financially or military. The degree of support varies according to the supporter's own political strength, both in the domestic and international spheres and is therefore influenced by its ability to deal with the benefits or losses of the outcome of cooperation with an exile government (Shain 1989: 111).

But in most cases, governments-in-exile are left alone with tentative gestures on their behalf which mostly serve as substitutes for diplomatic support. Nevertheless, even a vague acknowledgement in spheres of power becomes instrumentally important for validating the exile's claims of power because they lift up an exile community's confidence to continue its struggle and renews the hope to achieve the set goals. Any outside acknowledgement of the exile struggle is seen as more objective than an exile government's self-portrayal. The exile supporters' moral motivation may be a catalyst to activate additional operational support or other forms of official acknowledgement for an exile struggle. In this regard, any support, even supportive declarations services influence a government-in-exile's process of securing loyalty and support from the national community (Shain 1989: 110–12).

Host and home countries

A host country enjoys highest priority for an exile government because it provides the base for any exile activities, i.e. determines the political room of maneuver. It provides exiles with a base for physical survival through the provision of land and facilities for resettling. A host country is seen as a prerequisite for the exile's survival and the existence of a government-in-exile. Once a government decides to offer its hospitality, it is always in a position to limit the exiles activities. Any decision concerning the exiles' destiny is exclusively made by the host government and not, as often proposed, by the exile government itself. In general, the degree of pluralism in the host systems determines a government-in-exile's possibilities to influence the decision-makers of that particular country in its own interest. The host's involvement in exile politics varies from one case to another and primarily depends on its political system and official stance regarding the exile's conflict with the home government (Talmon 1998; Shain 1989; Iwańska 1981).

The relationship between host and exile governments may range from intimate friendship to animosity. There are enthusiastic host governments that support an exile government's struggle in ideological and/or pragmatic ways. In this case, an exile government may even exercise its own judiciary within the host's system. An example is the Spanish Republican exile government in Mexico, which was even allowed to use the Mexican governmental buildings to coordinate their activities against Franco. Furthermore, a host country may feel ideologically close to a government-in-exile but hesitates on a pragmatic basis, e.g. later seen in the exile Tibetan case in India. Such reluctance is rooted in a constant fear of revenge from the home government because of direct borders between the two countries and/or a relative political weakness of the host country. A third alternative represents a neutral host state. Such a situation is characterized by a government's tolerance of granted aid to the exiles by the host population, legal restrictions on the exile propaganda campaigns and limitations on the exile government's movements. Neutrality described the position of France in the early 1980s when it carefully scrutinized its policies towards the Iranian exiles in Paris and the Ayatollah Khomeini's regime. A more restrictive alternative in the host–exile relation describes a situation when a host country regards an exile government as enemy. In this case, exiles are only allowed to stay in camps, without being able to move from there or carry out any political activities. This was, for instance, the situation of the Vichy government which tried to convince the Spanish refugees in France to return home during Franco's rulership. Finally, Shain stated that a host country may provide a territorial base for an exile government against its own will. This is the case when a host country's domestic situation is characterized by instability or when there is a gradual process of the loss of parts of its own territory to a well-armed exile government, which aims to establish its own state on swathes of a host territory. This alternative of an exile–host relationship illustrates exemplarily the stay of the PLO in southern Lebanon since the early 1970s (Shain 1989: 121–3).

The importance of a host country for the exile's struggle is, unsurprisingly, realized by the home government, i.e. by the administrative structure the exiles try to overthrow, change or replace. Home governments mostly seek to eliminate exile opposition forces and often use diplomatic, economic and military constraints to discourage the host's support to suppress the exile government's activities or at least to reduce hospitality. On the diplomatic level, home governments often urge hosts to reduce their support for the exiles and portray exiles as illegal conspirators who misuse the right of asylum and work as minority against the host's national interests. To avoid any violence, a host country needs to invest material and human resources to foster its own domestic security and at the same time, give the impression that it discourages the exile activities (Shain 1989: 155–6). It can be concluded that the nature of the relationship between exiles and their host influences an exile administration's opportunities to interact with other political authorities.

International community

Since a government-in-exile is subject to constantly changing international developments, it needs to maneuver sensitively between different and sometimes conflicting political authorities to make sustainable alliances. Following Shain, a government-in-exile focuses in its quest for international recognition on three sources: enemies of the home government, political authorities that seem to be indifferent to the whole conflict and allies of the home government. Pointing attention only towards a single source contains the risk of total disillusionment because steady changes in international politics may cause a present supporter of an exile struggle to become a future opponent (Shain 1989: 125).

If an exile government is unable to address the governmental level of a potentially supporting country, it will try to find indirect access by appealing to lower ranked diplomats or approaching the civil society. It also may find supporters in sub-systems of a state or the international community who share the same goals. In this context, especially cultural, humanitarian and religious organizations, student associations, labor unions and political parties, are important for a government-in-exile (Shain 1989: 125). For the most part, these sub-groups lack knowledge about the exact circumstances of the exiles, as they focus on their programs on different issues. This makes them easily influenced by feeding them information suitable for the exile government's goals. As a result, they provide an exile government with effective aid by communicating the exile's moral and political views and, moreover, with financial help (Shain 1989: 118).

The UN especially became a main focus of many exile organizations, due to the growing importance of international organizations. UN resolutions are, for an exile government, of high symbolic importance because they legitimize and give weight in public opinion to the exile struggle, despite the UN's limited capacities to enforce and implement its decisions.

Exile governments mostly call for the international community's assistance through focusing on symbolically significant global issues. Universal myths are presented to the international community under the guise of 'archetypes of legitimacy', such as democracy, human rights, and self-determination (Shain 1989: 127; Appadurai 1996: 36)—a focus that becomes indispensable in contacting the UN through its specialized institutions and non-governmental agencies.

Foreign support tends to decline over time. Once an international patron realizes that the political system in the home country is established and unlikely to be overthrown and/or the exile struggle does not have any measurable success, it will limit its support. Furthermore, an authority may stop the assistance based on the insight that it does not benefit any longer from the exile's existence or the exile community has become an obstacle of its own political objectives. In such cases, support will only be continued when the popularity of a government-in-exile rises and therefore enhances the likelihood that the supporting authority can mobilize extra people and votes in the domestic political sphere (Shain 1989: 116).

To summarize, in its focus on the international community, an exile government needs to prove certain qualities of strength to motivate successfully other authorities to support its struggle. It is expected to have an undisputed leadership and popular acceptance among all compatriots. Especially, a constant provision of concrete evidence of a good relationship or at least the appearance of maintaining loyalties at home is crucial to get access to international financial, political, and academic spheres where a government-in-exile is able to promote its plight and political objectives. In contrast, exiles who lack such an intact relationship encounter severe problems in mobilizing outside support (Shain 1989: 79–80). Furthermore, it must convince the potential supporters that its political or military offers are necessary to achieve the exile goals as well as the supporters' political objectives (Shain 1989: 125–6). An exile government also has to promote organizational unity to attract international support and recognition. In this regard, an exile government needs to argue convincingly that it represents the will of the entire nation.

Additions to Shain's theory

Shain's theory emphasizes the difficult situation of exile governments in terms of national loyalty and international support. In their struggle to free their home country, they need to mobilize all members of the national community and different actors of the international community. But how can an exile government generate national loyalty and international support successfully? How important is the position of an exile leader in the context of the insider–outsider dilemma? Or, which policies are necessary for an exile government's ability to bridge the demands of both the national and international community? Shain's theoretical approach is insufficient to answer these questions. Only in the context of mobilizing the national Diaspora abroad did he outline James Wilson's organization theory, which focuses on organizations with voluntary membership and their instruments to mobilize their members to take an active part in the maintenance of the organizational structures and the achievement of the set goals. In my opinion, Wilson's theory provides an adequate in-depth framework to answer the aforementioned questions and, moreover, shifts the perspective from a description to an analytical study of the situation of exile organizations by looking at their investments of different political incentives to cultivate national loyalty and international support.

Exile governments and the investment of incentives

Taking up Iwańska's definition of governments-in-exile as 'formal organizations' (1981: 4) with a clearly definable membership, it is reasonable to look at the theory of political organizations in order to explain the exile government's functioning. According to Wilson's organizational theory, members of an organization with voluntary membership do not earn their livelihood as a result of their membership. His research findings are applicable to exile governments because their status in a host country is characterized by limited jurisdiction over people and territory, despite governmental claims and a lack of effective power. In most cases, exiles are obliged to live under host law and have no effective commitment towards an exile government-in-exile, e.g. a Tibetan who lives in Germany cannot be forced to support the Tibetan exile government in India. Generally speaking, exiles have only a moral bond, which makes the support of and membership in a government-in-exile voluntary. They are free to decide either to show their loyalty to the present ruler at home, the host government or the exile administration. Exile governments for their part, have no legal coercive instruments to force their people to actively support their structures and policies, while the host and the home governments are in such positions of power.

Wilson argued that political organizations with voluntary membership face various constraints regarding their maintenance and 'enhancement needs' (Wilson 1973: 13). Therefore, they need to adopt effective strategies to secure their organizational survival, because 'whatever else organizations seek, they seek to survive' (Wilson 1973: 10). Such striving in turn influences an organization's political objectives. But the maintenance of an organization is not merely a matter of its survival but also a process of producing and securing cooperative efforts through mobilizing its members. According to Wilson, incentives are invested to obtain compliance:

> For organizations to maintain themselves as systems of cooperative activity, they must find and distribute incentives so as to induce various contributors (members, donors, supporters) to perform certain acts [ranging from annual donations to services within the organisational structure].
>
> (Wilson 1973: 32)

The value of incentives is determined by the relative extent of demand on the members in return for the burden they have to carry to perform the asked accomplishments. Wilson distinguished in this context between four categories of incentives that are invested by organizations to motivate their present and potential members. First, there are material incentives, also considered as tangible rewards such as money, goods and services but also wages, salaries, tax reductions, improved property values, and gifts. These incentives can be readily priced in monetary terms and provide the receiver with exclusive and individual benefits. Second, there is the category of specific solidarity incentives that arise due to the act of associating with an organization, like honors, offices and deference. These are intangible rewards and not exchangeable on the regular economic markets, as they have little or no re-sale value. Their importance rather depends on the exclusion of certain members from an organization. Third, there are collective solidarity incentives that are awarded to all organizational members. They have the same characteristics as economic public goods, i.e. none of the members can be excluded. Examples are collective esteem and the appreciative time together. Fourth, Wilson mentioned the group of 'purposive incentives' that are intangible rewards, too. Their nature depends on the stated objectives of an organization and derives from the sense of individual satisfaction of having something contributed to the attainment of a worthwhile cause (Wilson 1973: 33–4, 36–51).

For an effective mobilization of the organization's present and potential members, organizations employ executive organs, which reduce internal strains of an organization as well as discrepancies between the tasks that need to be performed by the members and the incentives that are available for an organization (Wilson 1973: 31).

Summarized theoretical findings: the situation of exile governments

The combination of Shain's and Wilson's research findings describes a suitable approach to analyze how an exile government is able to secure its organizational existence and to reach the set goals. In this regard, I take Wilson's motivational concept of organizations to explain an exile-government's efforts to cultivate both national loyalty and international support for its exile struggle. Through the clever investment of certain incentives, an exile government can mobilize its present members, comprising all nationals it claims to represent. Furthermore, a government-in-exile needs to address potential members who are not yet actively involved in the exile struggle. According to such classification, the Tibetan government-in-exile must on the one hand cultivate loyalty of politically less involved exile Tibetans and those who live still in the homeland, and on the other hand mobilize the support of the international community as a whole including international NGOs, transnational organizations and individuals. Following Wilson's concept, members and potential members of an organization are asked to perform the requested acts that secure the survival of the organizational structure and contribute to the achievement of the set goals. In the context of exile governments, that would mean, supporting it operationally, diplomatically and/or morally and to participate actively in the exile struggle.

The investment of different kinds of incentives is based on the availability of certain resources, material (e.g. money, goods and services) and immaterial (e.g. ideology, information), which need to be generated by an exile government. In general, material resources in particular are difficult to obtain for a government-in-exile, first, because of the lost territory, it lacks the right to use resources that it possessed before the departure. They are now either in the hands of the present home government or used by insiders for their own political aspirations. Second, material resources in the host country may be already allocated between others, e.g. other exile authorities or the host government. The appearance of a government-in-exile may create or intensify competition, which in turn may lead to changes in the existing balance of power. Such an unpredictable situation makes the mobilization process from abroad exceptionally difficult. In contrast, immaterial resources are better available for exile governments because they can be easily generated, for instance, an ideology on which the pre-exile political system was based can still be used in exile. According to Shain, ideological commitment is seen as a primary source for recruiting followers in all strata of the national community (1989: 43–4).

To portray the problematic political situation of exile governments, I developed Figure 3, which summarizes the previously outlined theoretical considerations but also specifies the case of the exile Tibetan government-in-exile.

There are two main boxes within Figure 3. One describes the home country, i.e. the territory now under the effective control of an authority that a government-in-exile strives to replace. In the Tibetan case, this box describes

International Community

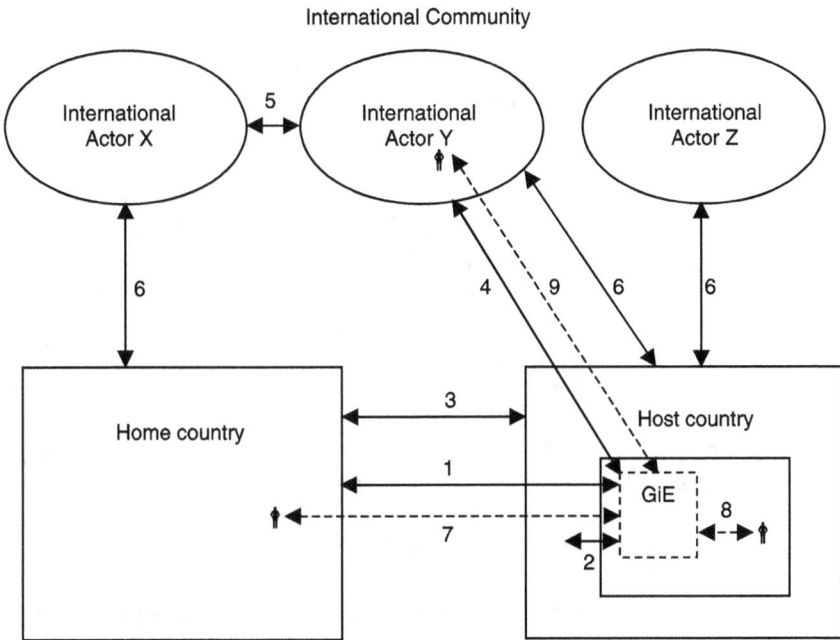

Figure 3 The political situation of a government-in-exile (GiE).

the People's Republic of China (PRC), including the area of the Tibetan Cholka Sum. The second box describes the host country, which serves as a territorial base for a government-in-exile; in the exile Tibetan context, India. The exile government, i.e. the CTA, is portrayed as the dashed-line box, indicating a general dependency on different political actors and the limited effective power regarding territory and people. The people of the national community the government-in-exile claims to represent, described in figures, are living in the host country, in the home country and in countries abroad. The international community, including sovereign states, transnational organizations, NGOs and individuals, are portrayed as the ovals (international actors X, Y and Z). The term 'International Community' above the ovals is not framed because it indicates its complexity and diversity.

The arrows between the different political actors describe interactions and relationships, which in turn illustrate the performance of certain acts according to the investment of incentives. Dashed-line arrows (Nos. 7–9) portray an exile government's efforts to gain loyalty among its national community while solid-line arrows (Nos. 1–6) illustrate a government-in-exile striving to cultivate international support and recognition. With the help of these arrows, the focus on exile governments in general and the CTA in particular in terms of national loyalty and international support, becomes clearer.

Arrow No. 1 shows the relationship between a government-in-exile and the present ruler at home. In the exile Tibetan context it describes the

relationship between the CTA and the Chinese leadership. I will not specifically look at this relationship in the empirical part of the book because it does
not illustrate directly the efforts of the CTA that are made to mobilize
national loyalty and international support. According to Shain, the interaction between an exile government and the present ruling forces in the homeland is at most characterized by tension and suspicion (1989: 59, 128–9).

Arrow No. 2 shows the relationship between a government-in-exile and a
host country, i.e. between the CTA and India. The host enjoys high importance in exile politics as it provides the base for the survival of an exile
government. A government-in-exile totally depends on the goodwill of the
host in legislative, executive and judicial matters. The framework for a host's
reaction towards an exile government is determined by its own political,
economic and social objectives. In this context, the main question in my
empirical part is: Why did India serve as host country for the exile Tibetans?

Arrow No. 3 illustrates the relationship between Host and Home countries,
which is related to the previously described arrows Nos. 1 and 2. Both countries are in a tense relationship, worsened when the host generously supports
a government-in-exile. The relationship becomes critical if there is a direct
border between the two countries, as is the case of the PRC and India. Such
pressure on the Host country may diminish the support towards a government-
in-exile (Shain 1989: 119–24). In this context, the question, why India served
as a host for the Tibetans, becomes ever more interesting.

Arrow No. 4 describes the relationship between a government-in-exile and
the international community. In general, an exile government needs to watch
and react to all international developments, including political maneuvers of
the present ruler of the homeland, its allies, potential supporters, and political counterparts of an exile government (Shain 1989: 145; Iwańska 1981: 4).
As previously mentioned, there is a high dependency of a government-in-exile
on international financial contributions. In the context of international recognition, governments-in-exile are often left alone with declarations and lip
services. Such symbolic gestures have a significant psychological impact on
the exile struggle as they are proven to be effective in the process of securing
national loyalty. Hence immaterial support contributes to the internal cohe-
sion of an exile government and emphasizes the reminder of a nation's existence (Shain 1989: 112). Looking at the exile Tibetan context, questions occur:
How does the CTA mobilize the international community to act on its
behalf? How and why does the international community react on the incentives that are invested by the exile Tibetan political elite? Who responds to the
exile Tibetan incentives?

Arrow No. 5 portrays the interactions between different political authorities in the international political arena. Such relations influence the exile
struggle indirectly. International interactions between different political
authorities will not be a particular focus of my empirical part but always play
a role in terms of their retroactive effects on the political maneuverability of
the CTA, the governments of India and the PRC.

The three arrows with the No. 6 show the relationships between different political authorities with the home and host countries. They are determined by the political developments that are portrayed as arrow No. 5. These relationships will not be part of my empirical presentation because they only indirectly determine the efforts of the CTA to cultivate national and international support.

The dashed-line arrow No. 7 describes the relationship between a government-in-exile and the people who stay back in the homeland, e.g. between the CTA and the Tibetans who live within the Chinese borders. These people are forced to support the present Chinese leadership. The relation between exiles and the people at home is discussed as an insider–outsider dilemma. To overcome and limit the upcoming discrepancies, both national groups need to stay in contact. Especially important are pre-exile organizational structures. Additionally, I will later look at the investment of incentives by the CTA to create new structures and communication systems to approach the national compatriots in Tibet.

Arrow No. 8 shows the relationship between a government-in-exile and the people who live in the same host country in which the exile administration is set-up, i.e. the exile Tibetans in India. These people are depicted in the illustration in a dashed-line box, which indicates their dependency on the host country. They can decide between their assimilation into the host population or living separated from the locals, whether they want to remain stateless or take a new citizenship, actively support the host government or participate in exile politics. Consequently, a government-in-exile is in a competing situation with the host government in the process to secure its loyalty. Especially those who are not actively involved in the exile struggle yet, need to be addressed by a government-in-exile's investments of the scarce financial and material resources. The allocation of financial and material rewards is either done as investment in human capital or as compensation for the involvement in the exile struggle. Material incentives are regarded as of minor importance among those who are already politically involved in exile politics because their activism is predominantly motivated by national commitment. Shain points out that especially after a long time in exile, these initial revolutionary energies may diminish in the majority because of a loss in hope and the inability to be successful in the near future (1989: 57–8). Such decreasing motivation is also a function of the status of the exiles in the host country regarding their social and economic position.

Arrow No. 9 portrays the relationship of a government-in-exile, with its national Diaspora abroad. In the Tibetan context, it describes the relationship between the CTA and the Tibetans who mainly live in Europe and North America. Especially for them, non-material incentives are more important, as they are mostly economically independent because of the living standard in their host countries.

To sum up, it can be stated that a government-in-exile finds itself in a critical position. To return home it needs to focus on the cultivation of national loyalty and to gain international support and recognition. Taking this into account, one question comes up: Is an exile government able to serve both interests at the same time? Shain did not reflect on this situation but it may become a problem if members of the national and international community have different and irreconcilable demands and objectives. In such cases, an exile government must perform a balancing act to serve both interests at the same time—a position that may either lead to an irritation among the addressees or to a ruinous situation for an exile government. To prevent the collapse of its own structure, an exile government may possibly face a dilemma to make cuts and compromises either among the national or the international community, which in turn influences the degree of the granted national loyalty and international support.

With regard to the empirical data, further issues are important: How can one distinguish between the efforts that are designed to mobilize national and international support and the policies that are carried out to return home? Shain did not offer an answer but it can be anticipated that a clear-cut distinction will be difficult. The cultivation of loyalty and support may become over time the 'real goal' of the exile struggle. Another striking topic describes the nature of leadership. Shain stated that in most exile cases, leaders of an organization fled while the lower ranks remained at home, either in detention or underground organized activities (1989: 78). Exile leaders try to maintain their pre-exile positions but are at most challenged by members of their own ranks or by countrymen who aspire to power. According to Wilson, leadership of an organization with voluntary membership is precarious because it does not enjoy effective power to mobilize the members by using coercive means (1973: 215).

In this context, the authority of a leader becomes important. Authority can be defined as legitimate ability to command and to be obeyed (Frechette 2004: 16). It can arise out of office, a principle that is adequate for obtaining routine performances (Wilson 1973: 219). But for sustained and demanding tasks, like the performance of certain favors for a large number of members of an organization, legitimacy out of office is insufficient. Here, the authority for leadership can be drawn out of personal qualities, expertise and personal fealty—characteristics that are the ultimate basis of authority. Furthermore, a leader can extend his legitimate status out of his commitment to the organization's objectives and his apparent possession of exceptional, even divine powers and qualities. According to Max Weber's concept of leadership, such a leader can be called 'charismatic'. But a charismatic leader who claims superiority by relying heavily on voluntary compliance must constantly prove his personal strength and perform 'heroic' deeds. If he fails to live up to the standards that justify his power, his established order and leadership become questionable. Then he may become the object of passionate hatred and his followers may soon abandon him (Weber 1976: 140). In the exile context, a charismatic leader like the 14th Dalai Lama can be a basis for a stable organizational structure that is less prone to crises over a long period of time.

Furthermore, it is likely that such leadership is able to unite opposing members of the national community (Wilson 1973: 219–22). In this context it is questionable, if the insider–outsider relationship becomes a dilemma because of the leader's divine qualities and heroic deeds he may be able to smooth upcoming conflicts.

In the following chapter, I take the theoretical findings as a basis for the analysis of the Tibetan exile context. From the theoretical viewpoint, it is essential to look at the CTA's policies to mobilize national loyalty and international support. The following questions are central: How did the CTA foster its claims to be the sole representative of all Tibetans during the decades in exile? and Which politics have been carried out to regain the homeland and how can they be explained and characterized?

4   Tibetans in exile: A portrait of the CTA

This chapter analyzes the efforts of the Tibetan government-in-exile in creating a base for its exile struggle to free the homeland. After portraying the reasons of the Tibetans for their departure, I give an account of the circumstances under which they have rehabilitated and resettled, mainly in India but also in other countries. In this context, I also look at India's motivation to serve as a territorial base for the Tibetans and the Central Tibetan Administration (CTA). In the center of the next section are the CTA and its efforts to resettle thousands of Tibetans and to establish an exile educational system. Next, I examine the development of the exile Tibetan struggle to regain the Tibetan homeland under the leadership of the CTA, from the early 1960s to the 1990s. The representative claims and the organizational structure of the present CTA is the subject of the following section, with regard to showing how the Tibetans in exile concentrate their energies on regaining their homeland. Next, I look at the role of the main exile Tibetan NGOs and how they fit in the political structure of the CTA. At the end of this chapter is an analysis of the present annual CTA budget, which gives detailed information about its policies.

Facts and figures rely to a large extent on the publications of the Tibetan government-in-exile. During the time in India, the CTA published several books and surveys on the challenges and problems of exilehood. The first extensive publications *Tibetans in Exile* were released in 1969 and 1981 (CTA 1969, 1981). The following publications of the years 1992, 1994, 2003 and 2004 focused on the implementation processes of various projects in the sectors of rehabilitation, economy, education, health, religion and cultural affairs, international affairs and institutional development (CTA 1992a, b, 1994a, 2003, 2004). An elaborated account of the demography of the exile Tibetan community in 1998 was published in 2000 (CTA 2000f).

Flight: reasons and numbers

Since the early twentieth century, towns such as Darjeeling and Kalimpong were already crowded by Tibetan aristocratic children who were sent to British missionary schools, but also by pilgrims and intermarried Tibetans. By the early 1950s, small numbers of Tibetans had left their homes, motivated by an increasing Chinese threat, and settled in Indian border areas, such as Sikkim,[1] Darjeeling and West Bengal (Arakeri 1998: 241–7). They belonged mostly to the Tibetan aristocracy or the upper Tibetan rural strata of traders and wealthy town dwellers.

With the arrival of the 14th Dalai Lama and his entourage in the spring of 1959, the number of Tibetans who poured into countries of the south Asian subcontinent culminated. The first big wave of Tibetans left their home-land between 1959 and 1962. During these initial years, the number of exile Tibetans grew to some 85,000 (CTA 1969: i). Their flight was mainly motiv-ated either by loyalty to the 14th Dalai Lama and/or by the fear of Chinese oppression. The Tibetans, mostly whole families, used traditional trade routes through Bhutan and Nepal for their escape. After these routes were increas-ingly controlled by Chinese border guards in the beginning of the 1960s, and some were even closed by the GOI because of growing political tension with the PRC, the Tibetans needed to take more difficult paths over snow covered 6,000-metre mountain passes. The dangerous and exhausting march to escape took an average of three weeks, mainly during night-time. This was because the migrants had a justified fear of the Chinese and Nepalese border guards, who would (if caught) send them to prison or back to Tibet. In addition, many women, children and elders died during the escape due to exhaustion (Subba 1990: 21–3). In his research, Tanka Subba reported a distorted age structure in exile and a predominant share of male Tibetans during the initial years. The male–female ratio was, in 1959, 70:30, an imbalance that did not last long however, as the sex ratio became balanced in the most reproductive age group of the 20–40-year-old Tibetans (Subba 1990: 24–5).

There are differing opinions on the exile Tibetans' social heritage. The CTA and a few scholars point out that the exiles came from all social strata (Subba 1990: 26; Forbes 1989: 27; Tethong 2000: 54–5). The CTA even specified that approximately 60 per cent of the Tibetans at this time had been either farmers or pastoral peasants (*News Letter* 1965: 4). In contrast, Chinese officials talk about a greater number of aristocrats and rich Tibetans (Methfessel 1995: 39). Regarding these data, one needs to consider that all information about the scope and scale of the exile community can also be used as propaganda instruments of one side or the other to prove its ideas on the Chinese takeover in 1959. The CTA may tend to show that people from all strata of Tibetan society were negatively influenced by the Chinese seizure of power and needed to leave the country. The Chinese in contrast, may rather illustrate that espe-cially the ruling strata realized that they were not needed any more in a Communist Tibet and therefore left the country. Such 'propaganda warfare' is in line with Shain's theoretical considerations (1989: 146).

Looking at the geographical exodus roots, the majority of Tibetans came from the central and southern Tibetan regions (70 per cent), while only 5 per cent came from the northeastern Amdo region and 25 per cent from Kham (Methfessel 1995: 37; Tethong 2000: 55). Tibetans from the eastern

Tibetan regions have been under-represented in exile for a long time; only in recent years have people from Amdo increasingly sought refuge in India. Such a share of the exile population does not represent the initial population figures of pre-1959 historical Tibet. In 1947, the Lhasa government estimated the population of the central part at 3 million, with the numbers for the eastern regions together at between 4 and 7 million (International Commission of Jurists 1960: 290). The under-representation of eastern Tibetans in exile can be explained by the relatively long distance between the eastern regions and the borders (Methfessel 1995: 37). But looking also at Tibetan history, the regions of Kham and Amdo mostly remained independent from the central government in Lhasa, in spite of ongoing attempts to incorporate them. Therefore, there may have been some reservations among the Khampas and Amdowas about the newly founded CTA, which portrays itself as the legal and sole successor to the pre-1959 Lhasa administration and claims to represent all people living in the area of Cholka Sum.

During the time of the Chinese Cultural Revolution, the number of newcomers in exile was constant but relatively small compared with the initial years. Chinese restrictive politics made the departure difficult for the people who wanted to escape concrete political oppression. From 1980 onwards, the number of exile Tibetans grew again because of a slow liberation in the PRC's Tibet policy. The opening of the Sino–Nepali border, in particular, resulted in a steady flow of Tibetans who intended to stay temporarily in India and Nepal. Renewed political turmoil and demonstrations in Tibet and the subsequent repression since 1987 (Schwartz 1996) led to a new growth in Tibetan migrants. At this time, mainly single people were leaving Tibet, rather than whole families. The CTA reported in 1994, that the number of new arriving Tibetans was steadily increasing. For instance, in 1992, approximately 3,774 Tibetans arrived in India and Nepal; in 1993, there were 4,477 (CTA 1994a: 41). According to other sources regarding the years 2000 and 2002, an estimated 3,000 newcomers annually arrived in India (*The Indian Express* 2002: 2). This shows that there are either certain difficulties in counting the new arriving Tibetans in the Indian subcontinent or the number had decreased again. Despite the exact numbers, the CTA classified all new arrivals in 1994 as follows:

1   *Political prisoners*: This group consists of those who had been imprisoned because of their political activities against the PRC.
2   *Monks and nuns*: Tibetans who have predominantly escaped religious persecution.
3   *Young children*: Many children are sent to exile by their parents so they can have a proper Tibetan education and to grow up in a free society.
4   *Youth*: Young Tibetans between the ages of 14 and 25 seeking a better education and job opportunities in exile.
5   *Pilgrims*: Especially during times when the 14th Dalai Lama gives initiations and teachings, many Tibetans leave their homes to go for

pilgrimage to the Buddhist sights in India and to see the 14th Dalai Lama. The majority return home after completing their pilgrimage.

6   *Family seekers*: Tibetans who come to exile to meet their relatives and friends. After receiving a blessing from the 14th Dalai Lama, they usually return to Tibet (CTA 1994a: 41–2).

Based on this categorization, the CTA identified, between the years 1989 and 1993, three major groups of exile Tibetans: 44 per cent of the new arrivals were young Tibetans between the age of 14 and 25, 45 per cent were monks and nuns and the rest consisted of lay adults (CTA 1994a: 44). This classification was out-of-date according to the data of the NGO's 'International Campaign for Tibet'. This organization closely works together with the CTA and stated in one of its brochures of 2002 that about 38 per cent of the new arrivals are young Tibetans, 24 per cent monks and nuns and around 40 per cent adults (International Campaign for Tibet 2002: 7). Again, data and counting seem to be problematic.

According to the statistics of the CTA, by 1998, there were around 122,078 Tibetans[2] living outside the political borders of the PRC. In India alone, there were 85,147 Tibetans. Additionally, Tibetans lived in other Asian countries, such as Nepal (13,720), Bhutan (1,584) and in the Russian Federation and Japan (together 109). In North America in 1998, there were around 7,000 Tibetans, in Europe 2,243, and in Oceania (Australia, New Zealand) 217 (CTA 2000f: 7).[3] In this context, it is important to note that the accuracy of the Tibetan exile population figures has varied since the initial years for two reasons. First, because of a lack of information about the scope and scale of the exile Tibetan community in general, and second, because of the use of the available data by the exile administration for its own political objectives. Tom Grunfeld stated:

> It is impossible to determine how many Tibetans actually left. Census figures are unreliable, and the situation is further complicated by the fact that it is advantageous to the refugee leadership to inflate the numbers of refugees. The greater the refugee population, the more proof that communist rule in Tibet was oppressive and rejected by the populace. Emigrating was seen as an example of people voting with their feet.
>
> (1987: 186)[4]

The official data only show all newly arrived Tibetans who are counted by the three CTA reception centers in Kathmandu, New Delhi and Dharamsala. In addition to these registered Tibetans, there are also uncounted unregistered Tibetans. Without valid papers from the host countries India and Nepal, they search for refuge in permanent or squatter settlements, get shelter at a friend's or relative's home or in monasteries. The existence of such 'illegal exiles' may serve as an additional explanation for a general exaggeration by the CTA and constantly varying numbers. According to the theory, one can also conjecture that relatively small numbers of Tibetan exiles are favorably for India because the smaller the number of exiles the less important is the exile community for the host regarding operational help. In this regard, India would limit the security threat on the northern frontiers and have little reason to discuss the topic of the Tibetan exile community with the Chinese. However, there is no scientific discourse on such an explanation but rather a general frustration about unreliable data (Grunfeld 1987: 186–8; Subba 1990: 39).

Those who stayed in Tibet have undergone significant changes regarding their social, economic and religious life. The CTA reported that:

> approximately 1.2 million Tibetans, about one sixth of the total population ... have died under detention, famine, prosecution and poverty. The casualties of the monastic population were especially high with the targeted destruction of Tibet's religious and cultural institutions. Widespread poverty, high morbidity, infant mortality and illiteracy; illegal abortions, controlled births and uncontrolled immigration from China are still characteristics of Tibet's demographics.
>
> (2000f: 1)

There is no doubt that the Chinese occupation had an immense impact on Tibetan life. This fact was already proven by two reports (in 1959 and 1960) of the International Commission of Jurists; a body with a history of CIA sponsorship (Sautman 2000: 63). This commission charged China with genocide in Tibet, based on Tibetans religious belief (International Commission of Jurists 1959, 1960: 3). Nevertheless, it has to be pointed out that the 1.2 million Tibetans who died as a direct result of Chinese rule in Tibet—a number that is constantly used in CTA publications as well as by international NGOs—is, again, hard to verify (Samuel 1993: 46). Patrick French summarized these difficulties by conducting research on that topic with the words: 'I was left with the unwelcome conclusion that this survey was a well-intentioned but statistically useless attempt to satisfy Western demands for data and tabulation' (2003: 292). He stressed the fact that the international community considerably influences the exile Tibetan publications and self-portrayal of the CTA's exile struggle, by collecting data and using statistics that can be easily utilized by potential supporters to emphasize their arguments.

The legal status of the Tibetans in India depends on the year of their arrival. Those who entered India before 1962, the year when India suffered from the defeat of the war at the Sino–Indian frontier, are officially considered as political refugees according to the aforementioned UN criteria. Nevertheless, India has not signed the 'United Nations Convention on Refugees'. Such refugee status provides the pre-1962 Tibetans in India[5] and their children with access to the formal Indian economic sector, such as job opportunities in the Government of India (GOI) and entrance to Indian universities (Scheidegger-Bächler 2001: 34). Those who entered India after 1962 are considered by

India as foreigners of Tibetan nationality—a status that entails several educational and professional disadvantages. To stay, Tibetans above 18 years of age need to hold a Registration Certificate (RC) that is issued under the Foreigner's Registration Act of 1946 (Universal Law Publishing 2003). For the registration form, see Appendix 2. This RC has to be renewed every year, which means that the GOI allows the Tibetans to stay only for one year, after which they need to extend their permit for another year. Tibetans are not supposed to be granted registration certificates, a practice that ensures that Tibetans are unable to settle permanently in India, but entails considerable insecurity for Tibetans regarding their investments in housing, employment, schooling, etc. Nevertheless, all exile Tibetans are free to apply for host country citizenship, in this case Indian, even though it is discouraged by the Tibetan exile government (see also Ch. 5). Accompanying advantages and disadvantages to the acquiring of a new citizenship have already been outlined elsewhere in this book.

Based on the theoretical implications of the terms 'refugee' and 'exile' and in our specific Tibetan case, I use the term 'exile Tibetans'. It describes best their situation outside their homeland, which is designed to struggle from a foreign base against the Chinese leadership in their homeland.

First years in exile: the role of the newly founded CTA

Most of the early Tibetan migrants in the 1950s left their homes to contribute to a starting resistance movement but also due to fear of the anticipated Chinese invasion. Officially they gave the reason for their migration to heavy flooding in Gyantse in 1950. Once in exile, they organized themselves into the Tibetan Welfare Association (TWA) which carried out the first Tibetan political activities from an exile base between 1954 and 1959. Consequently, this organization can be seen as the first exile Tibetan organization that focused on the struggle against the Chinese invaders. The TWA represented a link between the international political sphere and the happenings in the homeland as it lobbied the international community with petitions that were based on obtained information from inside Tibet. Furthermore, it organized the first exile Tibetan demonstrations in northern India and had contact with the USA, who were clandestinely operating inside Tibet by supporting the eastern Tibetan guerrilla forces. But despite its manifold exile activities under the unifying goal to fight the invading PLA, conflicts between TWA members appeared which weakened the organizational structure. Tibetan aristocrats were accused of not being dedicated enough in the struggle for a free Tibet and therefore failing in their position as political elite. With such criticism, the people from a non-aristocratic heritage caused a deep-rooted and sustainable uncertainty among the aristocrats. The TWA disappeared from the political stage with the arrival of the 14th Dalai Lama in India in the spring of 1959 and the proclamation of the Central Tibetan Administration of His Holiness the Dalai Lama (Tethong 2000: 46–8; Shakabpa 1967: 312–13).

The birth of the CTA can be determined as being the first meeting between the 14th Dalai Lama, aristocratic members of the dissolving TWA and Gelug dignitaries on 21 April 1959 in Mussoorie, a former British hill station in the north Indian Union state of Uttar Pradesh. The meeting was set to reflect the recent political developments in Tibet and the anticipated future in exile. Three days later, the 14th Dalai Lama and the Indian president Jawaharlal Nehru exchanged their views on the political situation at which event, Nehru first learnt about the Tibetan provisory government in exile. He responded emphatically that the GOI was not going to recognize an exile Tibetan government in India, first because India was still bound by the Sino–Indian agreement of 1954 and second, Nehru was unwilling to sacrifice the Sino–Indian relations for Tibet (Shakya 1999: 218–19, 224). He proclaimed three main factors that would determine the Indian foreign politics. (1) The preservation and maintaining of security and integrity of India; (2) the desire to maintain friendly relations with the PRC; (3) while at the same time India felt a deep sympathy for the Tibetan people, based on the Buddhist religion. The last point was given weight by the accommodation of the thousands of Tibetans in the Indian subcontinent and the generous aid that was granted to them by the GOI in the following years. But why did India still serve as host country for the exile Tibetans despite substantial reservations? According to Shain's theory, India's decision to accommodate the Tibetans was determined by its own political objectives.

When in spring 1959 the first big wave of Tibetans arrived, the Indian leadership showed, despite initial reservation, quite an interest in them. This reaction can be explained by Indian domestic politics at that time. Nehru's pro-China policy that focused on Sino–Indian friendship and was expected to reduce or at best neutralize the existing security threat from the PLA in Tibet, provoked many critics among the Indian public throughout the 1950s. Thus, the fleeing Tibetans were just proof enough for many Indians of Nehru's failed political course. Realizing that the majority of his countrymen sympathized with the Tibetans, Nehru took the chance and gave the Tibetan problem high priority on the Indian domestic agenda. The special attention that was pointed towards the arriving Tibetans, compared with exiles and refugees of other nationalities in India, was justified, as said before, by a religious Buddhist affinity between Indians and Tibetans (Norbu 2001a: 289–90; Chaturvedi 2004: 72–86). The rehabilitation of the Tibetans was entrusted to the Indian foreign ministry, which was headed by Nehru himself. In comparable situations, the ministry of the interior took care of such matters. The Tibetan issue was intended to be solved quickly to prevent an upcoming instability for the Nehru government because there was, for instance, the possibility of discontent among Bengali refugees in India who had reason to believe that the Tibetans enjoyed better treatment than them (Woodcock 1970: 415). Thus, the GOI took advantage of the thousands of newly arriving Tibetans to improve its political image in the domestic sphere. From a theoretical point of view, the situation illustrates the importance of the host population for the exile's treatment. Shain stated in this context:

> the more pluralistic the polity and the greater the variety of legitimate ways available to influence decision makers, the more likely it is that the state and society will influence each other in deciding how much and what kind of support to give exile organizations.
>
> (1989: 119)

In this regard, the Tibetans benefited from the Indian democratic system. Regarding India's external security, the GOI created at the end of the Sino–Indian War in 1962, a so-called Special Frontier Force (SFF). This 12,000-man strong elite guerrilla force, which was set-up to safeguard the Sino–Indian borderline to prevent and/or to conduct clandestine operations behind Chinese lines in the event of another war, consisted of a large number of exile Tibetans.[6] Their high percentage in the SFF was due to their ability to operate in high altitude and motivation to fight the Chinese. The establishing and training of the SFF was supported by Indian and US intelligence agencies. This shows that the Indian host took advantage of the exile Tibetans for their own security objectives, which in turn gives evidence to India's interest to serve as host country for thousands of Tibetans. Furthermore, the set-up of the SFF gives evidence of the US interest in an organized Tibetan force. In this regard, the exiles not only served the interest of the host country but also of a third power. During the decades, the SFF's initial objectives were shifted to a primary counter-terrorist and a VIP security force.[7]

On 29 April 1959, one month after his arrival in India, the 14th Dalai Lama officially proclaimed the CTA.[8] In the middle of June, he addressed the public for the first time in exile pointing out the Tibetan plight, accusing the PRC of the occupation of Tibetan territory and officially taking a stand in declaring the 'Seventeen Point Agreement' of 1951 null and void.

In 1960, the headquarters of the CTA was shifted on the initiative of the GOI from Mussoorie to Dharamsala (Dalai Lama 1996: 173–5). Since then, the entire administrative infrastructure has been located in and around Dharamsala, but in particular in a newly founded governmental district, called Gangchen Khyishong and the former hill station, the present tourist center of McLeod Ganj.[9]

In the beginning, the 14th Dalai Lama focused on two issues regarding life in exile: (1) the rehabilitation and resettlement of the steady flow of newly arriving Tibetans and (2) their education. These core points were subordinate to the main goal of the CTA exile struggle: the return to a free homeland. Such splitting of energies was necessary to overcome the unexpected difficulties in exile since the majority of the approximately 85,000 Tibetans who arrived in India, Nepal and Bhutan during the first years faced enormous problems in finding themselves in new cultural and climatic circumstances. The climatic and hygienic problems in India, especially, caused numerous

Plate 2 CTA complex in Gangchen Khyishong, India, 2003.

diseases among the exiles.[10] The CTA realized that only through the minimization of their daily hardship was it able to prove its position as the legal successor of the Lhasa government and representative of all Tibetans. As a result, the 14th Dalai Lama first set-up two departments to handle the resettlement and education of the exile Tibetans. Additionally, the CTA supported the ongoing guerrilla war inside Tibet to fight the Chinese (Grunfeld 1999: 292).

Rehabilitation and resettlement

In the spring of 1959, the GOI set-up two temporary transit camps in the Indian Union states of Assam and West Bengal, but the limitations of these camps were soon realized. The camp in Assam, for instance, was planned for a maximum of 9,000 Tibetans but by June 1959, three months after the 14th Dalai Lama reached India, already 15,000 people were squeezed into small bamboo huts and tents. Many Tibetans joined the local mendicant people and lived for months or even years on begging and small amounts of food predominantly distributed by foreign volunteers of international relief or Christian missionary organizations (Woodcock 1970: 413; Grunfeld 1987: 189–91). Another basis for living was on the selling of the few valuable belongings, such as jewelry and religious objects that had been brought from home to exile. These artifacts were sold on Indian markets in Darjeeling, Kalimpong and Delhi and pulled numerous Tibetan families through the first months (Woodcock 1970: 415).

Dawa Norbu remembered that '... the sons and daughters of Tibetan aristocracy and wealthy Tibetans, studying in colleges or working around Darjeeling, did not come to help us. Perhaps they were ashamed of us' (1974: 246). Norbu's statement shows that despite the difficulties in exile, the traditional social stratification was still in existence and, moreover, limited the interaction between the different social strata. While the majority of the humble Tibetans lived initially in transit camps, the clerics kept a low profile in exile sanctuaries and monasteries. In contrast to the Tibetan aristocracy, they helped their compatriots during the rehabilitation and resettlement (Karthak 1991: 16). However, in the following decades in exile, the monastic population showed the highest degree of change, as it found it needed to be actively involved in economic activities to secure its own livelihood instead of living on the donations of lay Tibetans, who had barely enough to feed themselves (Saklani 1984: 207).

Meanwhile Nehru's government was inclined to underplay India's role as host for the exile Tibetans in the interest of peace with the PRC. In addition to Indian domestic politics, the departure of thousands of Tibetans from their homeland still remained officially an external issue. To limit the security threat, India prohibited the CTA to struggle against China from Indian soil. The CTA reacted to India's restriction with an altered exile struggle, which did not directly focus on the regaining of the homeland. Since then, the CTA rather concentrated on the preservation of Tibetan culture and religion. One must also say that the reports of the International Commission of Jurists must have been alarming for the CTA and the 14th Dalai Lama, since they confirmed a successive destruction of Tibetan religion within the Chinese borders. Consequently, the initial exile Tibetan political struggle changed officially to the so-called 'Tibetan movement' to preserve culture and religion, where the numerous exile monasteries in particular played an important role as cultural and religious institutions. In the following section, I will keep the usage of the word 'struggle' instead of 'movement' in the exile Tibetan context because it refers more clearly to the theoretical considerations and the term 'exile'. The CTA's new political direction was not restricted but, moreover, provided the Indian authorities with a base for support. In 2003, the CTA described the goal of the exile Tibetan struggle as follows:

> The purpose of the Tibetans in exile is two-fold, viz., to seek justice for our homeland and, to preserve our identity and language by practicing our culture and traditions. The first purpose is dependent on many factors including international situation, political changes within China etc. that are beyond our control ... [while] the second purpose is not dependent on external factors and can be fulfilled by every Tibetans [sic] in exile, irrespective of gender, age and education, whether lay or monk/nun.
>
> (2003: 6)

To implement this new course, which did not directly focus on the freedom of

Tibet, the CTA created a Department for Religion in 1960. This department has been developed to the present day into a powerful institution within the CTA structures. It was manned by a large number of monk officials (Tethong 2000: 60) and financially backed up by 30 per cent of the CTA annual budget in the first 20 years of exile (McLagan 1996: 207). Additionally, the CTA set-up an office for information and publicity, and a branch office in Delhi, which focused on the relationship with the host country and the different actors of the international community.

Meanwhile, an increasing number of deaths of exile Tibetans caused by poor conditions in the camps urged the CTA to look for a new solution. Hence the 14th Dalai Lama requested the Indian administration give the Tibetans the chance to live and work in cooler places. In response, the GOI sent numerous exile Tibetans to the Himalayan regions to earn their livelihood as road workers (CTA 1969: 129–39). But this action plan did not work out to be a sustainable solution, as the CTA described the situation later:

> In the immediate years following His Holiness the Dalai Lama and the Tibetan refugees taking refuge in India, one of the more urgent needs was a long-term rehabilitation program that would serve to bring all the refugees into homogenous Tibetan communities large enough to allow them to perpetrate their language, traditions and thus preserve their national identity, and of course where they could secure food, shelter, medical care, education and a means of livelihood to develop economically self-supporting communities during their period in exile.
>
> (1994a: 3)

It is interesting that by that time, the CTA already anticipated an urgent need for a 'long-term rehabilitation program'. An UNHCR report about the situation of the exile Tibetans between 1960 and 1963 also showed that there was a need for a permanent solution for the Tibetans in South Asia (Holborn 1975: 720–5). This consideration was also portrayed in one of the speeches of the 14th Dalai Lama, who already stated in 1959: 'We will have to remain in exile for a longer period than expected. We will have to settle mentally as well as physically' (speech of the 14th Dalai Lama to the Tibetans in 1959, cited in Avedon 1997: 72).

Between spring 1959 and the middle of the 1960s, the international aid that was channeled into the Tibetan camps was dominated by a sense of emergency and international aid organizations focused first of all on the welfare of the Tibetan children (Norbu 2001a: 210). But once the likelihood of an imminent solution had faded, the numerous NGOs and volunteers gave their attention to a long-term and more realistic perspective to resettle the thousands of Tibetans coming into India. Most of the emergency help was organized by the Central Relief Committee for Tibetans (CRCT) under the leadership of Mr Acharyo JB Kripalani (Schweizer Tibethilfe Solothurn 1961: 247–51).

The second striking fact in the CTA quotation is that all exile Tibetans should be resettled into 'large homogenous communities'. As shown before, the exile Tibetans were from different geographical, social and religious backgrounds. But against the CTA's wishes, this was not fulfilled by the GOI due to its own security reasons. The Indians instead tried to scatter the Tibetans in different locations to discourage any unifying political activities. This strategy served the Indian interest with regard to avoiding a potential Chinese provocation but also it limited domestic quarrels: 'The widely separated locations were partly determined by the availability of land, but also in the interest of both harmonious foreign relations and a smooth internal development . . .' (Gombo 1985: 82). Furthermore, it was anticipated that it would undermine the development of a strong exile Tibetan nationalistic movement in the initial years, which could change into a political struggle, as the exile Tibetans now lived thousands of kilometers apart. For the Tibetans however, this non-assimilative resettlement provided them with an opportunity to preserve successfully their culture and religion to the present day: 'If Indians were accepting the Tibetan People on the same level as themselves, we might lose our identity and culture. But being resented and envied by Indians gives us stronger incentive to stay Tibetan' (Mr Gonpo Tsering cited in Ström 1995: 36).

In 1960, Indian authorities and the CTA planned to give arriving Tibetans the chance to live in permanent settlements. To realize such a plan, the GOI asked Sikkim, Bhutan and all Indian state governments to provide land for the Tibetans. Finally, Sikkim, Bhutan, the southern Indian Union states of Orissa and Karnataka, but also Himachal Pradesh, Madhya Pradesh and Uttar Pradesh in north India responded favorably (Norbu 2001a: 209; Arakeri 1998: 35–6). While in northeast India, the Tibetans leased the land from local Indians, the rest of the settlements in India were built on government property that was made available for a period of 99 years. In the latter case, the exiles signed a contract to pay annually around 50 Indian Rs. per hectare (interview with Mr Tsering Dorjee, Department of Home, Dharamsala, May 2006).

It is interesting to note that some Indian politicians expected an economic development of backward rural areas through the resettlement of the exile Tibetans (Goldstein 1975a: 162). Such anticipation is important in the theoretical context, as it proves Shain's assumption that a host country's interest in exiles is also linked to its own economic objectives. One can say that over the decades, the Indian economic expectations were fulfilled. For instance, numerous Indians found job opportunities in Tibetan households, monasteries and enterprises.[11] Indirect economic spill-over effects can be noticed in the tourist and public transport sector. Both segments expanded considerably because of an increasing number of Western tourists who annually come to India to visit the exile Tibetan settlements. One example for the impact of the increased tourism provides the changes in Dharamsala, which made a huge leap within recent decades and developed from an earthquake-destroyed British hill station to a tourist center. While in the 1970s and 1980s only two buses commuted daily between Dharamsala and New Delhi, today there are up to eight buses filled with tourists. The streets are jammed with traffic: buses, rickshaws and taxis. The entire place had changed with foreign funding: handicraft centers were set-up, Indian and Tibetan shopkeepers are in line with movie halls, restaurants, hotels and guest houses; monasteries and museums, cultural events and spiritual courses are offered weekly, starting from Tibetan cooking courses to yoga and meditation practice to meet the tourists' desires.[12] But also the supply of educational and health facilities expanded and the CTA summarized contentedly: 'Tibetan community enjoys a satisfactory infrastructure in terms of roads, toilet and drinking water facilities in comparison to surrounding Indian villages' (2004: 14).

According to Melvyn Goldstein, the economic development in and around exile Tibetan settlements did not have significant negative effects on the Indo–Tibetan contacts in the 1970s (1975a: 181). But during the last decades, the economic dominance of the Tibetans and their favorable treatment by the GOI in terms of financial and material transfers has increasingly caused animosity and jealousy among the locals, which partly lead to disputes and even killings (Methfessel 1995: 165). According to an Indian businessman, tax benefits and constantly growing international financial transfers cause the Tibetans to become increasingly richer. Additionally, Tibetans are known as cunning businessmen and traders who drive the biggest cars in town. But nevertheless, the Indians try to make profit out of the situation wherever they can (anonymous interview, 1999). To undermine any tensions between the locals and the exiles, the CTA has been striving to emphasize the importance of Indo–Tibetan relations. For instance, the 14th Dalai Lama constantly stresses in his speeches the friendship between the two nations and thanks both the GOI and the Indian people for their support of the exile Tibetans. For him, Indian support is now the '. . . key to regaining . . . freedom. No doubt, international support for our cause is increasing, and we do need it. But the most important factor is Indian support' (Tsering 1997: 14). Such statement illustrates the high importance of the Indian goodwill for the survival of the exile Tibetan struggle.

The first settlements were slowly established on the basis of financial support of the GOI. As many Tibetans formerly worked as peasants, it was natural to start with agricultural projects (*News Letter* 1965: 4). According to Tom Grunfeld, who cited some studies of Indian scholars, Tibetans were resettled according to their social and economic status:

> While all classes of Tibetans fled Tibet, it appears—if these studies are accurate—that the poorer classes are being relegated to the hotter, more economically depressed, more crowded agricultural settlements where education and employment opportunities are far below those in the northern refugee centres such as Darjeeling, Kalimpong, New Delhi, Dehra Dun, Dharamsala etc.
>
> (1987: 198)

Again, this statement stressed the importance of the pre-exile context, i.e. the social stratification of the Tibetan societies and its consequences. To work successfully in resettling the exile Tibetans, international NGOs realized the importance of coordinating their activities. Such an approach '. . . would minimize ad hocism inherent in relief operations, as various relief agencies act in separate ways in response to emergency situations overlapping their actions' (Norbu 2001a: 210). By 1963, the voluntary organizations summarized that their efforts had been less effective than assumed at the initial stage. As a result, almost all Western NGOs involved in the rehabilitation and resettlement process began to channel their funds through the hands of Indian agencies. Under Indian leadership, international helpers were able to identify basic needs and problems and systematically work together to achieve a long-term solution for the Tibetans in India. Thus, matters concerning exile Tibetans could be successfully conducted as interplay between the GOI, the international NGOs and the CTA (Norbu 2001a: 211; Goldstein 1975a: 162).

Slowly, the GOI delegated authority over the settlements in India to the CTA under the leadership of the 14th Dalai Lama. This automatic acceptance of the 14th Dalai Lama as spokesman of the exile Tibetans eased the communication between the GOI and the CTA. But according to Dawa Norbu, it also illustrated a concession of India's unwillingness or inability to recognize officially the CTA as Tibetan government-in-exile despite persistent pleas and considerable support by the Indian public, which increased even more after 1962. Furthermore, it was a gesture of respect towards the institution of the Dalai Lama, his moral authority and his leadership of an administrative structure. This official acknowledgement of the Tibetan leadership was a convenient and suitable solution for the GOI to support the exile Tibetans and respond to the Indian public. Consequently, the CTA got the affirmation of the legal right to exercise administrative control over all Tibetan settlements in India, suited to the Indian regulations of a non-assimilative resettlement (Norbu 2001a: 213). The shifted responsibilities from the GOI to the CTA was moreover a favorable decision for India because it still feared a Chinese attack. Shain mentions in this context that '[b]y providing shelter and support, the host state makes itself vulnerable to home regime reprisals, often exposing its own society to violence resulting from the political struggles of others' (1989: 120). Now, India was not in the first instance responsible for the exile Tibetans any more.

By 1965, members of the GOI, the CTA and foreign aid agencies founded the Tibetan Industrial Rehabilitation Society (TIRS) to rehabilitate Tibetans in agro–industrial settlements. These projects met the requirements of the 14th Dalai Lama to develop self-supporting communities. In the exile Tibetan context, agro–industrial means the settlements were initially based on tea estates, woollen mills, lime quarry, dehydrated lime-production, etc. For various reasons, most of the initial projects failed and the settlements were reorganized into handicraft-based settlements. Still, in 1994, 44.9 per cent of the Tibetan working population was primarily employed in agricultural activities, another 5.8 per cent in animal husbandry (CTA 1994a: 77). According to CTA publications, in 1998 there were in total 52 formal exile Tibetan settlements in India, Nepal and Bhutan, out of which 17 were agro–industrial settlements, 26 agricultural and 11 handicraft-based settlements. Besides, Tibetans, especially those who were not registered, also lived in scattered communities and various towns in India (CTA 2004: 40). The settlers in the handicraft-based settlements relied basically on carpet weaving as their economic base, a duty that met, according to the CTA, the requirement of the preservation of Tibetan culture and religion (CTA 2004: 24; 1969: 95–120). To sum up, one can say that the CTA dominated the resettlement progress through its access to international supporters and in its position to act on behalf of the exile Tibetans. In this regard, the CTA could prove its political position as Tibetan representative.

While one can say that in general, the resettlement process was smoothly implemented, Frechette's book *Tibetans in Nepal: The Dynamics of International Assistance among a Community in Exile* showed that there were and still are few exceptions. Here, international assistance organizations questioned the ideas of the CTA regarding resettlement, citizenship, schooling, etc. (Frechette 2004). One example in India, where a group of Tibetans challenged the authority of the CTA, demonstrates the founding of the organization '13 Settlements' in 1965. This organization consisted of individuals and regional groups from eastern Tibet under the leadership of 13 chiefs and religious dignitaries. These Tibetans were only partly willing to accept the organizational schemata of the CTA resettlement process. They refused the efforts of the CTA to assimilate them in the politically dominant central Tibetan structure, while at the same time denying their own traditions. Such homogenization strategy became obvious when Gyalo Thondup, who had acted as leading head of the TWA, increasingly gained political influence during the 1960s, mainly due to his outstanding foreign language skills and his personal relations to his younger brother, the 14th Dalai Lama. Gyalo Thondup and his followers tried to implement the homogenization ideas of the CTA on their own initiative and founded the first political party in exile, the Tibetan United Party (TUA). This party worked under the CTA and focused on the strengthening of solidarity and unity among all exile Tibetans through emphasizing similar ideals as the Chinese communists. The concept basically consisted of three main points: confiscating of private money to create a balanced economic base for all exile Tibetans, neutralization of traditional Tibetan class differences and unification of all religious sects (interview with Mr Chakzoe Ngawang Tenpa, TUA, Dharamsala, April 2003; Tethong 2000: 99–106). While the majority of exile Tibetans stood idly by, the Tibetans of the '13 Settlements' opposed the 1965 introduction of social, economic and religious reforms by the TUA. As a consequence of such opposition an informant remembers that '... the 13 groups were totally left alone without any help [from the rest of the exile community] to settle somewhere' (anonymous interview, 2003). According to Wangpo Tethong, the eastern Tibetans disagreed with the plans because of the existing different cultural and political traditions of eastern and central Tibetans. On the practical level, the eastern Tibetan chiefs intended to secure their traditional leadership within their communities and therefore encountered constraints to legitimate their role through economic power. Additionally, the eastern Tibetans wished to have their own interest group in future negotiations about the status of Tibet between the CTA and the Chinese leadership. The Tibetan historian Samten Karmay stated in this context:

> However, not all of the Tibetan refugees depended solely on the central administration [CTA] for their resettlement. Several people took the initiative to lead their own group. As they gradually settled down they developed their own policies which more often than not clashed with those of the central administration . . . There is no doubt that the most important undercurrent which brought this group together was the desire to counteract possible future danger based on the old fear of abandonment, i.e., that one day the Tibetan government in exile might enter into negotiations with China and sell out Amdo and Kham in order to gain independence for Central Tibet.
>
> (cited in Tethong 2000: 110–11)

The entire conflict, which caused many financial disadvantages for the eastern Tibetans in exile, ended in the founding of 13 CTA independent settlements in India, which were set-up with the help of international donors but still with the official agreement by the 14th Dalai Lama (Tethong 2000: 106–15; interviews with Mr Sedonyon and Mr Ugyen Tobgyal, Bir, April 2003). Furthermore, in 1971, all organization members and settlers applied for Indian citizenship, which was strictly opposed by the CTA for the sake of unity in exile (DeVoe 1987: 56; Goldstein 1975a: 180). As a consequence, the CTA entered into negotiations with the GOI to solve the dispute. The Indian authorities finally settled the matter after long discussion by stopping the social, economic and religious reforms of the TUA. In return, the settlers withdrew their applications for Indian citizenship. The leader of the '13 Settlements' was shot by an unidentified person, an assassination that has not been solved to the present day, but it was suspected that the murder came from within the exile Tibetan community (*Tibetan Review* 1978). Despite the official end of the exile conflict, the eastern Tibetan settlers and large parts of the Kham minority in exile refused to pay the annual 'voluntary freedom tax' to the CTA (see Ch. 5) until the 1980s to demonstrate their disagreement with official exile politics (interviews with Mr Sedonyo and Mr Ugyen Tobgyal, Bir, April 2003; Tethong 2000: 106–15).

This dispute illustrates first, the tendencies of separation based on regional differences. To minimize these inclinations among the exile Tibetans, the political elite has held considerable sway over all exile Tibetan settlements. While the regional diversity is still widely downplayed in the exile Tibetan community, it had been converted to the present day into a current Tibetan national problem in which outcome the CTA faces certain difficulties to create unity among all Tibetans. Second, the conflict shows the dependency of the CTA on the Indian host. Only through the intervention of the GOI could the differences be settled.

Map 2 shows the location of all Tibetan settlements in India and Nepal. It has to be mentioned that there is one additional exile Tibetan settlement with a Tibetan Muslim population, in Srinagar, in the Indian border region of Jammu and Kashmir, which is not depicted in Map 2.[13] As mentioned earlier, numerous Tibetans also live in scattered communities in Nepal and India.

Initially, the 14th Dalai Lama had planned to resettle and rehabilitate all exile Tibetans in India for the reason that they would be close to Tibet. This plan proved unfeasible mainly because of the land shortage in India, which became more acute as the Indian population grew. To lighten the burden of India and save his national compatriots from physical misery, the 14th Dalai Lama took action in revising his initial plans and focusing also on the resettlement of Tibetans outside India. Consequently, he wanted to give the exiles a chance for a 'proper existence and means to become self-supporting' (*News Letter* 1967: 8). Many Tibetans followed his idea and moved abroad from the 1960s onwards. This plan shows that the Tibetan leader and his administration were in the powerful position to decide about the resettlement of thousands of people.

Bhutan

Despite Bhutan being on one of the main flight routes from Tibet to India, only a few Tibetans decided to settle there in the first two years after 1959. Those who wanted to stay were welcome settlers, mainly because of the close ethnic ties between Tibetans and Bhutanese. In 1961, India closed its northern border to Bhutan because of an increasing political tension with the PRC, so many Tibetans were stuck in Bhutan on their way southwards. As the Bhutanese government was afraid to deal with the thousands of Tibetans in the country, a meeting took place in the following year in Calcutta between the Indian Political Officer of Sikkim, the Prime Minister of Bhutan and representatives of the GOI and the CTA. There it was decided that 4,000 Tibetans would be allowed to settle in Bhutan (CTA 1969: 162–72).

By 1973, tensions between the Bhutanese government and the Tibetan settlers arose, first because of a growing national consciousness in Bhutan; second, the privileges the Tibetan settlers had compared with the local Bhutanese population; third, because of the curious circumstances of the assassination of the Bhutanese king, and fourth, because of the Tibetans' non-assimilative way of living. All these facts led to general suspicion among the Bhutanese of the Tibetan settlers. A political reaction to this followed in 1974, when 28 Tibetans in Bhutan were arrested and accused of involvement in the Bhutanese king's assassination. Furthermore, all Tibetans on Bhutanese soil were

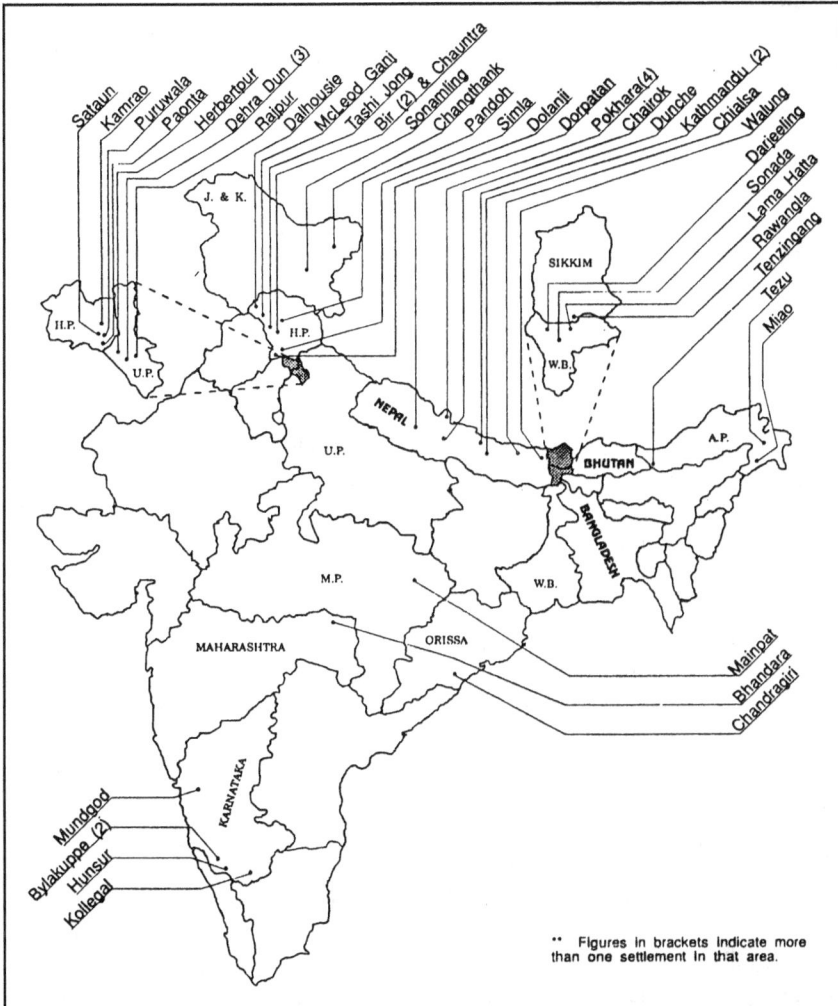

Map 2 Tibetan settlements in India and Nepal (*Source*: CTA 1994a: v). From *Tibetan Refugee Community: Integrated Development Plan – II 1995–2000*, page v, Planninng Council, CTA (1994). Reprinted with kind permission from the Planning Council, CTA.

requested to take Bhutanese citizenship with the threat of repatriation to the PRC if they did not do so.[14] As a consequence, in the following two years, three CTA-delegations went to Bhutan to discuss the matter of citizenship. The CTA put high importance on the question of new citizenship, which again substantiates Shain's theoretical considerations regarding the acquiring of a host country's citizenship. After numerous negotiation meetings, which were reported extensively in the exile Tibetan press and showed the interest of the CTA to play a superior role for the exile Tibetans,[15] 2,300 Tibetans finally applied for Bhutanese citizenship—against the will of the government-in-exile (Misra 1982: 30). The remainder of the 4,000 Tibetans were resettled in India. In 1998, the Tibetan population in Bhutan had decreased to only 1,584 Tibetans (CTA 2000f: 7).

Nepal

Nepal also represented a main transit country for the fleeing Tibetans. During the first three years, around 20,000 Tibetans arrived in Nepal, but most of them continued on to India. Those who stayed in Nepal were to a large extent originally from the Tibetan border areas. With the help of the UNHCR and several international organizations, the government in Kathmandu set-up 14 Tibetan settlements in cooperation with the CTA. But only 35 per cent of the Tibetans lived in one of these settlements. The majority were scattered in remote regions of the Himalayas near the Tibetan border (CTA 1969: 136–61). There they were either involved in cross-border trade or lived in poor conditions with little hope of a better future (Grunfeld 1987: 200). According to official numbers, there are at present between 13,720 and 30,000 Tibetans living in Nepal.[16] Unofficial statistics even put the number of Tibetans in Nepal as high as 100,000 (Moynihan 2004: 313). Again, the problems of getting accurate data about the numbers of exile Tibetans becomes apparent. Despite a geographical closeness and the similar landscape to the homeland, Tibetans in Nepal have a harder life than their compatriots in India, mainly due to unfavorable economic and political circumstances in Nepal. Job opportunities in Nepal are limited; several times, the Nepalese government has repatriated exile Tibetans to the PRC and since 1995, the authorities have not issued any new residential cards for Tibetans. This means that all Tibetans who arrived in Nepal after 1995 are illegal in the country, a status that entails tremendous consequences for the affected persons with regard to their standard of living and future prospects (interview with Mr Jigme Wangdu, CTA Office of Tibet, Kathmandu, May 2003). One way to ease their lives and, for instance, to become landholders, is to become Nepali citizens, but this option is strongly opposed by the CTA (Frechette 2004: 44).

Switzerland and other European countries

The events in 1959 in Lhasa and the departure of thousands of Tibetans from their homeland caused general sympathy in Switzerland for the Tibetan nation. Under pressure from the Swiss public and the request of the 14th Dalai Lama to accommodate Tibetan orphans in particular in Switzerland, the Swiss government took action in 1960 and granted asylum to 20 exile Tibetan children (Dalai Lama 1996: 181). They were placed with Swiss families or lived in the Pestalozzi Children's Village in Trogen. Between 1961 and 1964, another 160 Tibetan children were allowed to go to Switzerland. These were followed by 1,000 adults, who were mainly resettled with the help of the

Swiss government (which covered 75 per cent of the total costs), private sources and the Swiss Red Cross. In the 1980s, an additional batch of several hundred Tibetans arrived in Switzerland. In 1998, there were 1,538 Tibetans living in Switzerland—the European country with the largest number of exile Tibetans (CTA 2000f: 38).[17]

Besides the exile Tibetan population in Switzerland, there are also growing numbers of Tibetans living in other European countries, such as France (in 1998: 150 Tibetans), Germany (146), the UK (137) and Italy (75). Smaller numbers of Tibetans live in the Scandinavian countries, the Netherlands, Greece, Liechtenstein, Hungary and Poland (CTA 2000f: 38). The first Tibetans who came to the non-Swiss European countries were students and Tibetan scholars. No scholar has conducted research on exile Tibetans in these countries yet, probably because of the relatively insignificant numbers. According to my research findings, the number of exile Tibetans in the European Union (EU) has been growing in the last few years, which makes the CTA statistics of 1998 outdated (anonymous interviews, 2003).

North America

In 1998, exile Tibetan statisticians counted approximately 7,000 Tibetans in North America (CTA 2000f: 38). The first Tibetans who went there were members of a Tibetan Trade Delegation in 1947. A year later, the first Tibetan residents, religious dignitaries and members of the Tibetan aristocracy entered the USA (Dharlo 1994: 12). In the 1960s, the 14th Dalai Lama requested the Canadian and US governments to grant asylum to Tibetans, but without much success. Only six Tibetans were given work permits because they were hired by a US-company as lumberjacks in 1967; 21 Tibetans followed soon because of labor shortages. Over the years, the US government has allowed more and more exile Tibetans to stay in the country. Most of them were either students, religious teachers or scholars. After the massacres in Tiananmen Square and with the help of several TSGs, the US Immigration Act passed in 1990, gave 1,000 exile Tibetans the chance to immigrate to the USA and get US citizenship. Surprisingly, the granting of US citizenship to the Tibetans was not opposed by the CTA. The migrating Tibetans were rather anticipated to promote the Tibetan cause in the USA and consequently support the exile struggle (anonymous interview, 2006). There were far more applications for the 1,000 visas, so a lottery system was introduced for who could leave south Asia. According to rumors in Dharamsala, the selection process was unfair, giving CTA officials and their relatives and high skilled Tibetans preference. Even though there were many hardships during the first years, the USA has been ever since the most favored country for exile Tibetans (Gyaltag 2002; Messerschmidt 1976; Dale 1969). The younger generation in exile prefers to live at least temporarily in the USA. In this regard, the Dalai Lama's initial plans in the 1960s to resettle numerous Tibetans abroad developed to an accepted trend in the Tibetan community.

At the beginning of the 1970s, the Canadian government granted 500 visas to exile Tibetans. This decision was made mainly due to the good experiences that the Swiss government had published. According to Grunfeld, the Canadians carefully sorted out the Tibetans who were supposed to be settled in Canada: '... weeding out the poor and uneducated' (1987: 204), which illustrates that not all Tibetans were welcome to stay in Canada.

The set-up of an exile Tibetan education system

The first wave of Tibetans who entered the Indian subcontinent encountered unexpected difficulties regarding their educational skills, which were necessary to secure their daily survival. In the traditional Tibetan context, literacy was obtained either by family members or in the high strata of the society through the attendance of home or government schools. Additionally, there were few specialized schools teaching arts and medicine to the children of the wealthy. But the most important centers of education were the numerous Tibetan Buddhist monasteries. Consequently, the ecclesiastic community and the aristocrats were educated, while large parts of the Tibetan society, the rural population in particular, remained either illiterate or had only rudimentary knowledge (Goldstein 1975a: 160; Richardson 1984: 13–14). Katrin Goldstein-Kyaga revealed that only 67 per cent of the male and 21 per cent of the female Tibetans who came to India in the initial years could read and write Tibetan (1993). These educational lacks were soon recognized by the 14th Dalai Lama. Apart from the Tibetans' limited abilities to adapt themselves into the new environment, he interpreted the lack of knowledge and awareness towards international political developments among his people as one reason for the loss of the homeland. Consequently, from the early years in exile, the 14th Dalai Lama gave the educational sector top priority and pushed the set-up of exile Tibetan schools. Because of the initial financial constraints of the CTA, the implementation of this plan was only possible through the enormous support of the GOI and international NGOs. Additionally, the CTA faced numerous judicial difficulties, which needed to be rectified for the long-term existence of exile Tibetan schools as an integral part of the Indian system. With the founding of the Council for Tibetan Education (CTE), the 14th Dalai Lama set-up a special institution to look after the education of exile Tibetans. The CTE was headed by a Tibetan who was directly appointed by the 14th Dalai Lama. Such selection illustrates the priority of education in the eyes of the Tibetan leader but also represents a way of control for eventual intervention. The integration of the CTE in the Indian educational system was accomplished by the work of the Tibetan School Society, an independent body founded in 1961, which worked under the supervision of the Indian educational ministry. This interaction between the CTA and the GOI gives evidence of the importance of a friendly relationship between exiles and their hosts. The CTA stated in that context:

The Government of India reacted generously and under the steward-ship of the late Prime Minister, Pandit Jawaharlal Nehru, a special educational scheme was set-up for the Tibetan children. It was to become the backbone of the educational programme for Tibetan children and has been the mainstay of efforts in this direction . . .

(CTE cited in John 1999: 297)

At present, there are 80 Tibetan schools in India, Nepal and Bhutan, which are all supervised by the educational authorities of the host countries.[18] During the decades in exile, four different kinds of Tibetan schools have been developing, which differ in their funding and administration.[19] Most of the schools offer free primary education while further studies need to be paid for by the parents. If a Tibetan family is not able to afford the fees for secondary education, it can apply to the CTA for a sponsorship.

Approximately half of the 25,463 enrolled Tibetans study in residential schools.[20] While in the early years schools were only set-up in those settlements where the needs and the financial resources made such projects feasible, today they are spread all over the Indian, Nepali and Bhutanese areas where Tibetans settle. Primary schools can also be found in remote areas. This is one reason for a high school enrolment of 85–90 per cent for all Tibetans of school age. Additionally, some schools offer special educational opportunities for adults, for newcomers and for those who want to be trained in crafts. According to the CTA (2000f: 10–11) the literacy rate in 1998 was at 69 per cent (male: 42 per cent; female: 27 per cent). In a later evaluation in 2001, it was at 74 per cent. This was higher than the literacy rate in India, which was 65.4 per cent in 2001 (CTA 2004: 62). There are no independent and scholarly reflected data about the exile Tibetan literacy rate. Thus, following the CTA, the initially introduced literacy campaign has achieved its goals.[21]

Besides the Tibetan pupils, there are also local Indian and Nepali children enrolled in exile Tibetan schools. Such intercultural interaction is viewed by CTA officials of the Department of Education as an opportunity to create awareness of the situation of the Tibetans among the host population. But the decision of the non-Tibetan parents to enroll their children in Tibetan schools is not predominantly motivated by the idea of an intercultural exchange, but rather by their given economic and local constraints. They either live in remote areas where no other schools exist, in poor economic conditions, which do not allow the family to pay tuition fees, or the Indian and Nepali parents 'are attracted by relatively high educational standards in the exile Tibetan schools' (interview with Mr Tashi Rika, Department of Education, Dharamsala, April 2002). Nevertheless, the acceptance of the Tibetan schools by the host population and the attendance of local pupils provide the CTA with an opportunity to promote its political ideas in the host countries. From a theoretical point of view, the exile Tibetan educational institutions can be interpreted as material incentives that are not only invested by the exile administration to create national loyalty but also used to mobilize or at least sensitize the host population for the exile struggle. As mentioned previously, such a general understanding and resulting support for the exile situation among the host population was important for the Tibetans right from the beginning.

In contrast, there are also Tibetans who send their children to non-Tibetan schools. This happens for the most part among those who live in Western countries due to the simple fact that there are no specifically Tibetan schools. In such cases, the parents educate their children at weekends in Tibetan language and culture. Such private engagement is particularly enforced by the CTA through appeals and discussions to ensure that all Tibetans are in contact with their cultural heritage (interview with Mr Tashi Rika, Department of Education, Dharamsala, April 2002; Albers and Fuchs 1993: 44).

To summarize, the exile Tibetans have been successfully resettled and rehabilitated in India, Nepal and Bhutan but also in Western countries of Europe and North America. The CTA played a central role in the whole process—a position supported by the succession of traditional leadership and pre-exile loyalties but also by the GOI and Western aid agencies, which unquestioningly agreed to CTA dominance on behalf of all exile Tibetans. This international acknowledgement in turn emphasized the political status of the CTA within the exile Tibetan community and illustrates the importance of international humanitarian help. In the context of resettlement, it has to be pointed out that the CTA insistently discouraged the taking of new citizenship of the host countries. From a theoretical point of view, the CTA invested 'purposive incentives' to bar the Tibetans from taking a new citizenship. In the name of Tibet, exile Tibetans are called to remain stateless. One exception is the US resettlement program, where Tibetans were requested to support the exile struggle through the promotion of the Tibetan cause in North America.

The CTA also played an important role in the establishment of an exile Tibetan education system, a process that was, again, considerably supported by the GOI and international aid. The Tibetan government-in-exile has always functioned as the key institution that linked the exile Tibetan community, international NGOs and the host administration. Only through a close interaction of these different actors were the initial problems of the exile Tibetans regarding their educational skills overcome. Furthermore, the set-up of the Tibetan education system in exile showed exemplarily the high dependency of the CTA on the goodwill of the host country. Today, a close-meshed net of schools and the work of Tibetan officials in the settlements secure a high literacy among Tibetans in south Asia and therefore are responsible for the success of the exile Tibetan schooling system. Apart from the Tibetans, there are also local children who are educated in the exile Tibetan schools. This trend influences the contact between the exile community and the host population from the early school years. Tibetan parents in foreign countries are encouraged by the CTA to educate their children at home in Tibetan language and customs to bring all Tibetans in contact with their traditions and cultural heritage. This in turn serves the CTA's policy of the preservation of Tibetan culture and religion and therefore supports the exile Tibetan 'struggle'.

But in the context of education, one can ask: Why did the CTA set up its own schools instead of enroll the exile children into the already existing Indian, Nepali and Bhutanese schools? To answer this, in the early years in particular, the CTA faced enormous financial constraints and therefore it would have been less problematic to use the available capacities for basic education. I look at this topic from an analytical point of view in Chapter 5, after a further portrayal of CTA politics.

Regarding the exile—host relationship, the Indian host country profited in the domestic sphere in political and economic ways. The Nehru government improved the chances of its own political survival and its image among the Indian public through the resettlement of the exile Tibetans at a politically unstable time. Furthermore, an anticipated economic acceleration in rural and economically backward areas through the resettling of the exile Tibetans exceeded all expectations. Tourism in particular created manifold spill-over effects in the local economy, e.g. in public transport and the catering trade. Additionally, the Indian national economy profited from the export of high quality Tibetan carpets to Western countries, which increased the producer's income significantly but also transferred considerable amounts of foreign currency to India, which in turn had positive effects on the Indian account surplus (Banerjee 1982: 16). The presence of the Tibetans also influenced India's national security concerns. The long prevailing Sino–Indian conflict became acute with the arrival of thousands of Tibetans in India. The GOI used the Tibetans as instrumental in the reaction to the Chinese threat and Dawa Norbu summarized that '[t]here is no denying the fact that New Delhi used the Tibetan card whenever politics of Sino–Indian relation demanded it' (1996).

The exile struggle: changing politics

Since the founding of the CTA, the exile Tibetan struggle has been in a constant process of change regarding its focus in terms of international support, its goals and the pre-conditions to regain the homeland. Immediately after the 14th Dalai Lama's arrival in India, he profited from relatively wide international media coverage by promoting the plight of Tibetans through articles and TV reports. Tibet was brought back into the international political arena for the first time since the end of the Great Game. The Tibetan political elite in exile used this wide interest to lobby the UN, which finally passed three resolutions: in 1959 (No. 1353/14), in 1961 (1723/16) and in 1965 (2079/20) (CTA 1997: 4–6). There, the UN General Assembly expressed its concern about human rights violations in Tibet (Morris and Scoble 1990: 177). But the initial expectations of the CTA, that the UN would be in a powerful position to help them, was disappointed by the fact that the PRC was in such a dominant political position in the international sphere that the resolutions had no consequence on its activities in Tibet. Since 1971, the exile Tibetan efforts to raise awareness in the UN became increasingly complicated, first because the US Nixon administration altered its focus in the Cold War and stopped struggling against China, which had the side-effect that the USA lost interest in Tibetans and withdrew its support from them (Xu 1997: 1066). And second, in 1971 China was conferred its own membership into the UN. The permanent seat in the UN Security Council provided the Chinese leadership with powerful instruments to block any resolution on Tibet.

Besides the UN, the exile Tibetans had always sought to solve the Tibetan issue on a bilateral basis between Dharamsala and Beijing. These efforts were officially represented by numerous negotiations between the PRC and the exile Tibetans at a high political level, especially after the fall of Mao in 1976. The 14th Dalai Lama's elder brother Gyalo Thondup was invited to China several times to discuss the Tibet issue. Finally in 1978, Thondup visited Beijing with the Dalai Lama's approval. This event was followed by three CTA fact-finding delegations to Tibet in the years 1979, 1980 and 1984, accompanied by sporadic contacts between Beijing and Dharamsala. In the end, the Chinese leadership invited the 14th Dalai Lama to return for good, which he rejected in the mid-1980s (*Tibetan Bulletin* 1997b; Hilton 2003: 226). Since then, there have been constant contacts between the exile Tibetan leadership and Chinese officials but with inconsiderable outcomes.

The CTA changed its political focus at the beginning of the 1980s realizing that neither the UN was acting in the interest of Tibet nor the bilateral contacts with the Chinese leadership would bring the desired results. So the focus was then shifted from the UN to international NGOs. Since then, the so-called snowball effect, where one NGO was approached by the CTA and carried Tibet related issues to others, became the center of an exile Tibetan grassroots policy (interview with Mr Thupten Samphel, DIIR, Dharamsala, May 2002). The CTA reacted to political developments and looked for a more promising niche to generate support for the exile Tibetan struggle (Goldstein 1997: 75–8). According to Shain's theoretical approach, the exile Tibetans changed the packaging of their exile struggle as the Tibetan issue was no longer presented as a whole but rather split into different parts, which could be easily taken up by various international activists. Since the altered focus, it is difficult to make a distinction between the efforts to return to a free homeland and the mobilization of international support. Especially during the last two decades, exile Tibetans have taken up several Western political key issues, like human rights, non-violence, environmental protection, women's rights and peace (see Ch. 5). Through the presentation of these topics to an international audience, the exile Tibetans, with the 14th Dalai Lama in the lead, have been increasingly successful in terms of generating international financial support and awareness. The exile Tibetans have managed to create an impression as propagators of Tibetan Buddhism, as peaceful and friendly with a deep insight into religious practice (interview with Mr Thupten Samphel, DIIR, Dharamsala, May 2002). Despite the switch to the international grassroots level, exile Tibetans have still been lobbying the UN institutions in New York and Geneva through different Tibet offices.

At the same time, in the 1980s, the CTA also changed its pre-conditions for return home and therefore the goal of the exile struggle. Until the mid-1980s the CTA focused exclusively on an independent Tibet in the borders of Cholka Sum. The change of this goal found its beginning with a statement of the Chinese leadership in 1979 that was only willing to negotiate with the exile Tibetan leadership under the assumption that they would shift their focus from total independence to autonomy.[22] With regard to the Chinese requirement to enter into a dialogue, the 14th Dalai Lama, while addressing the US Congressional Human Rights Caucus, promulgated in 1987 the so-called 'Five Point Peace Plan'. This plan, seen as a landmark in exile Tibetan politics, formed the basis for the later Sino–Tibetan dialogue. The plan contains the following points:

1 Transformation of the whole of Tibet (including the eastern provinces of Kham and Amdo) into a zone of peace.
2 Abandonment of China's population transfer policy, which threatens the very existence of the Tibetans as a people.
3 Respect for the Tibetan people's fundamental human rights and demo-cratic freedoms.
4 Restoration and protection of Tibet's natural environment and the abandonment of China's use of Tibet for the production of nuclear weapons and dumping of nuclear waste.
5 Commencement of earnest negotiations on the future status of Tibet and of relations between the Tibetan and Chinese people. (CTA 1995: 12)

In June 1988, the 14th Dalai Lama elaborated on this plan in an address to the European Parliament in Strasbourg. In the so-called 'Strasbourg Proposal', the Dalai Lama explained his ideas of a future democratic and self-governing Tibet in association with the PRC. The Chinese authorities would be responsible for Tibet's foreign affairs while Tibet was to handle autonomously its internal affairs. The 'Strasbourg Proposal' was a turning point in exile Tibetan politics as the 14th Dalai Lama took the decision to aim the exile Tibetan struggle towards autonomy rather than independence, assuming that this was a general wish of his national compatriots.

To achieve an autonomous Tibet, the exile Tibetan political elite focused on a non-violent struggle. With the 12th Assembly of Tibetan People's Deputies (ATPD) (1995–2001), non-violence became, besides truth and genuine demo-cratic governance, a fundamental principle for the CTA to serve the Tibetan nation (CTA 2003: 5). The non-violent approach has since then become known as the 'Middle Path' or 'Middle-Way' policy of the CTA.[23] It was a clear and pragmatic appeal to the international community as a whole to prevent war and violent quarrels. Since then, the peace message has spread from Dharamsala all over the world through videos, tapes, radio programs and books. For the exile Tibetan elite around the 14th Dalai Lama, non-violence was and still is the only acceptable method to fight the Chinese. Over the years, it has developed into a powerful instrument for return to Tibet, which was especially emphasized by the international feedback, such as the awarding of the Nobel Peace Prize to the 14th Dalai Lama in 1989. In this regard, the non-violent struggle has helped to mobilize increasing support from 'guilt-ridden foreigners' (McGuckin 1997: 86; Pike 2001: 16). But the concept had no effect at the pragmatic level because international economic interests in the Chinese market and a relatively predictable power equilibrium in Asia, with China and India as the main actors, have been thus far the center of every political discussion rather than Tibet.

The 14th Dalai Lama's compromise in moving from independence to autonomy had no effect on the Chinese authority's willingness to negotiate either. Moreover, the Dalai Lama was requested to agree to the Chinese perceptions that Tibet had always been a part of China. This would have given the PRC an official legitimacy for their action and the Tibetan freedom struggle would have been officially over. In September 1991 the 'Strasbourg Proposal' was withdrawn by a newly elected cabinet of the CTA and with the Dalai Lama's approval because of a lack of '. . . sincere commitment to finding a solution to the issue . . .' on the side of the PRC (CTA 1995: 36–42, 54–6).

During the next five years, the exile Tibetan leadership considered different approaches regarding the question of Tibet. According to Barry Sautman, in 1993 the 14th Dalai Lama focused again on an autonomous Tibet but at the same time he affirmed that an independent Tibet remained the goal. So the 'Tibetans would settle for autonomy until their ultimate goal was achieved' (14th Dalai Lama, cited in Sautman 2000: 56). A year later, the exile Tibetan leader defined future Sino–Tibetan relations as a federation, whereby China would be responsible for Tibetan foreign affairs and defense. This idea was altered again in 1996 after an exile Tibetan referendum took place to decide about the final goal and policies of the exile Tibetan struggle. A referendum became necessary as there was growing frustration and impatience within the exile Tibetan community, first because of a lack of result in the 14th Dalai Lama's non-violent struggle and second, due to confusion about the final goal during the first half of the 1990s. Despite general international support of the Tibetan non-violence concept, there was still a large faction of exile Tibetans who would consider the use of violent acts to reach the final goal. In this regard, the CTA encountered considerable problems within the exile community and found itself with the problem of how to serve all interests—national and international. Recently, the 14th Dalai Lama emphasized again the concept of non-violence by announcing that '. . . he would resign the moment the Tibetan freedom movement took a violent turn'.[24] Such a conflicting situation has not yet been viewed by Shain, and therefore portrays a new theoretical problem in the context of exile governments. Because of its shaky political position, an exile government needs to maneuver carefully between the different and possible conflicting interests of the national and international community, to expand and maintain the support of both sides.

Because of the growing tension among exile Tibetans, the issue of clarifying the exile struggle was submitted on the 14th Dalai Lama's initiative to a referendum in 1995. The Tibetan people's choice was claimed to be essential in the decision about the future political course. The referendum was prepared for two years with a CTA campaign to instruct all exile Tibetans in four different CTA policy alternatives about which they were asked to decide. The first alternative was the 'Middle-Way' (lam uma), i.e. maintenance of the status quo in combination with an attempt to renew the dialogue with the PRC about genuine Tibetan autonomy. The second policy option described the struggle for Tibetan independence (rangzen), which would break with the existing basis of a dialogue with the PRC—a strategy equivalent to that of the first 20 exile years. The third choice was the struggle for Tibetan self-determination (rangthag rangchö) under the supervision of the UN. Finally, the fourth alternative represented the concept of Satyagraha (denpay utsug), the 'guiding philosophy' of Mahatma Gandhi to fight non-violently the British in India between the 1920s and 1940s (Tsering 1997a: 11–12, 21; Ardley 2002).

The electoral turn-out of the referendum showed that around 66 per cent of the participating exile Tibetans voted for the 'Middle-Way'. The total number of participants was not available for an outside researcher, but it has to be noted that the largest exile Tibetan NGO, the Tibetan Youth Congress (TYC), had called upon the exile people to boycott the voting. This was because in the TYC's opinion, the exile Tibetan community is not in a position to represent the opinion of the compatriots who still live in Tibet (Tsering 1997b: 11). In this regard, the TYC undermined the representative claims of the CTA. Consequently, it can be assumed that only a part of the exile Tibetan community went to the polls. Additionally, a few votes and opinions came from inside the PRC, which showed that Tibetans in the homeland knew about happenings in India. But there was no information on if they were called by the CTA to participate in the referendum. Despite the selectiveness, these votes were given great importance among the CTA officials and were interpreted as the will of the whole Tibetan community in the homeland. The election result, to follow the 'Middle-Way', was reworded in the following session of the ATPD, that the majority of the Tibetans were leaving the decision about the exile Tibetan policy to the 14th Dalai Lama. Furthermore, he was entitled to change the policy in the future according to international developments (interview with Mr Kelsang Gyaltsen, Special Envoy of the Dalai Lama to the EU, Berlin, March 2004; Samdhong Rinpoche 2002: 6). According to Frechette's research, the reinterpretation of the result was necessary because '. . . the Tibetan exile officials concluded that most Tibetan exiles are still not educated enough to decide how the exile administration should proceed' (2004: 167)—a decision that made the whole referendum questionable. The instrument of democratic elections was solely used to 'maintain the myth of return' (Frechette 2004: 165) but not to empower people. Since then, the CTA has followed the 'Middle-Way' as a basis for negotiation with the PRC, under the guiding principles of truth, non-violence and genuine democratic governance.

While the result of the referendum was clear for the exile Tibetan leading elite, it caused considerable confusion among the humble exile Tibetans. For the majority, the official change of goals of the exile Tibetan struggle from an independent to an autonomous Tibet was not in line with the wish to free the home country as soon as possible. They remained committed to a historically independent homeland (Ardley 2002: 178). Numerous Tibetans interpreted the changed focus as a step backwards, which in turn affected the political climate and perhaps also served as a reason for an obvious disinterest in political matters in exile (see Ch. 5). Consequently, the CTA's claim to enjoy the support of all Tibetan people to implement the Dalai Lama's compromise of autonomy has not as yet reached many Tibetans. Instead, they still follow the idea of independence, while of course at the same time granting their loyalty to the Dalai Lama. The vision of an independent homeland remains unspoken as an ideal among many exile Tibetans. In contrast, the term autonomy, put on the political table by the 14th Dalai Lama, does not enjoy widespread support. Thus, talking about independence in the exile Tibetan community is a taboo subject, while the conversation about autonomy causes conflicts and fears. Many exile Tibetans are confused about the way ahead, the strategies and policies for fighting the Chinese in their homeland and their situation in exile; in short, the 'flirting' strategy of the CTA provides many Tibetans no clear way to the future (Ardley 2002: 178; Taksham 1993: 16). Young Tibetans who are born in India and Nepal specifically do not agree with the moderate CTA political course. For them, the 'Strasbourg Proposal' and the Dalai Lama's compromise to negotiate with the Chinese leadership about autonomy rather than genuine independence further divides the exile community (Monnier 1993: 33).

Despite these obstacles, the 14th Dalai Lama claims that the majority of Tibetans in Tibet and in exile are still struggling for independence. Barry Sautman stated in this context that Tibetan '. . . emigré leaders are convinced that an explicit disavowal of independence will diminish their support and aid Diaspora forces who favor armed struggle and are endorsed by several Dalai Lama's brothers' (2000: 41). This shows that the exile Tibetan elite stresses on the one hand autonomy, anticipating that it is the only way to negotiate with the Chinese leadership. On the other hand, it encounters considerable difficulties within the Tibetan national community through the changed immediate goal of the Tibetan freedom struggle. To overcome this dilemma and bring the exile Tibetan struggle forward, while at the same time securing the loyalty of the national compatriots, the exile Tibetan political elite uses different languages. For instance, the 14th Dalai Lama uses the English language when he talks about the terms 'autonomy' and 'federation', while Tibetan is used for the term 'independence' (rangzen) (Sautman 2000: 31, fnt 1). Such distinction erases the fears in the communication within the Tibetan community because in discussions about the Tibetan future, Tibetans in the homeland and in exile use 'rangzen'. In contrast, at official meetings and in cases when English is needed (i.e. in front of potential sponsors of the exile Tibetan community, international NGOs or TSGs) the exile Tibetan leadership refers to Tibetan autonomy. Thus, language becomes a political instrument to secure loyalty of the Tibetan nation but also to react to present circumstances in the homeland. This in turn shows the vulnerability of an exile government, which needs to secure both national loyalty and international support.

In summary, it can be stated that the exile Tibetan struggle is, after decades, still alive. Moreover, the CTA optimized its functioning and secured its organizational survival. One can argue this is only due to several changes having been undertaken as a reaction on international developments; the CTA altered its focus from the UN to the international grassroots level, its goal from an independent homeland to an autonomous Tibet within China and its political course emphasizing a non-violent struggle. Such shifts were evidence of the vulnerability of the CTA in its position as exile government to international politics, which can be explained with Shain's theoretical approach that stresses the high importance of the international community. Therefore, the implemented policies to mobilize international support and to return home became indistinguishable. But these modifications have not been agreed upon by all Tibetans, especially not by the young generation. As a result, the CTA is in a problematic situation. On the one hand it needs to react to international political and economic developments and on the other hand it is asked to serve the national interests as sole representative of the Tibetan nation. Such discrepancies bring up a new theoretical viewpoint on the political focus of a government-in-exile that needs to serve national and international interests at the same time, which are conflicting. To bridge the gap between the demands of the present leadership in the homeland and those of the Tibetan community, the CTA uses for instance different language as a unifying instrument. This tactical effort portrays the difficult political situation of the CTA. It is constantly under pressure from the Tibetan national community for not achieving enough in reaching the final goal, an independent Tibet. But this goal was and is still not acceptable for the Chinese leadership, which in turn forced the CTA to alter it to emphasize its political position within the Tibetan community. Such change caused fears and disagreement among the Tibetans, who were not willing to support such policy and therefore the CTA. To overcome this dilemma and foster its political position, the CTA appeals at least superficially to all demands through the use of different language.

The structure of the CTA

The structure of the CTA depends on its representational claims. Therefore it is necessary to look at the set-up and political position of the CTA first before examining its political structure. Since its founding, the CTA has been portraying itself as the *de-facto* government of Tibet in exile, despite the fact that it neither rules over a defined territory nor over people—hence the CTA lacks the characteristics of a government according to 'political science'. The CTA exists as organization within the Indian Union and therefore depends on the goodwill of the host. In a self-portrayal the CTA formulated: 'The CTA is recognized by Tibetans, both in and outside Tibet, as their sole and legitimate government. It is also being increasingly recognized as the legitimate government and true representative of the Tibetan people by parliaments round the world' (2001: 1). This statement portrays the CTA as sole representative of the Tibetan nation, which enjoys national loyalty and is internationally recognized in that position. But the reality shows that the CTA lacks official international recognition and also struggles with the loyalties within the Tibetan community, as the following explanations illustrate.

The CTA's legitimacy to act in the name of the entire Tibetan nation is drawn due to a direct link to the former Ganden Phodrang government in Lhasa. Such linear succession of leadership was emphasized by the employment of the same personnel as in the pre-1959 structure in the newly founded exile administration. Around 45 lay and 80 monk officials of the former Tibetan government in Lhasa, activists of the TWA and a few young aristocrats with useful language skills formed the base for the organizational structure in exile. In 1959, the total number of CTA officials was 34, which had risen to 102 by 1965 (interview with Mrs Nangsa Chodon, Public Service Commission, Dharamsala, May 2006). The old elite's ability to communicate in English, taught to them in British missionary schools during their youth, provided them with the opportunity to interact with the outside world and hence to secure their positions of power. Through their education they were the only people within the exile Tibetan community who could handle the new challenges in exile. In addition to such language skills and intellectual capacities, a close and trustful relationship with the 14th Dalai Lama, based on former loyalties was also crucial for professional and social advancement in exile. Additionally, the traditional ranking of the government officials was basically continued (interview with Mr Thupten Samphel, DIIR, Dharamsala, April 2003).

The first symbolic event, at which all exile Tibetan officials were asked to show their loyalty to the newly founded CTA, took place at the end of 1959 in Bodh-Gayā, the place where the historical Buddha attained enlightenment. The meeting was planned to be a political and religious ceremony. The first Tibetan assembly, the Commission of Tibetan Peoples Deputies (CTPD), was installed, in which 13 deputies were intended to serve as exile Tibetan deputies, despite not being elected but rather descended from the Tibetan aristocracy and political elite of the pre-1959 administrative structure. Furthermore, the new officials showed their loyalty to the 14th Dalai Lama through an oath of allegiance and a prayer for his long life. This event marked the interwoven relations between Tibetan politics and religion and gave the oath a deeper meaning for the officials. From a theoretical viewpoint, one can

interpret such an event as an investment of specific solidarity and 'purpositive' incentives. The vows contained, for the first time, the Tibetan term Bö
Cholka Sum (Tibet of the three regions/provinces), which has been developed
since then into a cornerstone of exile Tibetan nationalism (Tethong 2000:
72–4). Tsering Shakya wrote:

> . . . Bod Cholka-sum has become deeply embedded in the political cul-
> ture of the Tibetan diaspora . . . [and] . . . crucial in forging unity among
> diverse refugee groups. But although the idea enjoys universal support
> among the exile community, it has no recent historical base and it is
> difficult to assess the extent of support it might enjoy inside Greater
> Tibet.
>
> (1999: 387)

Considering that the old elites of the central Tibetan government in Lhasa
became the new politicians in the exile Tibetan administration, it was not
surprising that the set-up of the CTA followed pre-1959 structures. Despite
their relative high education, the new exile Tibetan officials had only limited
knowledge about, and no experience with, any political system apart from the
Tibetan and Chinese political systems. Therefore in the early years, the exile
Tibetan officials copied some forms of the Chinese political practice, such as
monthly meetings of self-criticism. Such ideas were supported by the, at the
time, influential elder brother of the 14th Dalai Lama, Gyalo Thondup.
According to Jamyang Norbu, early Western travelers to Dharamsala who
were mainly Hippies and considered Mao's PRC to be a progressive state also
contributed to the implementation of communist ideology (1990: 15). Even a
Tibetan dance and drama show was invented, which was also remembered by
Norbu from Chinese propaganda, showing the unity and discipline of the
modern and progressive Tibetan nation (1990: 15; Tethong 2000: 78).[25] These
developments demonstrate that the international community and the home
country considerably influenced the exile Tibetan system in the initial years
of exile. It is interesting to note that the exile Tibetan political elite is still
fascinated by communist ideas. The 14th Dalai Lama talked on several occasions about the similarities of Buddhism and communism and high exile
Tibetan religious dignitaries traveled often to the Soviet Union and Outer
Mongolia, where they praised the achievements of the communist system
(*Tibetan Bulletin* 1991; *Paljor Bulletin* 2005b).

In the initial years of exile, many Tibetans saw the succession of leadership
in the exile administration as a natural part of the aristocracy's role in
Tibetan society. On the settlement level, the previous local Tibetan leaders
and chieftains, or CTA officials, were responsible for the effective functioning
of daily interaction between exile Tibetans, and acted as a link between them
and the Indian authorities. The continuation of the traditional Tibetan political structures '. . . possesses a high "adaptive capacity" and is the single
most important variable underlying the successful initial adaptation of the

Tibetans' (Goldstein 1975a: 169). Such patterns of pre-exile leadership and organizational structures were and still are instrumental for the success of the exile Tibetan community in terms of organizational unity, stability and the resettlement of thousands of exile Tibetans (Goldstein 1975a: 169; Norbu 2001b: 214–18; Arakeri 1998: 233–7). Additionally, the CTA investments in kindergartens, schools and meeting halls proved to be important '. . . to promote and maintain the idea of a unified and distinct Tibetan community in exile, loyal to the Dalai Lama and his administration, and poised to return to Tibet . . .' (Frechette 2004: 36) among the settlement population. In that context, Melvyn Goldstein mentioned that in 1975 the CTA controlled the monopoly of informational input among the Tibetan settlers in India (Goldstein 1975a: 178). Consequently, the founding of the CTA was a necessary step to concentrate exile Tibetan energies on the struggle against the Chinese.

The fact that no sovereign state recognized the CTA did not alter the position of the functioning *de-facto* legitimate leadership of the 14th Dalai Lama and his officials in the exile Tibetan community as a whole. From the beginning, they interacted with the GOI on behalf of the Tibetan community in exile and maintained small offices in the Tibetan transit camps, which contributed to the position of being the representatives and spokesmen of all exile Tibetans. As mentioned earlier, India accepted the Tibetan leadership and even enforced its position; most international aid organizations also tended to do so. Consequently, the 14th Dalai Lama and his ruling elite were welcome to participate in discussions on the problems of the exile Tibetans between the GOI and international NGOs. Only a few cases are reported where international authorities questioned the claimed rights of the CTA to decide on behalf of the exile Tibetans; Dawa Norbu mentioned the Swiss Red Cross and the Canadian immigration authorities, and when both countries, Switzerland and Canada, granted asylum to hundreds of exile Tibetans, the authorities sent their own officials to India to select Tibetans who were suitable to live in their countries. They refused to follow the recommendation of the CTA and therefore questioned indirectly the authority of the self-proclaimed exile Tibetan government (Norbu 2001a: 213).

The CTA structure and policies are characterized by the main principles of Buddhism and democracy, which indicate a combination of traditional values of the past with Western political concepts. This combination was outlined by the 14th Dalai Lama in the beginning of 1960. Western democratic concepts were introduced into the exile Tibetan political system by the 14th Dalai Lama on a top-down initiative, despite his interest in communism. The question why the Dalai Lama followed this secular concept will be discussed in Chapter 5, from an analytical point of view. According to Samuel Huntington, such an elite-led introduction of a democratic transformation process brings out more stable and crisis resistant political structures compared with transitions that are initiated by the masses. Furthermore, he assumes that a top-down transition serves, to a large extent, the benefits of the process initiating political elites (1984: 212). Huntington's analysis is proved by the present practice in Tibetan exile. The political authority is to a large extent entrusted to members of the present yabshi family, the family of the present Dalai Lama, or to its clansmen. They dominate key sectors of the process of decision-making and delegate authority either to members of that elite group or to their representatives.[26] Dawa Norbu wrote: '. . . the practice in Dharamsala has been for a few Yabshi-dominated hands to monopolize decision-making power on the crucially important issues and to monopolize popular involvement only cosmetically' (1991a). Lobsang Sangay revealed that in every cabinet between 1991 and 2001, at least one minister came from the Dalai Lama's family (2003: 125). Furthermore, Richard de Jongh commented that the Dalai Lama's power elite misuses the word democracy because it still dominates exile Tibetan politics through 'democratic' manipulation to perpetuate the existing patrimonial structures. The introduced reforms touch only the surface of Tibetan society but do not change the traditional system (Jongh 1995: 21, 65). From the political science perspective, the 14th Dalai Lama is no more than an '. . . unelected monk [who] holds little political legitimacy and certainly has no clear position in a democratic framework' (Ardley 2002: 88) but leads the exile Tibetan struggle to return to the homeland.

The introduction of modern Western ideas in the exile political system was not unanimously agreed by all exile Tibetans. From 1963, there were several open and hidden processes of disintegration among the political elite, which finally led to the resignation of numerous high officials from their posts, up until 1969. They either migrated to foreign countries or retired in India. Their official reason for such a step, which Wangpo Tethong[27] identifies as a taboo in Tibetan society, was given to their state of health but was also influenced by the political climate at that time. According to an informant, as an outcome of the aforementioned pro-communist course among the political elite in exile, Tibetan aristocrats even had to change their names (anonymous interview, 2006). In general, one can state that information about that time is sparse and needs to be given further attention. Tethong describes it as a period of political change, which was determined by hegemonic ideas of Gyalo Thondup (2000: 95–9). After the old officials had resigned, the empty posts in the exile administration were awarded to monks and traders who had partly served in the lower ranks of the Lhasa administration before their departure to India. Slowly, a new political elite was born, which, according to Tethong, better represented the whole exile Tibetan community regarding their regional, social and religious composition than the old one (2000: 139–40). Today, family and social background are no criteria to become a CTA official. Honesty, the level of education, patriotism, the will to work hard for the Tibetan cause and a peace-loving attitude are the important qualities of a person who is to become the political leader.[28] According to the CTA, there are no records that register the social heritage of the present officials. Exile Tibetan 'youngsters may not know where they descend from'. Because 'everybody is the same, there is no use of such information' (interview with

Mrs Nangsa Chodon, Public Service Commission, Dharamsala, May 2006). Indeed, it is important to note that every Tibetan, despite gender, religion, regional heritage or social strata is allowed to serve in the present CTA structure, a landmark in Tibetan political history. In this regard, today even a peasant can become an official through his dedication to the exile Tibetan struggle, a fact that was, apart from a few exceptions, impossible in the traditional Tibetan context. The only precondition is that the applicant needs to be officially a member of the exile Tibetan community, a status awarded to every exile Tibetan who supports the political position of the CTA as the leading administration in the exile struggle (see Ch. 5).

The democratic structure of the CTA was first constitutionally determined in 1963 in the draft of a *Constitution of Tibet*, a name that symbolizes the claim of the CTA to act in the name of the entire Tibetan nation. According to interviews with Tibetans, this constitution was elaborated by the exile Tibetan deputies on the basis of the limited experiences they had gained through their work in the first years in exile as well as by their political views, which were still characterized by formality and based on the political mentality of the old Tibetan way of thinking in classes and ranks. John Kenneth Knaus stated that an American, Ernest Gross, wrote the constitution following the US model (1999: 252). It is still controversial who actually wrote the constitution, as experiences with democracy were limited among the new Tibetan officials.

Nevertheless, the political position of the Dalai Lama remained untouched (CTA 1963: Article 29). He was in the position to exclusively appoint the deputies of the CTPD and the cabinet. Thus, the legislative and executive powers were condemned to act only symbolically without any power of attorney (Pardesi 1975). Christoph von Fürer-Haimendorf even asserted that the CTA still acted on traditional laws that have existed before the departure from the homeland (1989: 52).

The 1990s brought up several changes within the political structures in exile. The 14th Dalai Lama relinquished his power to appoint both ministers and deputies and instead called an extraordinary meeting to elect the cabinet until a new constitution could come into force. But surprisingly the exile Tibetans did not run for votes to become high officials within the CTA structures. They were filled with concerns and anxiety, a reaction that portrays their complete faith in the leadership of the Dalai Lama (Hortsang 2003). In 1991, a new constitution, the *Charter of the Tibetans-in-Exile*, came into power, which regulated a more differentiated CTA structure and was responsible for the set-up of numerous new institutions. But despite the additions at all administrative levels, the superior position of the Dalai Lama has remained to the present day (CTA 1991: Articles 19, 36). This fact shows that the traditional structure is partly still in use. It has to be noted that neither of the two documents, the 1963 constitution and the 1991 charter, has been approved by the Tibetans who still live inside the borders of the PRC but rather represent the political ideas of the exile elite.

The present (2006) CTA structure provides a high degree on institutional organization and is run by 685 officials (male–female ratio (%): 79:21) who work in the Tibetan headquarters in Dharamsala (interview with Mrs Nangsa Chodon, Public Service Commission, Dharamsala, May 2006). According to traditional Tibetan politics, the officials are still divided into ten ranks; half are designated for junior, half for senior officials (interview with Mr Tashi Norbu, Public Service Commission, Dharamsala, June 2003). They all act as links between the Dharamsala administration and the scattered Tibetans all over the world. Officials are entitled to appoint other staff locally, which creates a close-meshed administrative network all over the Tibetan settlements. Frechette found in her research that at the settlement level, appointment of government officials was not carried out according to their talent. Instead, '... [g]overnment officials usually appointed relatives when they could' (Mr Walter Jutzi, a Swiss intergovernmental official, cited in Frechette 2004: 47).

The duties of the CTA officials in Dharamsala comprise all bureaucratic work starting from the organization of national holidays and managing the government vehicles to the accounting of the CTA budget. In the CTA, both monk and lay Tibetans work together without an explicit division based on one's religious involvement as in the pre-1959 structures. The selection of new officials is carried out by the Public Service Commission according to the needs of the CTA, the applicant's loyalty to the exile administration, and the candidate's performance in a selection procedure: The examinations cover language skills in Tibetan and English, literature, politics and history. The final decision about a government post is made by the chairman of the commission (interview with Mr Tashi Norbu, Public Service Commission, Dharamsala, June 2003).

Pensions and salaries are small compared with the income arising from profit-making economic activities. Nevertheless, the vacancies in the CTA are popular among exile Tibetans in India and Nepal, partly because of several additional benefits that can be drawn. The earnings represent a permanent and predictable monetary flow that is enough to live on for many families (Roemer 2001: 34–5). Furthermore, CTA officials are entitled to send their children to a CTA kindergarten or to one of the CTA schools without payment. Additionally, the officials enjoy free medical treatment in CTA hospitals where they are treated first without queuing up, and where they are entitled to go once a year for a free general check-up (interview with Mr Tashi Norbu, Public Service Commission, Dharamsala, June 2003). They also have the opportunity to apply for further training and workshops, which both can take place in India or abroad and provide a good chance for professional advancement and a break in their daily bureaucratic routine in the numerous bureaus in Dharamsala. In these courses, predominantly Indian and foreign scientists and experts teach the qualities of leadership and decision-making. According to my fieldwork, exile Tibetan officials can also make contact with Western NGOs, researchers and donors during their working hours. Such personal connections to foreigners are highly valued in the exile Tibetan community and often lead to sporadic or frequent private support from the Westerners. But apart from the material benefits, working in the CTA is, for many officials, not so much a good job opportunity for earning money and status but more of a dedication and active struggle to free their country. Such chance for an active involvement in the Tibetan struggle makes the jobs attractive and considerably prestigious (interview with Mr Tashi Norbu, Public Service Commission, Dharamsala, June 2003; Edin 1992: 46). Despite such esteem, Tibetan officials are in the crossfire of a current generational conflict, whereby the younger generation of Tibetan officials, born in exile, is accused by the older officials of being less dedicated and motivated for the exile Tibetan struggle. Consequently, the initial spirit of the old officials who had the return to Tibet right before their eyes has vanished over time within the CTA structures (Samphel 1998: 15).

Looking at the exile Tibetan officials from a theoretical point of view, it becomes obvious that their loyalty to the CTA is determined by their ideological commitment but also generated by the CTA by investing certain incentives to serve in the exile administrative structure. According to Wilson's theoretical characterization of incentives, the CTA offers material (advantages in the health and education sector) but also immaterial rewards. The latter can be further subdivided into specific solidarity (access to Western supporters and further vocational training) and 'purpositive incentives' (Wilson 1973: 34) (individual satisfaction from an active participation in the exile Tibetan struggle, which in turn influences social status and prestige). In contrast are relatively small salaries, which can be interpreted in the context of the annual budget of the CTA as a general outcome of the financial constraints. In this regard, it can be summarized that the CTA invests certain incentives to the exile Tibetan people to work as officials. According to the theoretical considerations, such governmental work can be interpreted as loyalty of the exile Tibetan officials to the CTA and therefore provides a measure for loyalty of a person independent from one's ideological commitment.

Figure 4 illustrates the organizational structure of the CTA in 2004, which I explain in detail in the following sections.

The position of the 14th Dalai Lama

At the head of the CTA is the 14th Dalai Lama. He is the ruling institution and holds ultimate legislative, executive and judiciary powers—competences that are still determined by the Indian hosts. The Dalai Lama is serviced by a private office that handles all affairs regarding his person ranging from the management of thousands of visitors annually to the organization of his daily schedule. The 1991 democratic *Charter of the Tibetans-in-Exile* provides the Dalai Lama with controlling mechanisms to intervene in every governmental affair, reaching from the appointment of key positions within the CTA structure to the requirement that every political decision has to be signed by him

```
                          ┌─────────────────────┐
                          │   14th Dalai Lama    │
                          └─────────────────────┘
                                    │
  ┌──────────────────┐   ┌──────────────────┐   ┌──────────────────┐
  │ Supreme Justice  │───│   The Cabinet    │───│     Tibetan      │
  │   Commission     │   │    (Kashag)      │   │   Parliament     │
  └──────────────────┘   └──────────────────┘   │      (ATPD)      │
                                    │            └──────────────────┘
       ┌──────────────────────┐                          │
       │  Kashag Secretariat  │──┐   ┌──────────┬──────────┬──────────┐
       └──────────────────────┘  │   │ Election │  Public  │  Audit   │
                                  │   │Commission│ Service  │Commission│
       ┌──────────────────────┐  │   │          │Commission│          │
       │   Planning Council   │──┘   └──────────┴──────────┴──────────┘
       └──────────────────────┘
```

	Minister		Minister		Minister		Minister
Dept. of Information and International Relations	Dept. of Security	Dept. of Health	Dept. of Finance	Dept. of Education	Dept. of Religion and Culture	Dept. of Home

Environmental Desk. 13 Tibet Bureaus		TMAI and 37 branch clinics in India and Nepal, Delek Hospital and 66 other hospitals		80 Tibetan schools in India, Nepal and Bhutan		54 Settlements and Welfare Offices in India and Nepal

	Reception Centres Research and Analysis Section Documentation		SARD Section Business and Administration Budget Section Finance and Accounting Charitable Trust		250 Monasteries Cultural Centers: TIPA, LTWA, Norbulingka, CIHTS, Tibet House in New Delhi	

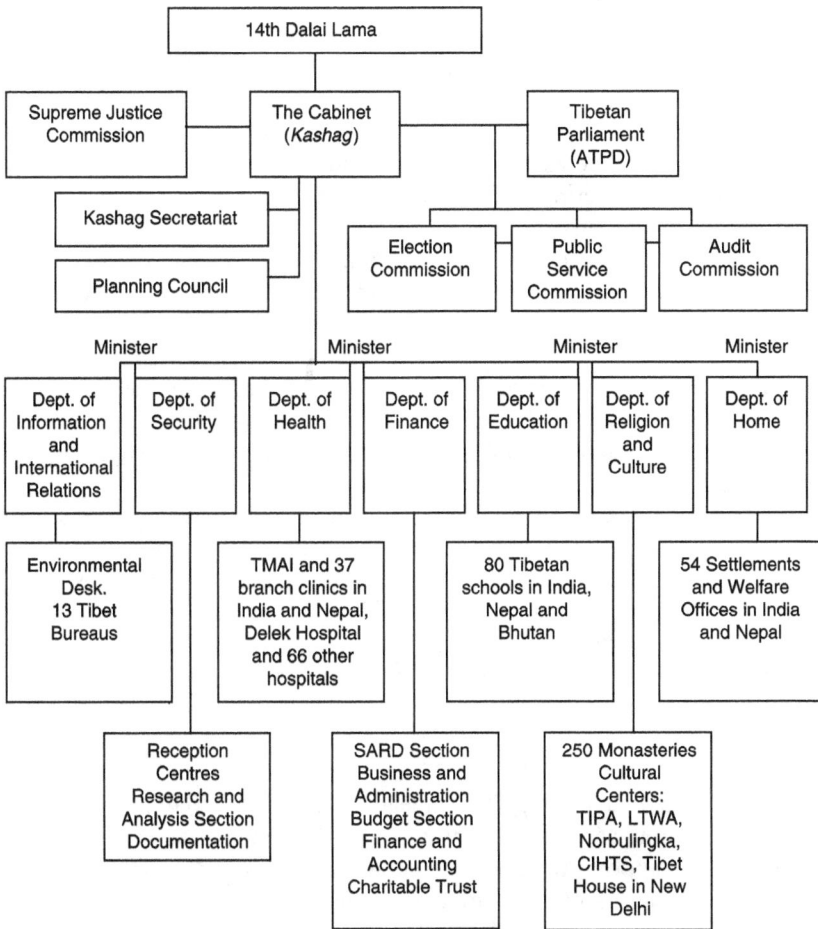

Figure 4 Organizational structure of the CTA (CTA 2001: 10–11).

before implementation. While in the historical context, the power of the Dalai Lama was sometimes rather weak, the exile situation describes a totally new situation with new challenges and the need for a strong political leadership. The introduced democratic ideas do not lower the status of the Dalai Lama, moreover, '. . . the Tibetan people's loyalty to him and his leadership remained as absolute and unqualified as ever' (Thinley 1996: 12). This loyalty to his political legitimacy of power lies in the traditional perspectives according to which he has a divine personality, as outlined previously. His decisions, both in religious and political matters, are assumed to be, without any doubt, in the name of all people's interest and every criticism that challenges his political authority is interpreted as anti-religious. Because of his religious superiority and strong ties to the CTA, any criticism towards the CTA is at the same time a questioning of the institution and power of the Dalai Lama.

Consequently, the Tibetan people's loyalty to the 14th Dalai Lama is to a large extent responsible for the political strength of the CTA as sole representative of the Tibetan nation. As Tsering Wangyal put it: 'Most Tibetans do and will continue to recognize Dharamsala [the CTA] as the only legitimate Tibetan Government as long as it is headed by the Dalai Lama' (1976: 4) The exile Tibetans totally rely on his decisions and consequently the decisions of the CTA. Lhasang Tsering said in that context: 'Our greatest strength is the Dalai Lama, but I think he is also our greatest weakness ... We Tibetans depend entirely on the Dalai Lama' (Monnier 1993: 35–6). In this regard, one can see that the position of the Dalai Lama within the Tibetan community is two-edged. On the one hand, his charismatic personality, and the history and tradition of this institution serve for Tibetans as proof of his superior position in religion and politics. On the other hand, his dominance and strong ties to the CTA hinder the democratic progress. The interrelation of democracy and Buddhist philosophy supports, in my eyes, the superiority of the Dalai Lama within the governmental structures, i.e. his political position is even more emphasized by its religious meaning. Additionally, the majority of Tibetans has received at least once in their lifetime, teachings and blessings of the Dalai Lama and has him as a root guru. They owe him respect in terms of a disciple–teacher relation, which makes criticism in the Tibetan context even more difficult (Mr Tashi Tsering, cited in Dixit 1991: 6).

Many exile Tibetans are unwilling to see that the Dalai Lama's political position is renounced, even though there is a general interest in changes of the present democratic set-up. This ambivalent situation was illustrated by the events in 1985, when the 14th Dalai Lama urged his compatriots in exile to discuss the issue of an elected Tibetan leader. But instead to limit his political power, no solution was found. Consequently, he promulgated that he was no longer going to appoint the assembly deputies and instead the exile Tibetans were asked to elect them. He addressed this idea to the exile community on the annual celebration of Tibetan Democracy Day, on 2 September 1985. The change was to be backed up by the 1991 *Charter of the Tibetans-in-Exile.* But the redrafting committee for the Tibetan constitution resisted the 14th Dalai Lama's appeal and instead asked him to remain in his position of power:

> Your Holiness is the eye and heart of the Tibetan people. Your Holiness is the soul of the Tibetan nation and its spiritual and temporal polity. The Tibetan people, both in and outside Tibet, look to your Holiness with absolute reverence and hope. No leader of a democracy enjoys as much trust from people as Your Holiness does. From this perspective, the existing system does reflect genuine democracy. Therefore, we appeal to Your Holiness not to ask us to constitute the committee. Instead, kindly, continue to take responsibility as our leader.
>
> (Petition of the Constitution Redrafting Committee cited in
> Hortsang 2003)

The quotation shows that the loyalty of the exile Tibetan people to the institution of the Dalai Lama was still unbroken. Moreover, the traditionally determined loyalty to this institution is, in the opinion of the Constitution Redrafting Committee, equal to a democratically legitimized leadership. With the topic of succession, the 14th Dalai Lama tried to sensitize his people for a prevailing contradiction of the traditional selection of new leaders by the tulku-system of rebirth and the introduced democratic ideas, which demand an elected leader. Furthermore, he aimed to prepare them for his death to prevent a breakdown of the exile struggle. From the theoretical point of view, the 14th Dalai Lama is, as mentioned before, an extraordinary and charismatic leader. His death demands, inevitably, a system that secures a succession of a charismatic leader (Weber 1976: 143). Such a system is only partly represented in the exile Tibetan democratic structures, which give space for elections but do not necessarily bring up a leader comparable with the current Dalai Lama. This is one reason why many Tibetans prefer the traditional system of reincarnation more than the democratic alternative.

The 14th Dalai Lama owns superior status despite existing differences along religious lines in Tibetan exile. While the Tibetan Buddhist Gelugpa sect has been in power since the seventeenth century, which has continued its religious and political supremacy in the exile context, the other remaining Tibetan Buddhist sects, members of the Bön religion[29] and the exile Tibetan Muslims are minor in their authority to decide anything at the high political level. They have built their own monasteries and formed their own communities. According to George Woodcock's research, they have been constantly complaining that they are less well off and are discriminated against by the ruling Gelugpa sect (Woodcock 1970: 414)—arguments that have been strongly rejected by the 14th Dalai Lama. During my fieldwork, I have felt no discrimination and observed that all monastic institutions are well off regardless of their religious affiliation. Nevertheless, studies of the Bön and Muslim communities are looked at with suspicion and regarded as less important by the CTA.

One well-documented example, which shows the power of the 14th Dalai Lama within the Tibetan community, describes the conflict over the worship of a Tibetan protector–deity, Dorje Shugden.[30] In the mid-1970s, the 14th Dalai Lama strictly advised his compatriots to stop the practice of Shugdhen on the advice of the state oracle, saying that it would damage the exile Tibetan struggle. The Dalai Lama's opposition to Shugdhen became louder in 1996 when the CTA prohibited the Shugdhen practice among all CTA officials and the entire monastic population that stood under its supervision. Additionally, the exile Tibetan laity was also called on to change its religious practice, otherwise '. . . it will harm the common interest of Tibet, the life of His Holiness the Dalai Lama and strengthen the spirits that are against religion' (CTA n.d. c: 34). This official prohibition led to religious tensions within the exile Tibetan community (Dryfus 1998) which culminated in the killing of a highly respected 70-year-old Tibetan monk teacher and scholar and two of his students in 1997 by Tibetan supporters of Shugdhen practice. The opponents of the ban claimed that the Dalai Lama was restricting religious freedom, applied for Indian citizenship and renounced the spiritual leadership of the 14th Dalai Lama (*Tibetan Review* 2000). Also Western Buddhists occasionally opposed the prohibition and accused the 14th Dalai Lama of religious intolerance. They interpreted his action as a breach of democratic freedom and tolerance of religious affinities, principles constantly emphasized by the 14th Dalai Lama in front of his Western audience (Lopez 1998: 191–6; Sparham 1996; Gruschke 1998). In Jane Ardley's opinion, the 14th Dalai Lama used his superior political position to solve a purely religious problem (Ardley 2002: 175–6). Even though the criticisms received extensive press coverage, they were only marginal and did not touch the position of the Dalai Lama; the incident exemplarily illustrates the complex involvement of Tibetan politics and religion. The 14th Dalai Lama was able to keep the Tibetans together and maintain his superior political and religious position in exile.

The 14th Dalai Lama also plays an important role for those Tibetans who live abroad. The Tibetan Diaspora abroad comprise of members of the early immigrants to Switzerland or to North America, of the first and second generation already born in the West and new emigrants to the West. With his extensive travels, the 14th Dalai Lama renews the national boundaries through religious teachings and discussions on the political future. Furthermore, he updates the Diaspora about the situation in the homeland and in Indian exile. According to Mary J. Gardner, he acts as a religious and political leader, but also as 'cultural mediator'—seeing him is, for many Tibetans abroad, a social happening and meeting of an 'old friend' (1999: 49).

For many Tibetans who still live within China's borders, the 14th Dalai Lama represents a political and religious leader who struggles for the Tibetan nation. His presence in the homeland was exemplarily documented in 2006 during the so-called Anti-Fur Campaign when the 14th Dalai Lama urged the Tibetans on the initiative of the Indian National Congress to stop wearing furs and wildlife skins as clothings (interview with Mr Thupten Samphel, DIIR, Dharamsala, May 2006).

> Despite the exiled leader's total absence from the state-controlled media, the message, couched in a mixture of environmental and Buddhist terminology, swiftly reached the Tibetan masses within Tibet and resulted in a success whose speed and thoroughness is unprecedented in nature protection.[31]

The appeal caused '. . . mass public fur burning in far eastern Tibet' and the detention of Tibetans being suspected to be '. . . under the effect of "foreign influences" while campaigning to destroy clothes made of fur' in China.[32] The TibetInfoNet, a non-profit and independent organization, summarized the happenings of 2006. After the Dalai Lama's statement:

... that seeing Tibetans wearing furs made him wish 'not to live any-more' ... [s]pontaneous fur-burning campaigns started within a few days all across Tibet until late Spring 2006. Apart from being one of the most powerful demonstrations of loyalty to the Dalai Lama within Tibet in decades, the movement eradicated the wearing of furs among Tibetans, at least for the time being, and fur trade prices have plummeted. In response, shops in Lhasa which used to openly display Tiger pelts switched to crude fakes made with dyed sheep skins, but this did not meet with much success. By summer 2006, a time for festivals and hence an important occasion for wearing fur, the movement had made fur garments so 'politically incorrect' that it had virtually disappeared.[33]

This example shows that the Dalai Lama has considerable influence over the life of the Tibetans in the homeland. With regard to the exile government's focus to preserve Tibetan culture and religion, the Dalai Lama's appeal is highly interesting because with his call, he undermined the official political course. On the one hand, Tibetans are called upon to hold on their traditions and wear traditional clothes (see also Ch. 5) but on the other hand, the use of traditional material (fur) is forbidden. Even though there were numerous discussions and a general confusion about the Anti-Fur Campaign, the 14th Dalai Lama was able to settle the upcoming conflicts and moreover, imple-ment his, i.e. the Indian's ecological ideas. In such a position, he is able to widen Shain's insider–outsider dilemma, since even different opinions about the CTA's political course can be smoothed over by him. Because of his divine personality, he is a unifying symbol for all Tibetans and remains an unquestioned leader, despite his present exile status. His authority underpins the legitimacy of the CTA as a continuation of the central government in Lhasa. Furthermore, the example gives evidence about the relationship between the Tibetan government-in-exile and the host government. The GOI is in the position to restrict the exile Tibetan activities for the sake of its own ecological objectives.

The legislature: the assembly of Tibetan people's deputies

Despite the 14th Dalai Lama being vested with sweeping powers, the CTA has a legislative organ, which fulfils, at least symbolically, the demands of a democratic system. During the 1960s, the assembly '... had no legislative functions, and since it was not influential in the appointment or removal of ministers of the Dalai Lama's cabinet, its role was essentially symbolic' (Norbu 1990: 14). But over time, the exile Tibetan legislature has undergone various changes. For instance, the initial CTPD was renamed the Assembly of Tibetan People's Deputies (ATPD), the initial number of 13 deputies has grown to 46 in 2004 and the election procedure was amended.

The founding of the Tibetan assembly in 1960 replaced the traditional secu-lar and ecclesiastic offices and removed the hereditary privileges of posting from the Tibetan aristocracy. Instead, the present ATPD serves as a symbol of an institutionalized exile Tibetan nationalism by following the idea of regional and religious quotas. At present, each region of the area of Cholka Sum (Ü–Tsang, Kham and Amdo) is represented by ten deputies out of whom there have to be at least two females. On the religious basis, each Tibetan Buddhist sect, Nyingmapa, Kagüpa, Sakyapa and Gelugpa, provides two deputies. Since 1976, there have been two Bön delegates (interview with Mrs Gyari Dolma, 13th ATPD, Dharamsala, April 2003). There are also two deputies who represent the exile Tibetans in Europe and one for those who live in North America.[34] Additionally, the 14th Dalai Lama directly nominates a maximum of three candidates.[35] The composition of the assembly emphasizes the claims of the CTA to represent all Tibetans, despite regional heritage, religious affinities or current place of living. With regard to such assertion, critical voices draw attention to the fact that the ATPD does not represent the will of the majority of Tibetans because those who still live in the homeland have no chance to communicate their opinion. Consequently, the assembly 'acts only symbolically as is not legitimated to decide about the future of Tibet' (anonymous interview, 2006). Looking at the territorial claims of the CTA one can see that the exile government even enlarged the political responsibility compared with the traditional polity of the Tibetan government in Lhasa. While the CTA declares to represent all Tibetans in the area of Cholka Sum, the Lhasa administration only controlled parts of the central Tibetan territory. From a theoretical point of view, such an extension of territorial claims by an exile government compared with the pre-exile situation is a new phenomenon that is not mentioned in the discourse yet.

Every exile Tibetan at the age of 18 and who is an official member of the exile Tibetan community (see Ch. 5) has the right to vote for their favorite candidate. Candidates must be at least 25 years old. According to a member of the exile Tibetan parliament, only those who 'make noise' are remembered by the people and therefore are elected. 'Otherwise people don't know about anything about politics'. One can get only little information about the candidates and their profile in the settlements, Dharamsala is in its function as exile capital an exception (anonymous interview, 2006).

To improve the contact between the politics in Dharamsala and the people in the settlements, the deputies are in contact with 38 local Tibetan assemblies that are found in the major Tibetan communities and represent the legislative power at the regional level, again, subordinated to Indian state law (interview with Mrs Gyari Dolma, 13th ATPD, Dharamsala, April 2003). The CTA deputies meet twice a year, plus in emergency cases they can be called for extraordinary sessions. Most members of the parliament do not live in Dharamsala, so in the absence of the majority, there is a standing committee.[36] The ATPD is empowered by the exile Tibetan charter to discuss the following matters: the election and impeachment of the cabinet ministers; the examination of cabinet decisions according to current valid policies and programs that are adopted by the assembly; laws, frame rules, regulations and policy decisions that will be enacted; the annual CTA budget and important national and international issues. Furthermore, it hears and debates public feedback, complaints, petitions and grievances and meets with envoys of international governments, parliaments, members of NGOs and with individuals to create awareness for the exile Tibetan struggle.

The two annual parliament sessions have been broadcasted since 2005 via television, so every Tibetan is able to follow the political process in Dharamsala. But despite long discussions between the deputies during the annual ATPD sessions, the 14th Dalai Lama is vested to make the final decision about any assembly decision and policy recommendation. All papers need to be signed by him to become an Act. Until spring 2003, the 14th Dalai Lama refused to sign only once. This was in 1991, when the position of the Dalai Lama within the CTA structure was discussed in the draft of the *Charter of the Tibetans-in-Exile*. Because of the need for the Dalai Lama's approval for any decision, some deputies of the 13th ATPD see the assembly as a powerless legislative body. In their opinion, this practice has both advantages and disadvantages. On the one hand, it ensures that all policy decisions are in line with the 14th Dalai Lama's political ideas, which is important because he is anticipated to be more knowledgeable about international happenings through his travels than any Tibetan deputy. On the other, the deputies have no full political responsibility, which affects their motivation to discuss any issue at all. So the legislative organ has developed more or less into a 'debating circle without relevance in *realpolitik*' (anonymous interviews with members of the 13th ATPD, 2003).

Indeed, the 14th Dalai Lama is head of the government but this post is more and more only theoretically. During recent years, his direct influence in exile politics has diminished and the ATPD became mature and more powerful. Nevertheless, there is still a considerable degree of dependency on the Dalai Lama among the Tibetan deputies. In this regard, the progress of the democratic transformation process of the exile Tibetan political system during the last decades is still questionable and not yet finished.

The executive: cabinet, departments and constitutional bodies

The Tibetan executive is subdivided into the Tibetan cabinet, its subordinated departments and constitutional bodies, which are headed by the 14th Dalai Lama.

The cabinet, kashag, is the main executive body of the CTA, which highly relies on the traditional structure of the Lhasa government, indicated by its name, structure, and functioning. The kashag consists of four ministers, the kalons, who are in number and name the same as in the pre-1959 Lhasa government. At present, they are directly elected by the exile Tibetan people for a five-year term.[37] The four ministers elect their chairman, or in Tibetan terminology, the kalon tripa, who acts in the position of a Prime Minister.[38] In

2004, all ministers shared their responsibilities[39] in the seven fields of exile Tibetan politics as shown below.

The kalon tripa was, in addition to his representative position as exile Tibetan Prime Minister, the head of the Department of Security and the Department of Information and International Relations (DIIR). The DIIR has the jurisdiction in promoting the exile Tibetan struggle and the present conditions in Tibet among all Tibetans and the international public. For this purpose, it publishes books, brochures and journals (in Tibetan, Hindi, English and Chinese) and also produces audio and video programs. Under the DIIR, since 1990, are an Environmental and Development Desk, which focuses on the promotion of Tibetan environmental issues in particular (see Ch. 5) and an Africa and Middle East Desk that aims for close ties between the CTA and the people living in these areas (CTA 1994a: 200–1). Further- more, there are: a Tibet Support Group Desk, a Chinese Desk (established in 1994), a UN and an EU Desk.[40] Through their specialization, they all support the work of the DIIR in a particular field. The DIIR also heads, at present, 13 bureaus worldwide—the so-called Offices of Tibet that function as CTA embassies. They are located in New Delhi (established in 1960), Kathmandu (1960), New York (1964), Tokyo (1975), London (1981), Geneva (from 1964 to 1991 located in Zurich), Paris (1992), Canberra (1992), Budapest (1993), Moscow (1993), Pretoria (1997), Taipei (1997) and Brussels (2001).[41] These bureaus lobby sovereign governments and transnational organizations, such as the UN and the EU, interact with members of the Tibetan Diaspora abroad and moreover organize the participation of exile Tibetan delegates in international conferences on human rights, ecological, population, develop- ment and women's issues (interviews with Mr Thupten Samphel, DIIR, Dharamsala, May 2002 and April 2003; Albers and Fuchs 1993: 40).

Three responsibilities fall on to the Department of Security: The safe- guarding of the 14th Dalai Lama, the monitoring of developments in the PRC and the registering of newly arrived Tibetans in Nepal and India with the help of three reception centers in Kathmandu, New Delhi and Dharam- sala. These centers have been specially set-up by the CTA to assist the new arrivals in finding employment, education, lodging and food. Such responsi- bilities show that the CTA is still in the position to act on the exile's behalf from the moment of their arrival. In this regard, the elaborated structure contributes to the fostering of the CTA's power position in the Tibetan com- munity as a whole. Furthermore, the reception centers are important for the CTA to gain information about present conditions in Tibet and the situation with the PRC. For instance, former political prisoners can give information on conditions in Chinese jails and the number of detained Tibetans. Add- itionally, they are able to identify arrested Tibetans and give information that can be added to the statistics of Amnesty International, the Tibetan Centre for Human Rights and Democracy or similar human rights NGOs. Former prisoners may be able to provide data about Tibetan resistance forces inside the PRC and their level of organization. According to a former Tibetan political prisoner and member of the Tibetan Gu-Chu-Sum movement, there is still a capacity of Tibetan resistance in the homeland, which is organized in small groups but hard for the exile Tibetans to identify (interview with Mr Yeshi Togden, Gu-Chu-Sum Movement, Berlin, February 2004). Additionally, there are numerous Tibetans who constantly move back and forth between the homeland and Nepal to gather news. According to an official of the Department of Security, the CTA has many contacts with people inside Tibet (anonymous interview, 2006). All the information is passed on to different CTA-departments or is directly handed to Western supporters. Since its founding in 1959, the Department of Security has been considered as one of the most important segments of the Tibetan administration that works with the help of Indian intelligence forces and Tibetan agents (interview with Mr Tashi Phentsuk, Department of Security, Dharamsala, April 2002).

The combination of the two departments under the leadership of the Prime Minister is, in my opinion, highly significant in terms of a theory of governments-in-exile. As mentioned previously, contact between the exiles and their compatriots at home and the national Diaspora are crucial. In the Tibetan context, the Prime Minister bridged all different groups of the Tibetan nation through the leadership of the security and international relation and information departments. Furthermore, he included international political players into the intra-Tibetan communication network. This made the Prime Minister a head of a global network, and all information between the Tibetans at home, in Asia and the Diaspora abroad was managed by him. Consequently, the Prime Minister of the CTA concentrated in 2004 key resources, which are crucial for the survival of the exile Tibetan community.

The second minister is responsible for the health and finance sector. The Department of Health administers 6 hospitals and 61 health centers in different Tibetan settlements. Additionally, it covers the costs of treatment for poor and needy exile Tibetans. A Tibetan Medical and Astrological Institute (TMAI) works under the auspices of the health department and provides Tibetans but also Indians and Nepalis with traditional Tibetan medicine. Because of a close net of health facilities that can even be found in remote areas, the exile Tibetan health system contributes to the close interaction between the exiles and local population of the host countries. Such contacts are, according to Shain's theory, most important for the exile's survival. Additionally, the TMAI functions as a political institution. It emphasizes the preservation of Tibetan culture through the promotion of the uniqueness of Tibetan medicine. Such an approach provides the TMAI with financial resources, which are mostly based on Western consumption of Tibetan medicine, but also creates international awareness of the Tibetan cause, which in turn supports the exile Tibetan struggle morally and financially (Kloos 2006).

The Department of Finance is subdivided into four different sections to meet the manifold tasks of the CTA: budgeting, administration, caring and fundraising (interviews with Mr Ugyen Chaksam, Department of Finance, Dharamsala, May 2002 and April 2003). Most important within the structure of this department is the Social and Resource Development Fund (SARD), which is responsible for international funds that have been granted for long-term projects (3–4 years) and investments over 5,000,000 Rs. The international monetary transfers to the CTA are generally initiated after a first meeting between the 14th Dalai Lama and a potential foreign donor, on the verge of international meetings. Then the Western delegation is invited to Dharamsala where the SARD staff enters into negotiations about a catalogue of projects that are needed and the objectives of the Western potential supporter. In this function SARD acts as the interface between international supporters and needy Tibetan exiles (CTA 2000e; interview with Ms Tenzin Chunkyi, SARD, Dharamsala, April 2003).

SARD also acts as key institution for the exile Tibetan NGOs to channel international funds from a particular donor organization to an exile NGO. This is because most exile NGOs lack an official registration according to the Indian Foreign Contribution Regulations Act (FCRA). Such FCRA registration is needed to receive foreign grants but is difficult to obtain and usually takes many years to be finally issued by the Indian administration.

The third minister heads the sectors of education, culture and religion. This combination refers to the pre-1959 traditional Tibetan context when Tibetan monasteries held the monopoly on education. In exile Tibet, the monasteries are still important institutions in the education sector, as shown in the exile Tibetan statistics. The majority of educated male exile Tibetans have participated in monastic education, while education in secular exile schools or professional training is less important in terms of number of students (CTA 2000f: 12). The Department of Education is subdivided into five sections according to its educational tasks: academics, sponsorship and scholarships, accounting, publication and project implementation.

The Department of Religion and Culture is responsible for the preservation and promotion of Tibet's spiritual and cultural traditions. In the initial decades of exile, until the 1980s, a total of about 40 monasteries had been rebuilt. At present, the department oversees more than 20,000 monks and nuns in around 250 monasteries and nunneries that have been set-up in India, Nepal and Bhutan (Tandzin 2004: 53; Gyatso 2004; Bangsbo 2004). The department is in contact with more than 700 Tibetan Buddhist centers worldwide, publishes religious and cultural books and organizes exchange programs for novices, who want to live and study for a period of time in other monasteries in India, Mongolia, Kazakhstan, etc. (Tandzin 2004: 66). Furthermore, it places new arrivals into monasteries and implements the policies and ethics of the 14th Dalai Lama in the monastic curriculum. It organizes public and monastic prayers for the Dalai Lama, which are traditionally performed to acknowledge his religious and political status (interview with Mr Phuntsok Gonpo, Department of Religion and Culture, Dharamsala, April 2003). Besides the religious tasks, the department also takes care of five CTA institutions in India: the Tibet House in New Delhi, the Tibetan Institute of Performing Arts (TIPA), the Library of Tibetan Works and Archives

(LTWA), the Central Institute for Higher Tibetan Studies (CIHTS) at Sarnath and the Norbulingka Institute for Tibetan Culture near Dharamsala. All CTA institutions work within the close political framework of the CTA as centers of cultural preservation. Åshild Kolås suggested that these institutions are modeled after Western perceptions and ideas of cultural preservation and consequently emphasize through their set-up the CTA's political approach on cultural preservation (1996: 59). The LTWA, for instance, opened its doors in 1971 to preserve and remind Tibet's cultural past. Its main objectives are the acquirement and conservation of Tibetan books and manuscripts and the providing of reading materials for studying and consultation. For this purpose, the LTWA contains a publication section, Tibetan and foreign language sections, a museum and study rooms for public religious instructions that are given by Tibetan religious dignitaries (CTA n.d. b). But despite its name as a library and archive, it developed over time into a center to protect, perpetuate and disseminate Tibetan culture. According to Jamyang Norbu, it turned into a place of worship and functions as a cultural institution for Western tourists as well as for exile Tibetans, even against the will of the director (1993: 17). A second example for such cultural transformation is TIPA, which travels around the world performing traditional dances, opera and folk songs. According to Tobden Tsering and Jamyang Norbu, the Tibetan culture is now more important for the West than for its own environment, the exile Tibetan community. Tibetan culture is largely preserved in exile because of the interest from the West (Mr Tobten Tsering cited in Pichler 2000: 101–2; Norbu 1993: 17–19). In this regard, the international community considerably influences Tibetan life in exile, which will be more extensively analyzed in Chapter 5.

The fourth minister is head of the Home Department, which takes care of rehabilitation of exile Tibetans. It oversees all Tibetan settlements and cluster units in India, Nepal and Bhutan, seeks to create employment and promotes self-reliance among Tibetan settlers. Since its establishment, the department has worked closely with the GOI and international aid organizations, which have spent a great deal of money supporting the exile Tibetan community.

Three constitutional bodies work officially independently from the rest of the executive field. First, there is the exile Tibetan Election Commission, which was established to secure free democratic elections. The commission and 65 local branch commissions worldwide supervise all elections within the CTA structures, such as the votings of the ATPD deputies, the local assemblies and the cabinet. Second, there is the exile Tibetan Public Service Commission, set-up to recruit, train, appoint and promote the civil servants of the CTA. Third, the exile Tibetan Audit Commission audits all accounts of CTA departments and its subsidiaries, such as schools, cooperatives and hospitals, etc.

The chairmen of all constitutional bodies and their assisting officials are directly appointed by the 14th Dalai Lama to ensure their independent work from the CTA. But looking at the position of the Dalai Lama as head of the exile government, it is obvious that the requirements of independent bodies are failing in this practice. Through such appointments, the 14th Dalai Lama has direct influence on the administrative infrastructure, which moreover provides him with insight into the elections, the CTA audits and the selection process of new officials. Such empowerment emphasizes the already superior power of the 14th Dalai Lama, as he is able to control, at least theoretically, all political and religious processes. Compared with Tibetan history, the present power over the constitutional bodies shows an enlargement of his political influence, which stands in contrast to his repeatedly promoted wish to diminish his political power but also with the exile Tibetan 'democracy'. Especially in matters of recruitment of new officials, the Dalai Lama expanded his power, while in the traditional context, this selection process lay exclusively in the hands of powerful monk officials or the finance department (see Ch. 2).

The judiciary: the supreme justice commission

The Supreme Justice Commission represents the Tibetan judiciary—a new invention in the Tibetan political context. It adjudicates all civil disputes within exile Tibetan communities and settlements but in all court decisions it is subordinate to Indian law. Moreover, it does not entertain major crimes and any case whereby enforcement is in contravention to the host's law. In its responsibility for law and order in the Tibetan settlements, the commission functions as an intersection of the CTA and the exiles because it accepts complaints and senses of injustice from the people (interview with Mr Tsering Tobgyal Dorjee, Tibetan Justice Commission, Dharamsala, April 2002). This link between the numerous exile Tibetan settlements and Dharamsala maintains the political position of the CTA because the exile administration is able to receive information about life in the settlements and react on it when necessary. The commission is led by a chief commissioner assisted by two officials who are all nominated by the 14th Dalai Lama and later approved by the Tibetan assembly. Again, the Tibetan leader is given control in judicial matters as the assembly is *de-facto* powerless. Some voices urge for a legal system of the CTA with an independent judicial institution. Responsible for the absence of such a system is in their opinion the existing inertia in exile and a traditional lack of interest in jurisprudential and legal aspects (Thinley 1990: 10).

In summary, it can be stated that during recent years the CTA has undergone several structural changes to optimize its functioning, to adjust to the changing political objectives and to foster its legitimized status as sole political representative of all exile Tibetans and those who still live in the area of Cholka Sum. In contrast to the traditional polity, the CTA even enlarged its territorial claims—a new phenomenon in the theoretical discourse. The CTA was set-up along the lines of pre-exile political traditions of the former Ganden Phodrang government, which supported its political position in exile. This development was backed up by the succession of leadership: former officials became the new political elite and the Dalai Lama remained as political leader. As charismatic political and religious leader, he enjoys the loyalty of all Tibetans. This in turn shows the importance of the pre-exile context in the situation of exile, which has also been stressed by Shain. The 14th Dalai Lama's position within the Tibetan community has, on the one hand, positive effects on the political credibility and stability of the organizational structure of the CTA. The Dalai Lama links all Tibetans despite their present place of living and thus widens Shain's insider–outsider dilemma. On the other hand, his superiority hinders a secular democratic transformation of the exile Tibetan political system as a whole—a topic that will be examined in Chapter 5 more extensively. The 14th Dalai Lama holds theoretically ultimate powers in the CTA, which indicates that the rest of the administration, the executive, legislative and judicative powers, functions to a large extent merely symbolically.

Through an elaborate structure, which is subdivided into numerous units, branch offices around the world and highly specialized sections, the CTA is able to reach all exile Tibetans in India, Nepal and Bhutan and also those who live abroad. Such a strategically well-considered set-up, which links all Tibetans, contributes to the political claims of the CTA as sole representative of all Tibetans. It provides the CTA with instruments to receive information about the exiles, to influence their lives and mobilize them to support the exile struggle. Additionally, the CTA structure eases the access to the international community, which in turn supports the exile Tibetan struggle worldwide and generates international support.

Exile Tibetan NGOs: their role in exile politics

Dharamsala also serves as the headquarters for different Tibetan NGOs, which additionally maintain branch offices in numerous exile Tibetan settlements. This chapter gives an overview of three exile Tibetan NGOs, the Tibetan Youth Congress, the Tibetan Women's Association and the Tibetan Centre for Human Rights and Democracy, which are most important in Tibetan exile regarding their present number of members and political relevance. It will discuss to what extent they fit in the overall political framework of the CTA and if they support or undermine the political status of the CTA within the Tibetan community.

Tibetan Youth Congress

The most important and largest exile Tibetan NGO is the Tibetan Youth Congress (TYC), with 20,000–23,000 members in 2002 (interview with Mr Karma Yishey, Dharamsala, April 2003). With its founding in 1970, it united numerous young Tibetans who represented the first generation in exile that had finished its course of education. The founders saw the TYC as a social welfare organization and a 'loyal opposition' to the CTA. Until the present day, the TYC aims to serve its country and people under the guidance of the 14th Dalai Lama, to promote and protect national unity and integrity by giving up all distinctions based on religion, regionalism or social status, to preserve and promote Tibet's religion, culture and traditions, and to struggle for the total independence of Tibet even at the cost of one's life.[42]

Taking the previously explained administrative structure of the exile Tibetan political system into account, the CTA was at no time open to accept any oppositional force. The whole political system was rather set-up to foster the superior status of the CTA instead of providing any political platform for opposition. Consequently, the CTA did not enthusiastically welcome the founding of the TYC, regardless of its intention to be loyal. Jamyang Norbu, who himself was among the founding members, explains the general skepticism of the CTA with a better overall knowledge among the TYC members compared with that of CTA officials. The exile Tibetan cabinet in particular, but also the security department, worked hard to undermine and discourage the initial oppositional and revolutionary power of the TYC members—with success—but the political involvement of the TYC never faded completely (1990: 14).

When the TYC was founded, it predominantly focused on social work in the exile community, which it has continued to the present day. In this regard, the TYC has been involved in the CTA resettling and rehabilitation programs and additionally carried out educational programs at schools, monasteries and local community centers to raise awareness for the exile Tibetan struggle, among exile Tibetans and recently also among the local Indian population (interview with Mr Karma Yishey, Dharamsala, April 2003). Through such work, the TYC tries to bridge the generations through the promotion of goals and values of the elders that are acceptable for young exile Tibetans. Over the years, the TYC has mutated into a springboard for politically interested young Tibetans and many of the present CTA officials and deputies used the TYC as a training ground for their positions (Aukatsang 1991; Dolkar 1995).

On the surface, the TYC backs up the official political course of the CTA, once again through its social activities, but also as an organization that politicizes the exile Tibetan community and the local population to develop a consciousness for the exile Tibetan struggle. But the TYC also challenges the CTA because it criticizes the 'unique Tibetan democratic system' as being nothing more than 'a combination of religious and secular affairs, which has little to do with Western democratic ideas' (anonymous interview, 2003). The TYC is also in favor with the idea of an independent Tibetan homeland instead of the official political course that focuses on genuine autonomy. Independence as the ultimate goal is taught among the exile Tibetans and moreover, the TYC called the exile Tibetans to withhold their participation in the 1995 referendum. Additionally, the TYC teaches the Tibetan and host population a more militant political approach than the CTA. It does not agree with the non-violent policy of the CTA because of its limited success to the present day. In this context, members of the TYC, who want to remain anonymous, compare the CTA's non-violent struggle with a non-action policy and reproach the CTA for misunderstanding Gandhi's philosophy. They further argue that the combination of politics and religion in the exile Tibetan context is a difficult mixture because every action to struggle for a free homeland, even self-sacrifice (for instance, hunger strikes or self-immolation) can be interpreted as a violent act (anonymous interview, 2003). According to the TYC, during recent years, the exile Tibetan struggle has become a victim of celebrity and Western fashion of non-violent means but has also lost its initial energy in fighting for an independent Tibet (Norbu 1997: 20).

The following example shows exemplarily that the TYC affirms Gandhi's philosophy in a different way than the CTA. In 1988, the TYC organized a hunger strike to death in New Delhi (Thinley 1998: 22; Ardley 1998) in response to a demonstration in Lhasa, which was one of the first protest demonstrations since the Uprising in 1959.[43] The hunger strike was strongly criticized by the CTA because it did not go along with the official non-violent course. But the organizers and participants justified their action as an obligation towards their Tibetan compatriots at home to demonstrate the exiles' willingness to sacrifice their life for the national struggle. In this regard, they showed that the Tibetans in the PRC were not forgotten and consequently stressed Shain's insider–outsider problematic. The critical intercourse in Dharamsala and New Delhi was highlighted by the self-immolation of the TYC member, Mr Thupten Ngodup. Since Ngodup's dramatic death, his photograph can be seen in any TYC office in India and moreover, he became a symbol in the Tibetan exile community for self-sacrifice to free Tibet. Even a memorial stone was built in Dharamsala to commemorate his martyr's death. In the context of resistance, Lhasang Tsering viewed human resources as the greatest benefit the exile Tibetans have to bridge potential misunderstandings between insiders and outsiders (Monnier 1993: 34).

The hunger strike and the self-immolation stand exemplarily for the still existing political energies of the TYC compared with the moderate course of the CTA. The incident can also be described as an outcome of a generational conflict in Tibetan exile. There is no unconditioned support of the CTA by the TYC. Moreover, the TYC and the CTA compete for support of the Tibetans inside and outside the PRC. Both organizations claim to represent all Tibetans. While the CTA widely promotes its policy and claims to be the representative of all Tibetans, the TYC declared that the majority of Tibetans inside Tibet struggle for an independent rather than an autonomous homeland and therefore support its policy (interview with Mr Tsultrim Dorje, TYC, Dharamsala, April 2003).[44] Nevertheless, the TYC works within the framework of the CTA structure bound by its loyalty to the 14th Dalai Lama but at the same time finds ways to circumvent the political lack of any platform for opposition within the CTA structures. Consequently, the TYC's political stand is ambivalent. On the one hand, it cushions potential tensions between the generations through political information campaigns during which it promotes the values and ideas of the older generation for the younger Tibetans. On the other hand, it challenges the CTA by following a different political goal and ways to achieve it.

In 1994, the TYC founded the National Democratic Party of Tibet (NDPT), which focuses on the strengthening of the democratic process initiated by the 14th Dalai Lama; the promotion and protection of national unity and the preservation of Tibet's cultural heritage. The party predominantly carries out education campaigns in exile Tibetan settlements, schools and monasteries to instruct people in democracy and the CTA policy but also holds contact with international TSGs. In general, the NDPT does support the political object-ives of the CTA rather than oppose them (interview with Mr Yeshi Phuntsok, NDPT, Dharamsala, May 2002; NDPT 2000).

Tibetan Women's Association

The second largest exile Tibetan NGO is the Tibetan Women's Association (TWA) with, at present, around 11,000 members. The first formal Tibetan women's organization was set-up by the Chinese PLA. Since the overthrowing of the Manchu dynasty in 1911, several women's organizations had to come into being calling for political rights for women, especially the right to vote. One of the most important of these organizations was the Lhasa Patriotic Women's Association (PWA), which was inaugurated in 1953. Following Alex Butler's historical account, the founding of the PWA was highly significant because it introduced a radically new concept in Tibet: organized political activities by women. This concept was taken up a few years later during the Tibetan Uprising in Lhasa (Butler 2003: 33–8). After 1959, a few women managed to escape to Kalimpong where they revived the organization. For the first two decades of its existence, the organization focused only on the preservation of Tibetan culture through the creation of educational and working opportunities for exile Tibetan women. The TWA maintained a low profile during the 1960s and 1970s when it opened three handicraft centers in India. There, exile Tibetan women produced voluntarily and without receiv-ing salaries traditional Tibetan clothing and carpets, which were offered to the CTA. The CTA in turn sold them for profit. According to a present member of the TWA, despite the limited amounts of such handmade products, this offering was for the women a suitable way of supporting the political struggle of the CTA (interview with Ms Pasang Dolma, TWA, Dharamsala, May 2002).

With the changing status of women within exile Tibetan politics in the 1980s, women were allowed to actively participate in politics and seats in the exile parliament were especially reserved (TWA 2005: 47–51, 65–70). The TWA was revived in 1984 by the initiative of the 14th Dalai Lama's family.[45] Existing projects were transformed into small business units, where female employees received small salaries on a profit basis. The TWA also shifted its focus more and more to the political sphere, in particular to the international community. The successful participation of the TWA at the Fourth UN World Conference on Women in Beijing in 1995 portrayed an important turning point for the organization. Tibetan women became known in the international women's rights arena as during the conference they had several opportunities for interaction with other international delegates and were able to raise awareness for the present situation in their homeland (TWA 1996). In the beginning, the CTA was not enthusiastic about promoting the exile Tibetan struggle in the light of women's rights, as it feared discussions about gender inequality of the traditional Tibetan perception. It was assumed that this may harm the exile struggle instead of support it. Consequently, the CTA's support of the TWA's international experiences was limited. But with the success of the exile Tibetan women and the increased international awareness the TWA could mobilize, the CTA changed its standpoint and accepted this angle to promote the Tibetan cause. In this regard, the Tibetan involvement in the UN conference helped considerably to re-frame and expand the exile Tibetan struggle as a whole through the innovative introduction of the Tibetan women's discourse (Pike 2001: 80). The years following 1995 were characterized by a rapid establishment of an international network with other organizations that emphasized women's rights and the TWA was able to set-up bureaus in India, Nepal, Switzerland, Great Britain, the USA, Canada and Japan.[46] As a result, the promotion and highlighting of Tibetan women's rights has increased besides other activities such as campaigns to boycott the Olympics in Beijing in 2008 and Chinese made products. Since 1995, Tibetan feminism has been used as another angle from which to promote the exile Tibetan struggle, but '. . . the Tibet activists "politicised" women's right in the sense that they linked women's rights to a nationalist cause for sovereignty, rather than to a social goal of gender equality' (Pike 2001: 92). During the last decade, the CTA directed struggle has been literarily 'feminized'. In this regard, the TWA supports the political position of the CTA in the international sphere through the promotion of a 'feminized' exile Tibetan struggle.

But despite a constant elaboration of the TWA's international focus, it also acts as a social organization, which performs community services such as childcare, help in finding jobs and educational opportunities for women and consultations in health matters. In such positions, the TWA functions as a social interface between the CTA and the exile Tibetan women in the settlements. In this regard, it supports the political claims of the CTA. Today, the TWA also works, as does the TYC, as a political training ground for the few female deputies of the ATPD (interview with Ms Pasang Dolma, TWA, Dharamsala, April 2003).[47]

Tibetan Center for Human Rights and Democracy

The Tibetan Center for Human Rights and Democracy (TCHRD) was founded in 1996 from a former Desk for Human Rights and Democracy that had worked under the DIIR. The change to a new judicial status was carried out in order to widen the possibilities of political action, because as an NGO the TCHRD was anticipated to have more room to act in the international sphere. While the CTA may be excluded from conferences because of its representative claim to be the government of the Tibetan nation, an NGO may not (interview with Mr Thupten Samphel, DIIR, Dharamsala, May 2002). In this regard, the TCHRD overcomes the limitations of the exile Tibetan government in maneuvering within the international sphere and consequently expands the CTA's access to the international community. Another reason for the change of status is given to the fact that an NGO does not necessarily need to be in line with official CTA policy.

Regarding the topic of democracy, the TCHRD is most active in the exile educational sector to promote the CTA's version of democracy. For instance, it organizes workshops in schools and publishes teaching material (interview with Mr Tenzin Norgay, TCHRD, Dharamsala, April 2002).[48] In the international sphere, the TCHRD specializes in the promotion of human rights in the Tibetan context. This topic became important with respect to the reports of the International Commission of Jurists and the shift from the UN to the international grassroots level in the 1980s. In this context, Tom Grunfeld pointed out that Jimmy Carter's coming into power in 1977 influenced the decision of the exile Tibetan elite to focus on human rights issues, because Carter was:

> pledging to carry out a foreign policy based on the principles of 'human rights' around the world. This led Tibetans to declare that, 'it is his special emphasis on the human rights issue that makes him a potential Messiah for Tibetans'.
>
> (1987: 198)

The CTA realized that the human rights discourse was an important tool for displaced and indigenous people in particular to change the political situation in their home territories—a relevance that had its beginning with the UN declaration on human rights in 1948 and became important anew in the 1970s. According to a TCHRD interview with the present exile Tibetan Prime Minister, human rights and environmental issues are regarded by the CTA as more important than the topic of Tibetan independence (interview with Mr Tenzin Norgay, TCHRD, Dharamsala, April 2002). Such a statement is surprising because the CTA struggle is officially pointed towards a return to the homeland.

For a successful promotion of human rights violations, the TCHRD needs internationally acceptable torture and prison accounts through which it is able to emphasize the cultural differences between Tibetans and Chinese. This in turn contributes to the CTA's course to preserve Tibetan culture and religion. In this context, the numerous imprisoned monks and nuns were viewed. Since the Chinese takeover, the monastic segment of the Tibetan population in particular has been repeatedly involved in Tibetan resistance activities that have caused imprisonment, torture or even death due to the tight control in the TAR (Schwartz 1996: 74–108). As soon as the monks and nuns are free they flee with the help of international human rights activists to the Western world, where they speak about their imprisonment, ranging from terrible torture methods to the plight of other prisoners and their health. Thus, there is a strong interrelation between Western human rights activists and the Tibetan former political prisoners. Because the topic of human rights is one of the key issues of the UN, it brought the Tibetans unexpected hearings in the USA and Europe. Such events provide the exile Tibetan elite with the opportunity to communicate its political objectives through the language of the Western world, using terms like 'human rights' and 'injustice' (Mountcastle 1997: 296).

Apart from the already mentioned exile Tibetan NGOs, there are other organizations, such as the Gu-Chu-Sum movement, which focuses on former political prisoners. It cares about their mental state after the flight, partly with the help of volunteer psychology students from all over the world who usually spend several months in Dharamsala, and it promotes former prisoners' experiences in the international arena, where it acts in a similar position as the TCHRD.[49]

I would also like to mention here the Tibetan Parliamentary and Policy Research Centre (TPPRC) in New Delhi—an exile Tibetan NGO that was set-up in 1991 on the initiative of the ATPD and the German Friedrich Naumann Foundation to '. . . build and clearly project the political image of Tibet and to promote political awareness among Tibetans' (TPPRC n.d.; interview with Mr Penpa Tsering, TPPRC, New Delhi, February 2002). Since its founding, it has published books and brochures on the structure of the CTA, its policies and the position of the CTA within international politics.[50] It also organizes workshops on the aforementioned issues to optimize the functioning of the CTA and also tries to push forward the democratic transformation. In this context, the TPPRC organized and managed the TV broadcastings of the ATPD sessions mentioned previously.

There are also numerous NGOs in the educational sector that have helped to set-up the elaborate educational structures, for instance, the Tibetan Children's Village (TCV), the Sambhota Schools or the Snow Lion Foundation.

Exile Tibetan NGOs: counterparts or supporters?

All exile Tibetan NGOs act within the CTA framework and support its official policy through their high specialization in various fields. Such support is due to the fact that they have all received the blessing and acknowledgement of the 14th Dalai Lama at the time of their founding. This approval provides them with a secure position within the exile Tibetan community but also defines an obligation of loyalty to the Tibetan leader and therefore also to the CTA. The gesture of blessing by the divine leader makes any opposing activity, which is not explicitly welcomed in exile politics, almost impossible. Consequently, all NGOs have firmly anchored in their programs the support of the Dalai Lama, his policy, the struggle for unity and the preservation of national traditions. In this regard, through the institution of the Dalai Lama all Tibetan NGOs are interconnected despite their various specializations. This becomes obvious as the NGOs work together on religious and political occasions. They plan demonstrations, perform prayers for the well-being of the 14th Dalai Lama and organize campaigns to boycott Chinese-made products or the Olympic Games in Beijing in 2008. A second argument that serves as interpretation for their support of the exile government is that all NGOs receive financial support from the CTA. As mentioned earlier, they lack the official FCRA registration and need to channel their foreign financial donation through the SARD section of the Department of Finance. In this regard, a totally independent functioning of the NGOs is almost impossible. According to the theory, the CTA invests both material (access to international financial transfers) and immaterial incentives (collective solidarity and 'purposive' incentives) to secure the NGO's loyalty. Most important is the official approval of the 14th Dalai Lama.

To implement the CTA's political objectives, the educational sector in particular provides all NGOs with a reason to be actively involved. They instruct their national compatriots in schools, monasteries and at the settlement level in community centers. Through their branches in almost every Tibetan settlement, the NGOs reach all social strata and consequently link the CTA work with ordinary Tibetans—a fact that is especially important because it also secures loyalty to the CTA among those who are illiterate, not in educational training, or religiously occupied. Hence, the exile Tibetan NGOs play an important role in creating unity among the exile Tibetan community beyond religious, regional and social stratification. This in turn supports the CTA's political position within the exile Tibetan community.

In the international sphere, the exile NGO's specialization and their non-governmental status provides them with a base from which they cooperate successfully with other activists. Through their links to international NGOs, the exiles have access to modern communication systems and political tools. Furthermore, international TSGs financially support the exile NGOs with donations, as the usual small membership subscriptions are not sufficient for most of the organizations' survival.

Regarding the support of the political course in exile, the only exception represents the TYC, which officially disagrees with official CTA politics, yet explicitly supports the 14th Dalai Lama. Because of the close ties between the Dalai Lama and the CTA, the TYC members find themselves in a contradictory situation by serving their compatriots in exile and in the homeland in struggling for an independent Tibet, even with violent means, and being loyal to the 14th Dalai Lama, who promotes insistently a non-violent exile struggle.

The annual budget of the CTA

The CTA faced enormous financial constraints especially in the early years of exile. While the GOI and numerous international NGOs granted substantial financial support to the thousands of Tibetans who arrived annually in India and Nepal to fulfill the new arrivals basic needs, funding for the CTA remained absent. Consequently, the 14th Dalai Lama was forced in 1964 to sell parts of the Tibetan state treasury, which had been kept in Sikkim since 1956.[51] The money of the sold gold was invested in the CTA structure and several programs as well as in the 'Charitable Trust of His Holiness the Dalai Lama', which was registered in India in 1964 (CTA 1969: x–xii). The trust funds were invested in company shares, bank deposits, etc. to cover the costs of running the CTA. But the returns of the initial investments were meager and the trustees decided to invest the remaining money in employment projects (CTA n.d. g: 8–9).

While there was an economic bottleneck in the early 1960s, the revenues of the CTA have been constantly increasing with the time being in exile. These developments are portrayed in Table 1. Because of incomplete and unrecorded budgeting in the early years of exile, this period cannot be exactly defined. Additionally, the development of project funds, i.e. extra investments from international NGOs, sovereign governments and transnational organizations to the CTA for the implementation of certain projects, was not available and therefore are not included in Table 1.

Table 1 shows that the annual revenues have been increasing over the last 47 years in exile, from US$42,000 to US$3,003,479.[52] According to the CTA alone, within four years (2002–6) the CTA budget had been increasing by 46.60 per cent (*Paljor Bulletin* 2005a). The enormous leap in the 1990s is attributed to the opening of seven CTA bureaus in Switzerland, France, Hungary, Russia, Australia, South Africa and Taiwan (interview with Mr Ugyen Chaksam, Department of Finance, Dharamsala, April 2002). This indicates that these CTA offices operate, in addition to their official work as 'Tibetan embassies', as fundraisers that successfully generate enormous unspecific project-orientated financial help around the world (Backman 2004: 209). Despite the absence of project funds, such financial growth disproves Shain's generalization about a tendency of decreasing international support for exile governments in time. The exile Tibetan case raises the question: How could the CTA maintain and even expand the international support over the years? According to the theoretical considerations, outside support only continues when the popularity of a government-in-exile remains high. Then the grants to an exile government enhance the likelihood for the supporting authority to mobilize extra people and votes in the domestic political sphere. This was the case at the end of the 1950s when the Nehru government actively supported the exile Tibetans. In regard to this theoretical remark, the initial question can be specified: Why does the CTA enjoy such broad popularity? But before answering this question, I will illustrate the annual budget of the CTA for the fiscal year 2003/2004.[53]

Table 1 Development of CTA revenues over time (interview with Mr Ugyen Chaksam, Dharamsala, 26 April 2002)

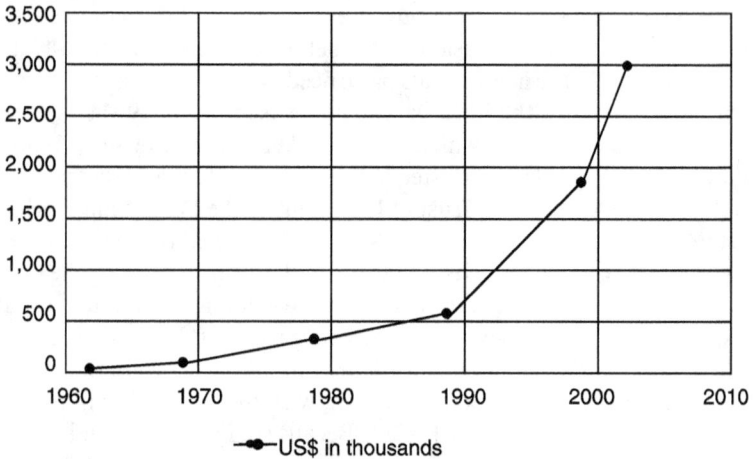

—●—US$ in thousands

	Early 1960s	1969	1979	1989	1999	2002
US$	42,000	66,667	307,662	554,682	1,858,071	3,003,479

The budget is annually made by the budget section of the Tibetan finance department, with the approval of the exile cabinet, assembly and the 14th Dalai Lama. The budget is split into revenues and expenditures, which are shown and explained in Tables 2 and 3, respectively.

The estimated revenues for the fiscal year 2003/2004 were 142,507,464 Indian Rs. They were drawn from the 14th Dalai Lama, the cabinet, the departments for religion and culture, home affairs and finance, the ordinary exile Tibetans, the finance department, the interest from the Copper Fund and the project funds.

The grants of the 14th Dalai Lama are drawn from the inheritance of Tibetans[54] but also gifts and donations. The total amount of the 14th Dalai Lama's treasury cannot be estimated because it is neither published nor did my interviewees give any detailed information. But the finance department assumes that the granted sum to the annual budget portrays only a small part of his wealth. One example of external funding of the Dalai Lama is pointed out by Michael Backman who cited an article in the *New York Times* of 1998 where the 14th Dalai Lama confirmed that he was on the CIA's payroll from the late 1950s until 1974. According to this article, he personally received during that time annually US$180,000 from the CIA. He transferred most of the money to the CTA to support its political activities, primarily to fund the Tibet offices in New York and Geneva. The CTA received from the CIA another US$1.7 million a year (Backman 2004: 208).

Table 2 Estimated total revenues of the CTA for the fiscal year 2003/2004 (interview with Mr Ugyen Chaksam, Dharamsala, 10 April 2003)

	Revenues	Indian Rs.	Percentage
1.	Grants of the Private Office of the Dalai Lama	18,000,000–00	12.63
2.	Grants of the Cabinet	63,500,000–00	44.56
3.	Departments (Department of Religion and Culture, Home Affairs and Finance)	4,575,684–00	3.21
4.	Annual voluntary contribution of all exile Tibetans	40,000,000–00	28.07
5.	Contribution of Department of Finance	3,000,000–00	2.11
6.	Interest from Copper Fund	3,080,000–00	2.16
7.	Administrative percentage from Project Funds	10,351,780–00	7.26
	Total revenues	142,507,464–00	100
	Deficit	4,517,156–30	
	Total operating budget	147,024,620–30	
	Project Funds	720,758,030–43	
	Total CTA budget	867,782,650–73	

Item two portrays the grants of the Tibetan cabinet. There are no data about the sources and kinds or total amount of the cabinet revenues. But interesting in terms of the scale of the grants is that the cabinet distributes almost 45 per cent of the total CTA revenues. This gives reason to the assumption that the executive body may also have an immense influence on the decision where the money is invested.

The third item describes a contribution of three CTA departments to the annual budget. This money comes from the departments' fundraising activities because apart from the aforementioned activities of the SARD section of the Department of Finance, all CTA departments can raise their own funds up to an annual sum of 5,000,000 Indian Rs and 2 per cent of these annual resources are requested to be donated to the annual CTA budget.

The fourth item shows a voluntary contribution, the 'voluntary freedom tax', of all exile Tibetans to the CTA. It is collected by the Tibetan People's Freedom Movement (TPFM), a CTA organization that maintains 96 branch offices in all Tibetan settlements. The TPFM was set up in 1972 on the initiative of politically engaged Tibetan intellectuals, members of the newly founded TYC and students of the CIHTS in Sarnath who were at the time all dissatisfied with the results of the UN-orientated CTA policies. As a result, the politically motivated exiles founded the first exile Tibetan people's organization, which exclusively focused on the struggle for a free Tibet, as the name TPFM symbolically indicates. But despite desirable political engagement, the movement was seen with skepticism by CTA officials. Wangpo Tethong even mentions that the critics of the TPFM had well-founded fears of the establishment of a 'shadow cabinet' of the CTA because, despite the young exile

Tibetans of the TPFM having a similar political orientation to that of the CTA, at the same time they criticized the political course of the CTA as being insufficient to regain the homeland (Tethong 2000: 126–8). Soon after, the founding of the TPFM was incorporated into the CTA structures after long discussions between the TPFM members and the CTA. Since then it has worked under the supervision of the exile Tibetan assembly. But during the time of existence, the initial political energies of the TPFM to free the homeland diminished. An evidence of these initial revolutionary energies represents a voluntary contribution on behalf of the CTA in 1973 initiated by the TPFM. The money was collected to support the exile struggle of the CTA to free Tibet. Today the TPFM works under the CTA cabinet and finance department and exclusively collects a voluntary contribution from all exile Tibetans (interview with Mr Lodrö Sampo, Dharamsala, April 2003).[55] A high ranking CTA official stated that the annual 40,000,000 Indian Rs. is a sufficient sum to cover the costs for the running of the whole administration (interview with Mr Thupten Samphel, DIIR, Dharamsala, April 2003). The importance of the exile Tibetan's financial support for the organizational survival of the exile government is also stressed in CTA publications (Chashar 2006). According to Shain's theory, such argumentation has a symbolic significance, as the CTA portrays itself as an administration that functions independent from any foreign power. 'They [governments-in-exile] will try to maximize the actual advantage of international assistancae [sic] while rhetorically downplaying their dependency' (Shain 1989: 129). But as shown in the following the revenues drawn from the voluntary contribution are not enough to cover all costs for the running of the CTA.

Budget item five represents a contribution of the Department of Finance, which is drawn from profits of the department's enterprises: manufacturers, travel agents, hotels and restaurants in India, Nepal and the USA. Because of a privatization campaign of the cabinet in 2003, this item has ceased since 2004.[56] Some 75 per cent of the privatization money is invested in the so-called Copper Fund, which is part of the 'Charitable Trust of His Holiness the Dalai Lama', and was especially created to manage monetary flows: to save and to reinvest the profits of the CTA business units. The interest from the stocks of the Copper Fund is listed as item six of the CTA revenues. The last budget item is an administrative percentage deduced from project funds.

The project funds amounted to 720,758,030 Indian Rs., which was around six times more than the whole operating budget. These funds have been administered since 2001 by the SARD section[57] and were invested in development projects that were initiated according to the CTA's need-based approach. That means that international aid runs exclusively through the CTA, which finally decides where the money is invested. Marie Dorsh DeVoe argues in this context that loyalty to the CTA is an essential part and unwritten criteria for an aid recommendation. So if parts of the exile Tibetan community (whole settlements, groups like the '13 Settlements' or schools[58]) or an individual do not fulfill the loyalty requests in the opinion of the CTA, they will be excluded from foreign aid (DeVoe 1983: 10). Ann Frechette wrote:

> Like many other exile organizations worldwide, the Dalai Lama's exile administration uses control over economic resources to enforce its decisions. Its access to economic resources derives from its position as middleman in the provision of international assistance. The Dalai Lama's exile administration uses its middleman position to tax fellow exiles (thereby gaining access to additional economic resources) and to regulate schools, monasteries, businesses, health care centers, publishers, and research centers.
>
> (2004: 152)

This in turn means that the CTA fosters its own political position within the Tibetan community through the monopoly on and exclusive access to international aid agencies, NGOs, governments and transnational organizations (for instance, Norwegian Church Aid, Heinrich Böll Foundation/Germany, Danida/Denmark, Tibet Fund/USA or the EU) that are willing to support the exile Tibetan community as a whole.

While in the initial years in exile the Tibetans relied predominantly on Indian aid, today the exile economy depends to a large extent on international aid, which is represented by the enormous budgetary item of project funds. The monetary transfers continually improve the standard of living of the exile Tibetans. There are many Tibetans who live in better conditions than the local Indian and Nepali population. According to a study on exile Tibetans in northern India '... 25.29% characterized themselves as previously "very rich", 20.0% as "rich", 40.0% as "middle", 14.71% as "lower middle". None thought of themselves as "poor" ' (Grunfeld 1987: 198). Such economic self-perception causes a loss of credibility of the Tibetan plight among the host population but also among the Western visitors of the exile Tibetan communities. Consequently, there is a paradox: the economic surplus above the subsistence level based on international aid takes considerable ground to support the exile Tibetans more and more. Nevertheless, the international monetary transfers, mainly described in the project funds, increase annually. In this regard, the exile Tibetans fall theoretically victim to their wealth by not fitting into the anticipated picture of displaced people or refugees. This causes a certain degree of skepticism among Western visitors and agents regarding the demanded aid by the exile Tibetan community (Roemer 2001; Mountcastle 1997: 312).

Another critical aspect regarding the international financial help is the absence of an independently functioning exile Tibetan economic sector and a widely communicated economic self-sufficiency (*Paljor Bulletin* 2005c,e). Unlike other authors (Saklani 1984; Goldstein 1975a; Norbu 1994; Frechette 2004) I argue that the economic success of the Tibetans is since so far limited. The only exceptions in the economic sphere describe the development of the carpet manufacturing sector in Nepal in the 1980s and 1990s and the Tibetan's ability to generate international financial assistance. But a well-functioning and self-sufficient economy could be not established yet (Roemer 2001). My research findings are proved by the official unemployment rate, which was 18.5 per cent in 1994 among all exile Tibetans in India and Nepal between the ages of 16 and 50 years (CTA 1994a: 76). In 1998, 74.1 per cent of all exile Tibetans in India and Nepal were considered as non-workers, meaning people who are not economically active, including students, seniors, disabled, children and unemployed exile Tibetans. Furthermore, those who are economically active are to a large extent involved in the informal sector (CTA 2000f: 13–15)—a problem that is encountered by the CTA home department during its constant search for income opportunities and Tibetan welfare. In this regard, I state that the exile Tibetans are skilled enough to mobilize enormous international help but not to create a self-sufficient economic sector. Moreover, international support hinders the CTA's intention to develop a self-supporting economy and maneuvers the whole exile Tibetan community into a high dependency on international support; in short it creates a *rentier* mentality.

Adding annual revenues with project funds, the estimated annual budget of the CTA for the financial year 2003/2004 was 867,782,650 Indian Rs. The annual deficit was 4,517,156 Indian Rs, i.e. the annual expenditures exceeded the revenues by the amount of around US$ 93,000. The estimated expenditures of the CTA for the fiscal year 2003/2004 are shown in Table 3.

The total amount of 867,782,650 Indian Rs. was estimated to be spent in politically related affairs, the running of the administration, education, social welfare, health, religious affairs, other social welfare and judicative and legislative affairs.

The biggest part of the total annual expenditures is listed under the term 'politically related affairs'. This item was not further specified by the finance department, only that it comprises all political goal-orientated activities of the CTA, including the work of the cabinet, the DIIR, the CTA offices abroad

Table 3 Estimated total expenditures of the CTA for the fiscal year 2003/2004 (interview with Mr Ugyen Chaksam, Dharamsala, 10 April 2003)

	Expenditures	Indian Rs.	Percentage
1.	Political related affairs	286,765,269–86	33.05
2.	Administration	208,552,011–32	24.03
3.	Education	128,948,812–80	14.86
4.	Social welfare	109,472,998–41	12.62
5.	Health	56,666,753–00	6.53
6.	Religious affairs	33,221,291–00	3.83
7.	Other social welfare	27,368,787–40	3.15
8.	Judiciary and legislative affairs	16,786,726–94	1.93
	Total	867,782,650–73	100

and the CTA security department. Regarding the division of responsibilities between the four cabinet ministers (outlined earlier), it is obvious that the Prime Minister controlled in 2004 the biggest part of CTA expenditures because he was head of all matters in item one (in Table 3). Such unequal allocation compared with the other sectors also emphasizes the importance of the contacts to the Diaspora abroad and the people in the homeland regarding monetary flows. According to the finance department, the expenditures for such politically related affairs have been constantly increasing during the last years (interviews with Mr Ugyen Chaksam, Department of Finance, Dharamsala, April 2002 and April 2003).

The second item of the CTA expenditures is for administration, comprising all costs for the running of the finance department, the CTA computer center and the constitutional bodies. The listed 208,552,011 Indian Rs. clearly exceeded the revenues of the contribution of the exile Tibetan community with 40,000,000 Indian Rs., which the CTA official called a sufficient basis for its functioning.

Item three illustrates the importance of the exile Tibetan educational sector, which since the initial years in exile has always been portrayed in relative high expenditures compared with other sectoral activities. Around 16 per cent of the budget (items four and seven) are spent on new arrivals and the social welfare of the exile Tibetans in India and Nepal. There is no information available about the difference between these two items.

Relatively small were the expenditures for the health sector of the CTA (6.53 per cent of the annual budget) and for religious affairs (3.83 per cent). The limited money given to religious affairs is unexpected considering that the preservation of Tibetan culture and religion is one cornerstone of the exile Tibetan struggle. It can be explained by the fact that a considerable share of the necessary funds has been cushioned since the 1970s by Western sponsors who started their financial help after the first Tibetan religious teachers left India and Nepal to bring Tibetan Buddhism to the West (McLagan 1996: 205–8). This shows the international approval of that political course apart from the Indian restrictive frame. There are no data about the exact amounts of Western support for Tibetan Buddhism. Also unclear is whether the small Bön and Muslim communities receive Western aid or if the foreign monetary transfers are split between all different religions.

The exile Tibetan assembly and supreme justice commission receive 1.93 per cent of the annual budget. While the expenditures for the annual parliamentary sessions and the standing committee can be anticipated to be comparatively small, the judicatory sector is not yet well-developed.

To sum up, one can see that in the annual CTA budget of the fiscal year 2003/2004, the contributions of the 14th Dalai Lama, the exile Tibetan cabinet and various CTA departments were relatively small compared with the most important item, the project funds of the international community. They were six times higher than the total operating budget. This amount portrays the high dependency of the CTA on international financial support. Such dependency has a considerable impact on the exile community, as there is no need to develop an exile Tibetan economic sector. This in turn finds expression in the high unemployment rates among the exile Tibetans. Nevertheless, most exile Tibetans live in relative wealth compared with the local people—a situation criticized by and confusing for Western visitors. Another symbolically important budget item represents the annual voluntary contribution of all exile Tibetans. The estimated amount of 40,000,000 Indian Rs. was interpreted by a high ranking CTA official as a sufficient sum to cover all costs for the running of the entire administrative structure. Such a statement can be disproved by looking at the expenditures of the annual CTA budget.

The expenditures of the fiscal year 2003/2004 were orientated on political relevance for the CTA. In the forefront were the work of the cabinet, the DIIR and the security department—executive sectors that were all headed by the exile Tibetan Prime Minister. In this regard, his power within the CTA was backed up by 33 per cent of all CTA expenditures. This item was followed by the running of the administration and the educational sector. Social welfare, the health sector and religious affairs enjoyed only minor importance in the annual expenditures. Equally treated were the judiciary and legislative affairs, which portrayed their relative insignificance in the CTA structure.

Interesting in terms of the political position of the CTA is that all monetary flows run through the CTA. The CTA is in a monopoly of 'middleman' position in terms of access to financial resources, which mainly come from the international community. Such exclusive access fosters the political position of the CTA to decide about allocation of financial resources.

According to the research question of how the CTA fostered its claims to be the sole representative of all Tibetans over the decades in exile, the amended theoretical framework provided an adequate instrument to answer it with regard to the organizational structure of the CTA. It became clear that the political position of the CTA to act on behalf of the entire Tibetan nation as its sole representative is determined by the pre-exile political structures in Tibet, the institution of the Dalai Lama, the CTA's structural set-up, the unofficial acknowledgement of the Tibetan movement and the CTA by the international community, including the host country India. These factors favorably influence the superior political position of the CTA within the Tibetan community and foster its representative claims. But how do certain exile Tibetan policies contribute to the political position of the CTA as the sole representative of the entire Tibetan nation?

In previous discussion, I have focused on overall CTA politics, such as the changes in the political course in exile Tibet and the promotion of human and women's rights through the various exile Tibetan NGOs. I illustrated that the CTA policies have been changing over time according to international developments, which made the shaky political position of the CTA clear. But some questions still remain:

In the context of the first efforts of the CTA to get settled in India, I stressed the importance of education in exile. Despite the CTA facing enormous financial constraints in the early years of exile, the 14th Dalai Lama enforced the establishment of an exile Tibetan educational system. Instead of making such immense investments, the exile Tibetans could have attended already existing Indian or Nepali schools. Additionally, it became clear in the previous examination that there is no functioning economic sector in exile, which would provide employment for the thousands of well-educated exile Tibetans. So why did the CTA set-up its own schools instead of enrolling the exile children in the already existing Indian, Nepali and Bhutanese schools? And how is the educational system used by the CTA to foster its superior political status?

While examining the position of the exile Tibetan NGOs, it became evident that the promotion of democracy, human, eco and women's rights have been increasingly used to raise awareness in the international community for the exile Tibetan struggle. The exile Tibetan Prime Minister stressed the importance of these universal rights in the exile Tibetan struggle, and he even put these topics above the political goal of the exile Tibetan struggle, the return to a free homeland. So the question remains: Why does the promotion of human, eco and women's rights in Tibet enjoy such a high priority in the CTA, while the main goal of the exile struggle is to regain the homeland?

In the context of the annual budget, I showed that the amount of available money has risen over the years. While a functioning economic sector is absent, the exile Tibetans in India were extraordinarily successful in mobilizing international monetary resources. This is interesting in regard to Shain, who stated that the monetary base of exile organizations is in general limited and even decreases over time rather than grows. Only in cases when an exile community contributes somehow to the domestic politics of a supporting state, its government may continue the support of the exiles. As the CTA increasingly relies on international help, two questions come up: How can the CTA maintain and even expand international support over the years, as illustrated in the development of the annual budget? And why does the CTA enjoy such broad popularity?

In the portrayal of the structure of the CTA it has become obvious that it aims to function according to Western secular concepts of democracy. The democratic ideas, introduced by the 14th Dalai Lama in 1960, have not been fully implemented until the present day. Particularly critical, is the role of the Dalai Lama within the exile democracy, who derives his legitimacy out of the traditional tulku-concept of reincarnation. So why did the CTA apply insufficiently the secular democratic ideas within the exile Tibetan political structures?

In the following chapter, I systematically analyze and characterize exemplary CTA policies with the viewpoint of the mobilization of national and international support, which will provide a basis for answering these questions.

5 Theoretical characterization of CTA policies

Based on the amended theoretical approach, all CTA policies can be characterized following the question: How do the policies contribute to an exile government's mobilization process of national loyalty and international support? As an exile government depends on the support of present and potential members, it needs to use the available resources in a tactical way to secure its own organizational survival and to return home. According to Wilson's assumptions, special importance is given in this context to the investment of material or immaterial rewards. Immaterial or so-called soft resources, such as ideology and cultural attraction, are particularly important in an exile context because an exile government's situation in a host country is characterized by a general loss of effective control over people and territory and consequently over material resources.

Mobilizing support of the national compatriots and international patrons is a challenging task for an exile government also because of its geographical distance to a large number of people it claims to represent and its limited abilities to reach the international community. Thus, there is a need for a well-functioning communication network. In the Tibetan context, one can anticipate that the CTA, located in north India, faces certain difficulties in the process of mobilization of national loyalty. As already mentioned, the Tibetans in India were resettled in a non-assimilative way, scattered throughout the whole Indian sub-continent.[1] Additionally, while numerous Tibetans live in Nepal, Bhutan, Taiwan, and in North American and European countries the majority still reside inside the Chinese borders. Consequently, the CTA needs to invest various incentives to mobilize all geographically separated members of the national community. Additionally, potential international supporters must be addressed from the north Indian base to foster the CTA's claimed position as legal and sole representative of the Tibetan nation. This is because the Tibetan question cannot be solely examined as a Sino–Tibetan problem. International political agents are not just neutral observers but also shape the entire debate between the two administrative bodies that claim to represent the Tibetan nation and territory.

In the following analysis, I refer to the CTA's efforts to create national loyalty and international support. Therefore, I look systematically at the concept of membership in the exile Tibetan community, the educational course in exile Tibet, the political use of Tibetan Buddhist religion, the promotion of universal rights and the implementation of democracy. In this context, I analyze the use of different incentives according to Wilson's categories, the reaction of the approached people in terms of a successful mobilization of support for the CTA and upcoming discrepancies. This analysis goes beyond Shain's research and will demonstrate that both foci, mobilizing national loyalty and international support, are interdependent.

Membership in the exile Tibetan community

With the loss of the Tibetan homeland, the CTA, as exile government, is challenged to create unity among all members of the Tibetan community. One instrument that is used is the so-called 'green book'—a name that derives from its outer appearance: a green hard cover booklet, the size of a passport. In Tibetan it is called the freedom booklet, rangzen lakhdeb (Sangay, L 2003: 126–7; Frechette 2004: 170). This document is issued by the CTA to every exile Tibetan with Tibetan parentage and shows Tibetan citizenship even if a particular Tibetan holds identification papers that are issued by the hosting government. The 'green book' is a membership card of the exile Tibetan community and comparable with a passport. While in India and Nepal it is used as traveling document and identification paper, it is also required when an exile Tibetan wants to travel abroad. Then the person needs to apply for an Identity Certificate (IC) at the GOI. But before the Indian Passport Office can proceed, the CTA checks the application, too. For a successful passing of the application, an exile Tibetan needs to submit a birth certificate, the 'green book', a valid Registration Certificate (RC) and a recommendation letter from the settlement officer in charge. When all submitted papers are checked by both entities, the CTA and GOI, the Tibetan receives, usually after one year, the permit to travel. Such practice shows an interaction between the CTA and the GOI regarding the exile Tibetan's traveling activities. The CTA is entitled to participate in the decision-making of whether an exile Tibetan is allowed to travel or not. Additionally, the procedure illustrates the interest of the GOI in a stable exile Tibetan community directed by the CTA, which acts as responsible authority for the Indians regarding all matters of the exile Tibetan community. This strengthens the CTA in its position as representative administration for all exile Tibetans.

According to the theoretical considerations, the concept of an exile membership is also important for the CTA in the context of competition with the host country for support of the exile Tibetans. The acquiring of Indian citizenship is actively discouraged by the CTA. Already in the 1960s, the exile administration urged the Indian authorities to refuse any exile Tibetan application. Since then a Tibetan in India needs to hire a lawyer and file a lawsuit to get Indian citizenship. As a result of these formalities, money and time-taking procedures, most Tibetans in south Asia remain stateless, despite considerable disadvantages that derive from such status. Exceptional cases found Jayanti Alam and mentioned that Tibetans who live in Darjeeling '. . . since many generations . . . consider themselves Indians, and they have Indian citizenships and jobs . . .' (2000: 20). Ann Frechette found in her research that the taking of the host country's citizenship is also controversially discussed among the Tibetans themselves. In some Tibetans' opinion, a new citizenship means '. . . disloyalty to Tibet and the Tibetan cause'. Others, who think more pragmatically, argue that '. . . real citizenship implies political loyalty, as citizenship that facilitates business is only a practical agreement' (2004: 130), i.e. the improvement to someone's life in exile through the acquiring of a new citizenship can be tolerated. Melvyn Goldstein stated in the context of new citizenship:

> The Dalai Lama Government [CTA], however, has maintained the position that Tibetans taking Indian citizenship would diminish the strength of the refugees' claims to Tibet. Taking Indian citizenship therefore is considered as a renunciation of Tibetan cultural and national aspirations and is actively opposed. It is obvious, however, that a consequence of this policy (whether intentional or not) is the greater dependence of the refugees on the Dalai Lama Government. Because as individuals Tibetans are stateless 'guests' of the GOI, their strength lies in their collectivity, and it is precisely the role of the Dalai Lama and the Dalai Lama Government to organize and represent that collectivity.
>
> (1975a: 180)

Based on my research, the status of the exile Tibetans is another indicator for measuring the exile Tibetans' loyalty to the CTA, as statelessness is seen by the CTA as a crucial precondition to preserve Tibetan national identity and consequently the claims of the CTA as sole representative of the Tibetan nation. In this regard, Goldstein's indirect question, whether such policy is carried out intentionally or not, can be clearly answered with the fact that the question of citizenship is important for the CTA's organizational survival and therefore used strategically. For many exile Tibetans, the 'green book' is a symbol of being a member of the Tibetan nation and refers in this regard to the theoretical advantages of citizenship, which implies a source of an individual's national pride. Consequently, it functions as a symbol of cultural and political existence that is shared with the other holders of the same citizenship. In this regard, the CTA cleverly solved the problem of displacement among the exile Tibetans who suffer from the loss of the Tibetan homeland and citizenship. Instead of taking the citizenship of the host or home country, the majority of exile Tibetans remain stateless with an 'exile Tibetan citizenship'—a status that is not internationally recognized but has a considerable impact on the psychological situation of the exiles. Moreover, one can anticipate that it also positively influences the exile Tibetan's opinion to struggle successfully for a free homeland because, according to Shain's theory, without a new citizenship of the host country the chances to return are enhanced. This in turn improves the relationship between insiders and outsiders: The exile Tibetans show their compatriots who still live in the homeland that they left their homes to struggle for the national cause instead of improving their individual standard of living through the taking of new citizenship in their host country.

But this membership in the exile Tibetan community is not granted unconditionally by the CTA, as the following explanations illustrate. In return for community services and identification, the CTA expects that all exile Tibetans contribute voluntarily a fixed amount of money, the so-called voluntary freedom tax, to the exile Tibetan administration. The name derives out of the idea that the 'money is used to free Tibet', i.e. in the beginning period to gain an independent and since 1989, an autonomous homeland (interview with Mr Lodrö Sampo, Dharamsala, April 2003). This payment is considered to be affordable by every exile and is symbolical, as a contribution to the exile Tibetan struggle under the guidance of the CTA. The contribution follows a graduated system whereby a minimum amount of money is fixed according to age and income, above which every exile Tibetan is free to pay more. For instance, exile Tibetans in India, Nepal and Bhutan between the age of 6 and 18 are requested to pay annually a minimum of 36 Indian Rs. to one of the TPFM offices; exile Tibetans who live in these countries and are above 18 years are asked to contribute a minimum of 46 Indian Rs., while those who earn a regular salary should transfer at least 2 per cent of their gross or 4 per cent of their basic salary to the CTA. There is no fixed amount for individual businessmen yet, but they usually pay more than the minimum amount.[2] Exile Tibetans living abroad are requested to donate through one of the exile Tibetan committees that are set-up in every country with a Tibetan population or one of the CTA offices.[3] Here Tibetans between 6 and 18 years are asked to pay a minimum of US$36,[4] Tibetans above 18, unemployed or in the educational process US$46, semi-employed Tibetans US$71 and full employees US$96. Based on total monetary terms, one can say that the exile Tibetans living abroad contribute more than those in India, Nepal and Bhutan (interview with Mr Ugyen Chaksam, Department of Finance, Dharamsala, April 2003).

According to the amount of contributed money, the exile Tibetans receive different stamps, which need to be stuck into the 'green book' to give an exact account of the years and amount of payments. The stamps depict Tibetan national symbols and, the more a Tibetan contributes, the more sophisticated becomes the design on the received stamp. Because the contribution is collected to free Tibet it lies in the symbolic nature of such a tool to design stamps in relation with the goal. For instance, the stamp for 20 monetary units shows the design of a Panda bear, for 250 a yak and for 25,000 the homeland Cholka Sum.[5] The voluntary contribution also has social effects because with a growing amount of contributed money the social status and reputation of the individual increases within the exile Tibetan community.

This result is emphasized by the CTA through the practice of granting special honors to the most generous exile Tibetans at special ceremonies or national holidays. According to an official of the finance department, such publicity is mostly granted to Tibetan businessmen in Nepal and India (interview with Mr Ugyen Chaksam, Department of Finance, Dharamsala, May 2002). Such esteem can be theoretically categorized as specific solidarity incentive that arises due to the act of associating with an organization. It is not exchangeable and its value depends on the exclusion of certain members of an organization.

The Department of Finance interprets the payment as an opportunity for every exile Tibetan to support the CTA apart from his/her daily duties, place of residence, profession or income (interview with Mr Ugyen Chaksam, Department of Finance, Dharamsala, May 2002). Such support may create feelings of satisfaction among the Tibetans of being at least indirectly involved in the exile Tibetan struggle. Such emotional satisfaction is categorized by Wilson as 'purpositive incentive' (Wilson 1973: 34). It depends on the stated objectives of the organization and derives from the sense of individual satisfaction of having contributed something to the attainment of a worthwhile cause. But particularly in the Asian host countries, where the material survival for many exile Tibetans is determined by social and financial constraints, the refusal of the payment may result in isolation, economic hardship and exclusion from the political process in Tibetan exile because:

> only those who show that they are up-to date on their taxes are able to enjoy certain privileges such as the right to vote, eligibility for jobs in the CTA and eligibility for immigration programs (for example to the US in 1990).
>
> (Mountcastle 1997: 123)

Such exclusion from active participation in elections, from work in the CTA structures and the CTA immigration programs, shows that the CTA is in a position to sanction those who are not holders of the 'green book'. In this regard, the small booklet becomes a powerful instrument for the CTA to foster its own position in terms of support of the exile community.

Most important in this context is the mediation of donor aid. As the CTA holds power since the beginning years in exile over the distribution of financial resources drawn from international supporters, it passes on such money in exchange for the exile Tibetan's allegiance to the CTA's politics. Those Tibetans who fail to support the Dharamsala administration are excluded from international help, for example, they are unable to get a CTA scholarship to study at a university abroad. Margret McLagan considered aid as a CTA negotiation tool and control mechanism in India and Nepal as '... recipients or potential recipients [are obliged] to show political deference to their own government before their needs as refugees will be addressed' (1996: 224).[6] Frechette put it as: 'International organizations provide the exile administration with the resources it needs to entice fellow Tibetan exiles into compliance with its decisions' (2004: 157). Anonymous interview partners in India, Nepal and some Western countries told me that the material benefits have minor importance compared with the aforementioned psychological effects.

According to the CTA, the majority of exile Tibetans pay the requested amount of money annually. But there are also those who are reluctant to pay. Unsurprisingly, data about the number of these renegades are not available, only that their number is higher among members of the Tibetan Diaspora abroad compared with the exile Tibetans in Asian countries (interview with Mr Ugyen Chaksam, Department of Finance, Dharamsala, May 2002). Those who are reluctant to contribute money to the CTA, who I have spoken to during my fieldwork, have doubts about the exile politics and therefore refuse to support the CTA with a donation. This was also illustrated in the example of the above-mentioned '13 Settlements'. Because the renegades are at best in a materially independent situation, they neither suffer from material disadvantages nor from their status of not being officially part of the exile Tibetan community. They rather enjoy their freedom and moreover develop a feeling of unity in opposing the general opinion (anonymous interviews, 2003). In this regard, the voluntary contribution is a quantitative measure of loyalty for the CTA. The regular payments portray a general acceptance of the CTA as legitimate representative by the exile Tibetan people. So the payment provides every Tibetan with a chance '. . . to demonstrate support to the exile Government and confirm his or her exile status' (Bhattacharjea 1994: 8). This fact is also proved by the interpretation of the annual contribution as a sufficient financial basis to run the CTA. But it needs to be considered that especially those who suffer economic shortages mainly caused by unemployment in the Asian countries, are in no position to decide voluntarily about their contributions because their unwillingness to pay would deepen their financial constraints. Consequently, the 'voluntary contribution' can be considered as a tax payment to the CTA. Even though the CTA has no power to impose directly any sanctions among those who do not pay, there are indirect constraints especially among those who are in a difficult economic position. Frechette summarized in her research: 'The exile administration has no coercive means to force Tibetan exiles to pay their taxes. It encourages them to do so by making access to international resources contingent on tax payments' (2004: 159). But also in the context of a political opposition within the CTA structures, I put forward the following hypothesis: Those who are reluctant to contribute are critics of the CTA and are therefore excluded from the exile Tibetan political process. This in turn gives evidence to the reality that the CTA does not tolerate any opposition within exile 'democracy'.

Furthermore, the involvement of Indian authorities, who require the 'green book' as a necessary document in their decision about allowing exile Tibetans to travel, fosters the legal status of the CTA and shows an interest in the loyalty of the exile Tibetans in India to the CTA—a fact not considered by Shain.

If, for some reason, the 'green book' becomes necessary (for travels abroad, etc.) for an exile Tibetan who is reluctant to follow the CTA requests, it is possible to purchase such a book illegally in Nepal without contributing any money to the CTA at all. Such a supply of forged 'green books' in a market situation portrays a considerable demand for such books. According to anonymous interviewees, there are even numerous Nepali people who got these books in the initial years or have purchased them to become members of the exile Tibetan community. With such membership, they anticipate certain advantages (like material and moral support from the international community). Frechette also emphasized this fact by pointing out that the Sherpa and Manangi people in Nepal use 'green books' to apply for scholarships for their children in CTA schools (2004: 170 n: 20).

As with the 'green book' for individual exile Tibetans, the CTA initiated in 1992 a 'brown book', specially created for exile Tibetan Institutions (NGOs, departments, business units). The requested amount by the CTA for government-run businesses is at the moment 15 per cent of the net profit. Tibetan departments that raise their own project funds are requested to contribute at least 2 per cent of the net project fund (see Ch. 4). In return, the institution receives a 'brown book' that is not, like its green counterpart, linked to any special material benefits. It is rather attached with symbolic importance for the institutions that support the exile Tibetan community (interview with Mr Ugyen Chaksam, Department of Finance, Dharamsala, April 2003).

The only institutions exempted from the 'tax' are the monasteries. Such exemption is striking because the CTA constantly lacks financial resources, yet the monasteries operate successfully as business units in comparison with many government or private enterprises. The establishment of new cultural institutions and a renaissance of religious and artistic production provide the monasteries with considerable economic power (Roemer 2001: 39–41, 46–7; interview with Mr Phuntsok Gonpo, Department of Religion and Culture, Dharamsala, April 2003), which, surprisingly, is not taxed by the CTA. The reason for such 'tax-exemption' of the exile Tibetan monasteries can be explained in different ways. First, the traditional patterns of the pre-exile situation are still important in the exile context. With the existing pre-1959 *status quo*, the CTA follows its traditions supporting the special status of the Tibetan monasteries in Tibet before 1959. This is further emphasized by the worldwide promotion of the preservation of Tibetan culture and religion. Second, there is a powerful monastic lobby within the exile Tibetan administrative structure. Many religious dignitaries work in high official positions or are consulted for political decisions.[7] A member of the exile Tibetan parliament said that the monk deputies always protest when the lay parliamentarians want to discuss the privileges of the monastic community. He thinks that they 'don't want to lose power' (anonymous interview, 2006).

Such appointment of the traditional political elite in key positions refers to the theoretical importance of leadership in the pre-exile context (Shain 1989: 78). Third, exile Tibetan monasteries shoulder a great amount of the costs of the newly arriving Tibetans in India and Nepal because, as mentioned before, between 24 and 45 per cent of the new arrivals are monks and nuns. They all need to be placed in one of the exile monasteries where they receive shelter, food and education. The special treatment of the exile Tibetan monasteries in terms of taxation emphasizes Eric McGuckin's argument that monastic power reaches far beyond religious and cultural preservation to elicit monetary resources (1997: 75). Fourth, Wilson's theory stresses the investment of incentives to certain members of the organizational structure to motivate them to act on behalf of the organization. This group of tangible rewards includes services, money and economic goods but also tax reductions. In this regard, the CTA secures the support of the monasteries by awarding them a special status in exile.

Following the examples of the 'green and brown books', the CTA gives non-Tibetans who regularly donate to the CTA the opportunity to obtain a so-called blue book. While in the beginning years of exile, some Westerners successfully applied for 'green books' to contribute to the Tibetan government-in-exile the number of international supporters grew with the time (Frechette 2004: 170 n: 20). To meet the wishes of the international patrons the CTA introduced in the 1990s the 'blue book'. The 'blue book' holder is not entitled to draw certain material benefits from it, but rather obtains immaterial benefits in terms of officially being part of the exile Tibetan struggle (interview with Mr Ugyen Chaksam, Department of Finance, Dharamsala, April 2003). According to Wilson's organization theory, such benefits can be classified, first, as collective solidarity incentives and, second, as 'purpositive incentives' (1973: 34) that provide an individual satisfaction due to the contribution to the attainment of a worthwhile cause.

Through the invention of three different books that all have a common meaning—membership in the exile Tibetan community—the CTA addresses the exile Tibetans, exile Tibetan institutions and non-Tibetans. While the exile Tibetans who live in the Indian subcontinent draw tangible and intangible advantages from such membership, the exile Tibetan institutions and non-Tibetans benefit from 'purpositive incentives'. Because of the employment shortages in Asia, the annual voluntary payments have a tax character, which in turn secures the exile Tibetans' loyalty to the CTA and therefore fosters its political position. This is moreover supported by the GOI, which entrusts the CTA to decide on the exile Tibetans' behalf because of its own domestic political objectives. With the 'green book' in particular, the CTA counteracts the general problem of exile's denaturalization. It provides the exile Tibetans with a source of identity and membership in the exile Tibetan community. Shain did not attach great importance to the concept of an 'exile citizenship', neither did Iwańska, who mentioned, that the Polish and Spanish governments-in-exile issued passports (1981: 60). In this regard, the 'exile citizenship' represents a unique and fascinating form of an exile government's action, which first, provides the members of the exile community with a source of national identity and second, fosters the position of an exile government in terms of its representative claims.

Educational opportunities

In this chapter, I answer the following question: Why did the CTA set-up its own schools instead of enrolling the exile children in the already existing Indian, Nepali and Bhutanese schools? According to Margaret Nowak, the 14th Dalai Lama saw the following advantages in the education of his compatriots in exile: to create happiness among his people, to eliminate superstition and to preserve and promote Tibetan culture and religion (1984: 100–2). One can say that apart from the personal benefits of being educated, the exile Tibetan educational system was intended to play an important role in the political struggle of the CTA to regain the homeland under the guise of the preservation of Tibetan culture and religion.

From the political science point of view, the educational sector is one of the key elements for a government to create loyalty among people and to improve the political culture of a society (Ilchman and Uphoff 1997: 254–5. According to Wilson's organization theory, I classify the investments in education as tangible rewards. The main research question in this context is: How is the educational system used by the CTA to foster its superior political status?

As mentioned in Chapter 4, the present exile Tibetan school system is highly faceted compared with the initial years in exile. But despite the schools differences in funding or administration, the majority have a close link to the CTA. One exception is the Dorji School in Nepal that challenges the CTA in its decisions.[8] But in general, the two main educational authorities, the Department of Education and the Central Tibetan Schools Administration (CTSA), are directly linked to the 14th Dalai Lama through their secretaries and an auditor general.

> The links in the chain between the Tibetan children and their leader, His Holiness the XIVth Dalai Lama, are two: the Council for Tibetan Education, which is the official body of the Tibetan Government-in-Exile; and the Central Tibetan Schools Administration (CTSA), an autonomous body under the Ministry of Education of the Government of India.
>
> (CTE, cited in John 1999: 299)

The Tibetan pupils are also daily reminded of the Tibetan leader because his photos are pinned on the walls in every classroom. Furthermore, the pupils sing that they are thankful to attend schools, which would not be possible without the engagement of the 14th Dalai Lama (anonymous interview, 2006). Such close links in the course of education secures the pupils' and, later, the adults' loyalty to the Tibetan political and religious leadership. The exile Tibetan education system aims that all Tibetan children are educated in both Tibetan traditional and modern subjects to raise the new generation's confidence in economic, cultural and political ways with a clear emphasis on Tibetan culture and identity. The CTA described its aims as followed:

> The very purpose of establishing Tibetan schools is to prepare our children to face the challenges of the modern world, grounded firmly in our traditional values. As a result, though we have lost our country, we have not lost our identity.
>
> (CTA n.d. f: 3)

This statement illustrates that the educational course emphasizes the CTA's focus on the preservation of Tibetan religion and culture within a context of modernity. The CTA aims to raise literacy among the countrymen so they can manage their daily lives in exile. Because of the importance of the preservation of Tibetan traditions, the pupils, who are to a large extent born in India and Nepal, are familiarized with the exile Tibetan struggle under the lead of the CTA. In the center of the educational course is the creation of a Tibetan identity and therefore an understanding for the exile status from early childhood onwards—to be a foreigner in a host state.

Principally, the curriculum in all exile Tibetan schools in India follows Indian (in general the host country's) guidelines set by the Board for Education. This ensures that all pupils in India reach a certain level of education, which provides them with the opportunity for a higher course of education and to study at Indian schools. Such guidelines expose the involvement of the host country in the exile Tibetan activities and show that the exiles are not free to decide on school curriculum. But apart from the regular Indian program of study, pupils in exile Tibetan schools are taught compulsory subjects, such as Tibetan history, literature, opera, dance and music. In this context, it has to be mentioned that Sino–Tibetan history in particular is highly politicized. According to the 14th Dalai Lama, '[a]s to history, we . . . take what we need, adopting what we need, and disregarding what we do not like' (14th Dalai Lama, cited in Sautman 2000: 35).[9]

While the CTA focuses on the passing on of Tibetan religious and political ideas, it is interesting to note that there is no subject such as 'Tibetan religion' or 'Buddhism' in the official school curriculum. This is because, according to Indian guidelines, it is particularly left aside to prevent any discrimination, which is important in a multi-religious country like India. Instead, the pupils are taught 'Civics', comprising general knowledge in political structures and secular philosophy. The banning of religion in schools is awkward for the CTA, as religion is an integral part of exile Tibetan life (interview with Mr Tashi Rika, Department of Education, Dharamsala, March 2003) and, moreover, part of the preservation of Tibetan traditions. The exile Tibetan schools circumvent the Indian guidelines through daily prayers and ceremonies on a practical level. In this regard, Tibetan boarding schools, religious ceremonies and prayers are an integral part for the pupils in their daily schedule. There are morning prayers and assemblies where national symbols like the national anthem, flag and school uniforms are used to create nationalistic feelings but also daily songs to praise the 14th Dalai Lama. Furthermore, the pupils participate in national holidays through the performance of national music and dance or in demonstrations. The participation in such rituals is given reason by the CTA by the widespread practice that the children only visit their families sporadically because of the distance between school and home. This creates, according to Gudrun Ludwar's study, a loss of practice in Tibetans' religious and traditional patterns (1975: 175–8). At the intellectual level, there are frequent visits by monks in the schools, who teach the basics of Buddhist philosophy to the pupils in the afternoons (Nowak 1984: 81). They are also taught about the universal value of their religion (McLagan 1996: 215). In this context, it is seen that the Tibetan traditional centers of education, the monasteries, are still involved in the exile Tibetan educational system. Not only a large part of the literate exile Tibetan population in India and Nepal enjoy a monastic education (16.7 per cent) (CTA 2000f: 106), the exile monasteries also participate in the secular educational process. This fosters their position within the exile Tibetan society and also supports the political position of the CTA, which relies to a large extent on traditional leadership.

In addition to Buddhist doctrine, in their free time, the pupils are also taught exile Tibetan political ideas. So-called outside instructors, like TCHRD employees, teach the CTA's principles of non-violence, truth and democracy, the Tibetan version of history and about the present situation in the homeland with a special emphasis on human, eco and women's rights (Boyd 1999: 105). Katrin Goldstein-Kyaga even mentioned so-called 'peace zones' that are set-up in every exile Tibetan school. The pupils who quarrel are sent to these zones to solve their problems peacefully (2003: 97), though I could find no proof of the existence of such zones during my own field studies.

Through the additional educational measures, which go beyond the official guidelines of the host authorities, the Tibetan educational system passes on nationalistic ideas to the new generation. Modern Tibetan history and Buddhism are especially used to create a Tibetan identity. Robert Ekvall recognized five criteria that are important for Tibetans to affirm their cultural self-consciousness: religion, folkways, language, race, and land. He considers religion as the most important criteria in the Tibetan context (Ekvall 1960: 376),[10] and the difference between 'believers' and 'non-believers' is used in exile Tibetan schools as a basis for a Tibetan collective identity. Historically, the main distinction between Tibetans and non-Tibetans was made on the basis of religion. Believers of the Tibetan religion were literally called 'insiders' (nangpa) while the others were called 'non-believers' (chipa) regardless of a person's birthplace. This collective identity can be witnessed during the teachings and initiations of the 14th Dalai Lama, where regional and sectarian differences no longer exist (Shakya 1993: 9). Åshild Kolås stated that the religious and regional discrepancies between the pupils are downplayed, while the conflict between Tibetans and Chinese is constantly accented. The differences between exile Tibetans and local Indians are not communicated at all (1996: 58). In my opinion, such differentiation refers to the exile Tibetan struggle against the Chinese because with the creation and maintaining of an own identity and therefore a clear distinction between Tibetans and Chinese, there is a clear picture of the exile's counterpart. In contrast, the local host population is integrated in the exile struggle simply because the exiles depend on the goodwill of the host country in terms of tolerance and providing political shelter. In this regard, the CTA fosters its own status in enforcing a Tibetan identity and motivating the members of the exile community to support its politics.

Such a process is even more influenced by the present CTA practice of granting scholarships, as the following examination illustrates. For higher education and specialized training, every exile Tibetan can apply for scholarships either to Indian authorities or the CTA. Between 1995 and 2002, the CTA granted 2,044 scholarships in India, and between 1982 and 2002, 367 abroad.[11] No other authority awards more scholarships to exile Tibetans than the CTA. In the year 2002, the CTA granted 330 scholarships in India and 65 abroad. There are two CTA committees that select for suitable students: the Scholarship Committee, which handles scholarships within India, and the Second High Scholarship Committee (SHSC), are responsible for universities abroad. Both committees are chaired by high CTA officials, the SHSC even by the exile Tibetan Prime Minister.

Scholarships are only exceptionally granted for an academic degree but more often for vocational training. This is due to the CTA's view that vocational training provides better opportunities to serve the exile Tibetan struggle and therefore is seen as more valuable. So exile Tibetans study abroad with the approval of the CTA, for instance, in water management, construction, nursing or teaching (interview with Mr Tashi Rika, Department of Education, Dharamsala, March 2003). The procedure of sorting out the hundreds of applicants is handled carefully, especially in cases for a scholarship abroad. In addition to an excellent academic background, potential recipients need to prove previous community services and the payment of the annual voluntary contribution to the CTA (and their parents and/or spouse).[12] There are similar requirements for a CTA sponsorship program, where the CTA acts as the link between Western people who are willing to sponsor an exile Tibetan child or a needy Tibetan family.[13] According to the details on the 'green book', this practice shows that material incentives of the CTA are linked with the exile Tibetans' support of the CTA. Only through the annual payment and community services is an exile Tibetan given the chance to receive financial support for education, regardless of his or her academic skills. Furthermore, the CTA links a scholarship to a binding commitment to support the exile Tibetan struggle. After finishing the training, the recipient of a scholarship has the obligation to serve, for a limited period of time, in the exile administrative structure. Consequently, the scholarship program provides a key factor for the CTA's efforts to secure the exile Tibetan's loyalty in the educational course.

Around 80 per cent of the students who were given a scholarship follow this obligation, while the remaining 20 per cent, mostly those studying abroad, do not. They refuse on the spot to return to Asia, despite appeals either made by the CTA or by exile Tibetan organizations (for instance, the CTA or the TPFM offices). But the CTA has no coercive means apart from calling on them in the name of the national cause. Such losses in human capital make the hard selection process understandable (John 1999: 312; Wangyal 2000: 21).

On my question on the loss of bright students, the CTA Department of Education reacted unexpectedly. My interview partner saw in the brain drain a positive development because the migration would help to promote the exile Tibetan struggle in the Western world (interview with Mr Tashi Rika, Department of Education, Dharamsala, April 2002). The secretary of the DIIR adds that Tibetans who migrated to the Western world would 'feel more rootless' and become 'more a Tibetan', which in turn increases their desire to be more politically involved in the exile struggle (interview with Mr Thupten Samphel, DIIR, Dharamsala, April 2003). But this viewpoint was toned down by further arguments that those who never return to India may be less dedicated to the exile Tibetan struggle and rather act out of self-interest to improve their individual livelihood. They are interested in money-making and business (interviews with Mr Tashi Rika, Department of Education, Dharamsala April 2002 and Mr Thupten Samphel, DIIR, Dharamsala April 2003). This shows in my opinion a withdrawal of loyalty of parts of the educated youth, who focus rather on their own well-being than on the exile struggle of the CTA (CTA 2004: 14). Moreover, those I have talked to and who want to remain anonymous complain about a considerable frustration and helplessness about CTA politics and the failed results in the Tibetan freedom struggle until the present day.

The development of brain drain is emphasized by Indian restrictions for exile Tibetans and their children who arrived in India after 1962 to study at Indian universities. Not being permanent Indian residents, they must apply for admission, which makes the entrance for higher studies difficult. There are exceptions for exile Tibetans who got a CTA or Indian scholarship and those whose parents came to India before 1962. Otherwise, an exile Tibetan needs to take Indian citizenship. But as mentioned before in several passages, the taking of new citizenship is a sensitive issue and actively discouraged by the CTA. There is an expected acceleration of losing Tibetan identity and a simultaneous assimilation in Indian sub-cultures (Tsering Thondup 1990: 12). This would undermine the CTA struggle to preserve Tibetan religion and culture and limit the exile Tibetan loyalty to the CTA. Consequently, the young exile Tibetans' ambitions to study and improve their education level are in contrast with CTA politics. With the taking of Indian citizenship, the Tibetan youth automatically opposes the official exile political course. So they have the choice either to follow the CTA course and remain as non-Indian citizens or apply for Indian citizenship to have a chance to proceed with a higher education independently from the CTA scholarship program. Apart from the CIHTS in Sarnath, the CTA has not established any institution for higher studies yet, and plans for such a project have remained unsuccessful for decades (Tsering, Thondup 1996: 24).

Another bottleneck interrelated with the educational system and brain drain in the exile Tibetan community is the lack of employment opportunities. Because of the before mentioned absence of a functioning economic sector in exile, the CTA is unable to create sufficient employment opportunities for young graduated Tibetans and other specialists. Thondup Tsering stated that there is:

> absolutely no link between supply of human resources by the educational institutions with the actual requirements of the Tibetan community both quantitatively and qualitatively. Nobody seems [sic] to be working towards ensuring some reasonable parity between the supply and demand. This is reflected in the way scholarships are given and the total chaos and mismatch between manpower and employment situation in our community.
>
> (1996: 25)

Free vacancies in the CTA structure and job opportunities in the exile Tibetan community are limited. This lack of employment either leads to brain drain (Dorjee 1993) or to the situation of highly de-motivated students who are already looking for income opportunities at the secondary level (Gupta 2005: 196–7). This trend is even emphasized by the motivation of 72 per cent of the exile Tibetans to use their education first of all to improve their personal standard of living and to achieve economic self-reliance. As a result, education is influenced by the 'lack of any immediate benefits' (CTA 2004: 65).

In contrast, only 28 per cent of the exile Tibetans view education as necessary to fulfill '. . . community-based values such as serving the community, carrying forward the vision of His Holiness the Dalai Lama, and contributing towards Tibetan freedom struggle' (CTA 2004: 14). This shows that the exile Tibetan education system partly failed in terms of securing loyalty among the young Tibetans during the educational course. There is a tendency in exile that in the forefront of the opinion of many exile Tibetans are their daily economic survival and personal wealth rather than community service and the exile Tibetan struggle (Shastri 2006: 21). These developments explain a high drop out rate of nearly 50 per cent at primary and middle school levels and an unemployment rate of 16.9 per cent among the 16–25-year-old exile Tibetans in 1994 (CTA 2004: 14; 1994a: 85).

The problematic situation in the education sector does not only have an impact on the pupils and students but also on the teachers in the exile Tibetan schools: teachers are of both local (Indian or Nepali) and Tibetan heritage. Since the 1990s, the CTA has been struggling with a lack of well-trained teachers because of brain drain. For instance, in the 1990s approximately 250 Tibetan teachers migrated from Asia to North America when the USA permitted 1,000 Tibetans to settle there. Additionally, the CTA carried out an unbalanced policy in providing only few incentives to motivate Tibetans to become teachers, through limited numbers of scholarships during the period of studying and small salaries at the end of the educational course. The problematic situation became even more drastic during the 1990s with a change in the educational course, by introducing Tibetan language as teaching medium in the primary level, when the CTA realized the teachers' importance in the process of preserving the Tibetan traditions.[14] Since then, exile Tibetan teachers who are able to teach sciences, technology and mathematics but also traditional dance and music in a proper Tibetan language are rare. In contrast to these developments, the employed Indian teachers are considered by the CTA as unsuitable to fulfill the exile Tibetan standards of education. Thus, despite a general lack of Tibetan teachers, the CTA focuses on a reduction of Indian teachers (John 1999: 321–2).

These developments in the scope of teachers are in conflict with an increasing number of students. Besides a steady growing exile population, the educational opportunities in exile also attract many Tibetans who live within the PRC borders. There, Tibetan parents increasingly send their children to India for education—a situation that is portrayed in the above-mentioned exile Tibetan statistics, which show that large parts of all new arrivals are between the ages of 14 and 25. The situation in the lessons in the exile schools is even worsened by the fact that the majority of the exile Tibetan teachers are unable to speak the Chinese language or the different local Tibetan dialects that are spoken by the new arrivals. In this regard, the passing on of knowledge and skills becomes difficult and sometimes even impossible (anonymous interview, 2006).

Many of the young Tibetans return home after the educational process to find a job in the PRC. Their knowledge in languages (Chinese, Tibetan, English and Hindi) and at least basic skills in reading and writing advantageously influence their job-finding process, yet the fact of being educated in the exile system may cause suspicion and disapproval in the PRC. According to the CTA, the steady flow of young Tibetans between the homeland and exile provides a chance to promote exile political objectives inside the Chinese borders. With regard to Shain's and Iwańska's theoretical considerations, such contact between insiders and outsiders is most important for a well-functioning relationship in terms of the achievement of the goal of an exile struggle. Kevin Garratt found in his research that the CTA actively encourages Tibetans to return home in '. . . an attempt to relieve pressure on relevant Tibetan educational institutions rather than merely seeking to hold the line in Tibet itself' (1997: 47).

Besides a personal development through the improved level of education, young Tibetans carry CTA ideas and political viewpoints to their village or nomad tent. They are encouraged by the CTA to teach their families basic knowledge and, above that, a critical view on their life under the Chinese administration and of the contents of the political work in exile (interview with Mr Tashi Rika, Department of Education, Dharamsala, April 2002). So with the incentives of a free primary education in exile and a secondary education with Western sponsorship, the CTA fosters its superior position and the loyalty of the students who are thankful for the educational opportunities. Moreover, their parents and friends at home study the political course of the CTA and are linked to the exile Tibetan struggle even if they live in remote areas of the homeland. So the investments in the education system are useful to secure the loyalty of the Tibetans in exile and the people at home. The encouragement of the young Tibetans who intend to return home is emphasized by a blessing of the 14th Dalai Lama, a ritual for all new arrivals, which is for all Tibetans a lifetime highlight. Additionally, the 14th Dalai Lama shows with such ceremony that he has not forgotten his national compatriots back home.

In summary, the educational course is used by the CTA to foster its superior position among the Tibetan exiles who are still of school age, and therefore gives reason for the enormous investments in the educational sector right from the start in exile. Tibetan culture and religion are major foci of the educational course in the exile Tibetan schools in South Asia to create a Tibetan identity. To the CTA's regret, these specific Tibetan subjects are officially excluded from the Indian schools and therefore need to be taught compulsorily through outside instructors and through the participation in national holidays and daily rituals, like prayers and singing of the national anthem. Crucial factors in securing loyalty are the scholarship and sponsorship programs of the CTA, which foster the CTA position through the monopoly on financial resources and access to international universities. Only those who are bright, politically active in supporting the official CTA policy and pay the voluntary contribution to the CTA annually benefit from grants and the allowance to study at universities abroad and in India. Furthermore, the educational system also attracts many Tibetan parents who live within the Chinese borders to send their children to one of the exile Tibetan schools. Many of these students return home after finishing their educational course and contribute to the exile Tibetan struggle by passing on their knowledge of CTA politics to their parents and friends inside the PRC. In this regard, they link the exile Tibetan community with the Tibetans in the homeland, which is, according to the theory of exile governments, most helpful in minimizing upcoming discrepancies between the two communities. This in turn supports the position of the CTA as the representative of all Tibetans. The importance of the educational sector in the exile struggle is not mentioned by Shain and therefore represents a new focus in the theoretical discourse on exile governments.

But the exile Tibetan educational course also contains many problems, such as high drop out rates in schools, a lack of highly skilled human resources because of brain drain and little dedication to the exile Tibetan struggle, and also high unemployment among the youth. These developments may have weakening effects on the position of the CTA as the number of people who actively support the exile Tibetan struggle is limited. After decades in exile, many of the Tibetan exiles care now more for their individual wealth than for their return to the homeland.

Tibetan Buddhist nationalism

In this chapter, I look at the phenomenon of nationalism, and how the Tibetan exile government's emphasis on nationalistic ideas can help to mobilize national loyalty and international support. The importance of nationalism in the context of an exile government's struggle against the present home government is stressed in the theoretical context (Shain 1989: 131, 145). But no elaborate comments on that issue are made by Shain. In this regard, I clarify his overall theoretical finding.

In the following sections, I examine the major and officially celebrated traditional holidays and newly created ceremonies and symbols, which foster the CTA's political position by inducing a feeling of unity among the participants. Furthermore, I show how Tibetan nationalism is used to motivate the national Diaspora abroad, in particular to take an active part in the exile Tibetan struggle. Then I illustrate the reaction of the international community to the promoted Tibetan nationalist image and how it contributes to the political claims of the CTA.

The source of Tibetan nationalism is predominantly described by Tibetan Buddhism. Following the argumentation of Åshild Kolås, Tibetan Buddhism provides several idioms for the political discourse in Dharamsala. There is, for instance, the aforementioned distinction between 'insiders, believers' and 'non-believers' that is widely used in the educational course. This distinction is also important for the uneducated, old or newly arriving Tibetans. Such religion-based differentiation is at present combined with a definition of a secular Tibetan identity along geographical lines, which distinguishes between Tibetans (böpa), Chinese (gyami) and Westerners (inji). This secular concept of a Tibetan identity runs along the lines of a Western terminology of nationhood and in this regard, appeals to an international audience (1996: 51–66). Because of a close link between Tibetan nationalism and religion, most Tibetan national symbols are related to Tibetan Buddhism. In the opinion of the 14th Dalai Lama, Tibetan religion and consequently also religious rituals are '. . . helpful in keeping Tibetan patriotism alive' (1991: 12).

Tibetan national symbols appear to everybody who enters an exile Tibetan settlement in Asia, in the form of colorful prayer flags that are tied around trees and roofs, mani stone walls, reliquary monuments (chörten), small altars and Tibetan monasteries. Stepping into someone's house, an altar, pictures of the 13th and 14th Dalai Lamas and other religious dignitaries can be seen. The religious practice is still an essential part of every exile Tibetan's life. Additionally, there are numerous traditional religious rituals that are officially celebrated and are part of an annual celebration calendar,[15] like monastic cham dances, which dramatize transition, Tibetan New Year celebrations (losar) or the mönlam chenmo, the great prayer where religious power takes over from the secular (Ström 1995: 204–5).

According to Morton Grodzins, the creation of a ceremonial calendar is a promising tool to evoke national sentiments among the members of a nation because ceremonies and rituals decrease differences among people (1956: 61). Moreover, they support the process to distinguish the participants of the rituals from others who are excluded. Therefore rituals and ceremonies help to create a self-perception and identity (Wulf 2001). Such interpretation applies to Wilson's collective solidarity incentives, which are invested by an organization to motivate its members to play an active part in the organizational structures. The advantages for the members to belong to an organization derive from the feeling of association, which is one of the most important psychological needs of exiles.

The ceremonial calendar in exile Tibet starts with a three-day celebration of the Tibetan New Year at the end of February or the beginning of March, which is highlighted by a CTA-organized celebration. During this time, all CTA offices and Tibetan shops are closed. It is interesting to note that the lunar cycle, which also determines the dates of the Tibetan New Year, is still in use among exile Tibetans, despite the current Gregorian calendar in India. While the secular events are dated after the host's Gregorian calendar, the numerous religious celebrations are determined by the traditional Tibetan lunar calendar—a practice that refers to the traditional Tibetan context and therefore bridges Tibetan past and exile present.

The New Year celebrations are followed by a national commemoration of the Tibetan Uprising on 10 March, 1959 in Lhasa. The official commemoration takes place in Dharamsala, while similar celebrations on a smaller scale are organized in all exile Tibetan communities worldwide. The Uprising represents the beginning of Tibetan exilehood and therefore 10 March portrays a central rite of exile Tibetan's patriotism and honors emotionally the Tibetan people's revolt in Lhasa. In the following, I briefly sketch the 43rd celebration in 2002, which I witnessed. Margaret Nowak and Christiaan Klieger gave similar accounts on the 10 March commemorations of the years 1977 and 1987, respectively (Nowak 1984: 151–5; Klieger 1992: 60–4). Comparing the different accounts on the central ceremony one can say that the event roughly follows a similar protocol.

The 43rd commemoration took place at the main temple of the Gelugpa Namgyal monastery, right across the 14th Dalai Lama's residence. Numerous Tibetans and armed Indian security people ensured that nobody entered the place with unwelcome items (cameras, arms, knives, etc.). Such high presence of security forces shows in my opinion a certain sensibility of the exile

Tibetan and Indian authorities about potential assassinations or quarrels during the ceremony. The security people showed the mixed crowd of around 2,000 Tibetan people and Western tourists their assigned seating, which roughly followed the social strata of traditional Tibet, when the precedence and status of people was defined on the basis of whether a person is sitting or standing, the proximity of each position to the 14th Dalai Lama and the size of the chair or cushion. Furthermore, Christiaan Klieger witnessed a dominance of the secular faction compared to the pre-1959 composition (1992: 61). The ceremony started at 9a.m. with a traditional orchestra and a dance of TCV pupils dressed in traditional clothes. The crowd rose from their seats when the exile Tibetan Prime Minister, followed by the 14th Dalai Lama, entered the location. Then the Prime Minister hoisted the national flag while the crowd of exile Tibetans was singing the Tibetan national anthem; a prayer song which emphasizes non-violence and was composed by the 14th Dalai Lama (Goldstein 1975b: 23). It was followed by a marching band that accompanied another patriotic song, the more militant 'Song of the People's Uprising'.[16] The singing was followed by a mass prayer, after which the Prime Minister and then the chairman of the ATPD spoke to the crowd. Third to speak was the 14th Dalai Lama, who followed a printed speech that had been handed to the audience.[17] These annual speeches of the exile political elite are held in Tibetan and always stress the topics of Tibetan history, Tibetan resistance within the PRC and the exile struggle of the CTA. Furthermore, there are thanks to the Indian host population and the GOI for their support, which illustrates once more the importance of the host country (CTA 1995). The 2002 commemoration was highlighted by a presentation of a statue of the 14th Dalai Lama that had been designed by a Chinese artist who lived in New Zealand. The whole ceremony ended after three hours with another TCV performance. Then the 14th Dalai Lama left. Next the crowd started a CTA organized demonstration, following Gandhi's peace marathons (Pathak 2004b: 87), to the town of Dharamsala, five kilometers away. Tibetans and Western tourists waved Tibetan flags[18] accompanied by the shouting of English slogans, like 'Chinese get out of Tibet', 'Free Tibet', 'Tibet belongs to Tibetans', 'Long Life to the Dalai Lama', etc. Additionally, a few Indian flags were visible and some curious locals watched the shouting crowd from their doors and balconies. At the final destination, more speeches were given.

During and after the demonstration, I interviewed several young Tibetans about their opinion of the commemoration. All interviewees stressed the importance of the demonstration and their chance to give voice to their emotions, which otherwise is not welcomed by the CTA because of the non-violent exile struggle. The youth had been looking forward to this event for weeks.[19] According to the interviews, there is a general frustration among the young people about the non-violent struggle of the CTA and an emotional potential for more radical and sensational ways to promote the Tibetan cause. From a political science point of view, the whole commemoration stresses the different problems that are encountered by a government-in-exile.

Plate 3 Demonstrating young exile Tibetans on March 10, Dharamsala, India, 2002.

First, it emphasizes the relationship between insiders and outsiders. Through the religious and secular rituals, the CTA honors annually those who have sacrificed their lives for the Tibetan national struggle in opposition to the Chinese invaders. It keeps the historical events alive and renews the actuality of the existence of two separate nations: the Tibetans and the Chinese. Second, the ceremony creates a feeling of unity among all Tibetans who are involved in the struggle against the Chinese authority in Tibet. It strengthens their energies and confidence to return once to a free Tibetan homeland. Third, the event stresses the existence of an exile Tibetan community and its relationship to India. Fourth, the commemoration links the exile Tibetan community with present and potential supporters from Western countries. The non-Tibetan audience comprises free Tibet activists and curious tourists with some knowledge of the Tibetan struggle and the political circumstances that led to the present situation. In this regard, the CTA is able to maintain and expand Western operational and moral support for its struggle, which in turn fosters its superior position in terms of political and financial power within the exile community.

Two days later follows the commemoration of the Tibetan Women's Uprising in 1959 in Lhasa. This time the main ceremony takes place in New Delhi where exile Tibetan women march on the official Indian parading ground, Rajpath, from India Gate to the parliament complex, shouting free Tibet slogans under the leadership of the organizing TWA, which has a close relation with the CTA. Additionally, the TWA also organizes gatherings and commemorating ceremonies in all exile Tibetan settlements. These events specially address the exile Tibetan women to show their support of the exile Tibetan struggle and therefore their loyalty towards the CTA through active participation in a demonstration. Furthermore, they link the exile Tibetan women with their female compatriots who still live in the homeland. In this regard, the commemoration of the Tibetan Women's Uprising strengthens the relationship between all Tibetan women. According to Butler, the annual women's demonstrations represent an authenticating symbol of the TWA that is perceived as a direct descent from the women's demonstrations in 1959 (2003: 52–5). Such unifying symbols linking past and present (Smith 1992: 438) are important for a well-functioning insider–outsider relationship, which is, according to Shain's theory, important for the organizational survival of an exile government and the achievement of the goals of the national struggle.

These two secular political events are annually followed by the traditional mönlam chenmo series of religious instructions when the nationwide monastic population would fill the streets of Lhasa. With the help of their monastic force, the Lamas would take power from the civil magistrate of Lhasa and symbolically install ecclesiastical martial law for 21 days. The mönlam chenmo was introduced in 1409 by Tsongkhapa to preserve and protect Buddhism in Tibet. This rite of precedence of Tibetan religion is taken up in exile by a series of public teachings on Buddhist philosophy by the 14th Dalai Lama, which attract thousands of tourists annually because, first, they provide a chance to meet the 14th Dalai Lama and, second they are free (comparable instructions are costly in the West). Such tourist invasion provides many advantages for the local and Tibetan tourist businesses. Furthermore, the numerous tourists present, for the CTA, an opportunity to raise international awareness about the exile Tibetan struggle and mobilize support. Through the service of religious instructions, the Tibetan political leadership is able to cultivate loyalty among the exile Tibetan community to the exile struggle because of the close links of religion and politics.

Margaret Nowak pointed out that both the 10 March commemoration and the mönlam chenmo instructions are examples of the existence of the Tibetan paradigm of chösi nyiden, the combination of religion and politics (see Ch. 2). Each event focuses on another part of the Tibetan strata. While the secular people and laity renew their claims to free Tibet at the Uprising commemorations, the ecclesiastic stratum takes over power during the mönlam chenmo (1984). Christiaan Klieger stressed in this context the important role of the 14th Dalai Lama during both ceremonies:

> March 10 and Mon-lam represent the dynamic of change and continuity, the outward and inward, the profane and the sacred, the nation and the religion. The unifying symbol bridging both events is the Dalai Lama, the king and god, the active agent between this world and the next.
>
> (Klieger 1992: 67)

So the core symbol of the Tibetan nation is the institution of the Dalai Lama. His dual position as a human and a God makes him superior. In this regard, he uses a wide repertoire of symbols for his own presentation. Following Klieger's argument, the 14th Dalai Lama's success lies in his ability to manipulate '. . . a complex of meaning and present appropriate segments of this [secret mysteries of another world] to his people and the world' (1992: 76). In this regard, the significance of this office as the Tibetan national key symbol has not changed.

In the Tibetan ceremonial calendar the annual birthday celebration of the 14th Dalai Lama is on 6 July. It is celebrated by all Tibetans and their world-wide Western supporters and, in this regard, links the Tibetan nation with the international community. This illustrates the importance of the international community to participate actively in exile Tibetan ceremonies to promote the exile Tibetan struggle.

The event is followed by Tibetan Democracy Day on 2 September, the day when the first assembly was founded in 1960. The date is officially celebrated with a central ceremony in Dharamsala organized by the CTA. In the center of this celebration are speeches by the 14th Dalai Lama where he usually stresses the progress of the exile Tibetan struggle and the topic of democratization in the exile Tibetan community.

In my opinion, all these exile Tibetan national ceremonies are created to support the close link between Tibetan secular affairs and religious symbolism, but also to evoke unifying feelings among all Tibetans. Interesting is the mix of secular and religious ceremonies. Numerous exile Tibetans do participate in the events (CTA officials are obliged to do so) but I can make no general statement about percentages within the exile population. Those I have talked to and who are reluctant to join in the ceremonies are skeptical about the CTA politics. This indicates that the participation in the CTA organized events goes in line with the support of the exile Tibetan struggle of the CTA and therefore is another instrument to measure the degree of national loyalty.

During all ceremonies one can see religious and secular symbols, which are either rooted in Tibetan Buddhism or copied during the period of British presence in Tibet in the early twentieth century. At this time the Tibetan political elite imported numerous Western symbols of nationhood like a national flag, anthem, emblem and passports. While these symbols were known and used in the pre-exile period only by the Tibetan political elite, they experienced a renaissance in the exile context through their use by the CTA. Today they are widely accepted by all Tibetans, both in exile and in the homeland, who consider them as necessary tools to emphasize their struggle to free Tibet. The success of the nationalistic course of the CTA is illustrated by the following statement of the exile Tibetan historian Tsering Shakya:

> The prerequisite paraphernalia of nationalism, such as the flag and the national anthem, have been introduced. Most Tibetans in exile are now

socialized into thinking of themselves as a homogeneous group through schooling and group rituals such as the celebration of the 10th March Uprising, or the Dalai Lama's birthday in July.

(1993: 11)

In addition to these national symbols and ceremonies, there is a dress code for Tibetan officials at all exile Tibetan national holidays. They are obliged to wear the national dress (chupa), since 2005, without fur of wild animals, while the ATPD members are dressed according to customs of their represented Tibetan region or religious sect. During daily office hours, male Tibetan officials are dressed casually or in suits, while their female counterparts are requested to wear their chupa. This particular obligation for female officials is viewed critically among the young generation of women and many of them are not happy with such unequal treatment (anonymous interviews, 2003). In contrast, the older generation of Tibetan women in exile like to wear their chupa daily. In my opinion, this difference in the acceptance of a national dress code among women describes, on the one hand, a variety in the national consciousness between those who fled Tibet and those who were born in exile. On the other hand, it portrays a development of habits between generations, e.g. the older generation feels comfortable wearing a chupa while the young Tibetan women view it as a restriction of their freedom. They prefer a Western dressing style, which they can only enjoy outside their office hours. This questioning of the young exile Tibetan women to follow the official dress code shows that their link to the Tibetan traditions is different from that of the older generation, which in turn limits the response of the young generation of women in exile to the nationalistic instruments by the CTA.

Furthermore, Tibetan nationalism has been enforced by the CTA through the introduction of the central Tibetan Lhasa dialect as the national language, the promotion of ethnic endogamy and high birth rates, the discouraging of assimilation with the host population and the taking of new citizenship. Again, the Tibetans react differently to the CTA efforts. The Lhasa dialect, for instance, is widely spoken in public and in schools, but at home the Tibetans talk their native regional dialects. Regarding the topic of birth rates, one can see that, while the population increased in the beginning years of exile (Goldstein 1975a: 184) the total fertility rate of the exile Tibetan community has declined over the last decades, from 4.9 between 1987 and 1989, to 1.7 in the years 1999–2001. This present fertility rate is considered by the CTA as too low. Main factors for low birth rates are the increasing orientation of the younger generation towards a Western lifestyle (postponing of childbirth to the 30s, use of contraception, one-child families, etc.) and the host countries' policy (in Asia: TV spots and advertisements for two-child families) (CTA 2004: 31, 2000f: 24–8; Nowak 1984: 95). The factors show that the CTA policy to motivate the exile Tibetans to be more reproductive, fails because of limited control over the young exile generation, which has grown up outside the homeland and is highly influenced by their host countries and a Western lifestyle. Additionally, it illustrates the high dependency of the CTA on policies of the host state.

Tibetan Buddhist-based nationalism is also employed by the CTA to motivate the Tibetan Diaspora abroad, in particular to take an active part in the exile Tibetan struggle. Shain stated that material incentives are considered as minor due to the abroad-living Diaspora's relatively stable economic situation. In contrast, symbolic and religious means play a more important role in creating nationalistic feelings and in mobilizing them into taking an active part in the exile struggle to free their home. One instrument used to encourage Buddhist-based nationalism abroad is the religious centers. Their importance as key institutions to keep the national identity alive had been copied by the CTA from the Jewish experience. The first contact of the 14th Dalai Lama with a Jew took place right after his arrival in India in 1959, when a Jew from Poland gave advice on several projects to ease the life of the exile Tibetans and especially on the foundation of a Tibetan children's home (Dalai Lama 1996: 190–1). The first official contact between the CTA and Jews was in 1990, when a delegation from Israel visited Dharamsala. A member of the delegation wrote about the reasons for the visit: that the exile Tibetan political elite was eager to know '. . . the secret of Jewish spiritual survival in exile' (Kamenetz 2000: 31) because '. . . in the Dalai Lama's eyes, and to many of the Tibetans, Jews are survival experts' (Kamenetz 1994: 3). The Jewish delegates emphasized in their speeches the topic of religious symbolism in the educational process, within households, families and in schools. They also gave weight to the use of prayer and study centers abroad that are set-up to function as meeting points for members of the foreign Diaspora and stressed the importance of the work with religious texts to link past and present. This Jewish approach in particular opened a new perspective to the CTA to use religious topics among all strata of the exile Tibetan community to mobilize national commitment (Kamenetz 2000: 31). Furthermore, it emphasized the CTA's focus on preservation of Tibetan culture and religion as overall exile Tibetan policy, which shows that the interaction between different exile communities is fruitful and inspiring for both sides. They support each other on a moral basis, but also with operational support.

Exile Tibetan nationalist developments based on Buddhism have always been linked to a wider field of international relations, which are the center of the following explanations. At present, Tibetan nationalism is tied to foreign consumption of goods and images for two reasons: first, because freedom of religion and the expression of one's own history serve as key scenarios in Western society. The first Tibetans who came to the West wore maroon robes and seeded interest in Tibetan Buddhism at the grassroots level. Because the Tibetan clergy was the main target of the Chinese invaders, the Western world warmly welcomed these exile Tibetan scholars (Mountcastle 1997: 283). Second, Tibetan Buddhism in the West spoke of a lack in universal values and sense of life in industrial societies—a fertile ground for the creation of meaningful approaches for managing one's own life (Berger 1980). These two reasons show the promotion of Tibetan Buddhism in the West and the transmission of a certain image of Tibet, which is based on Tibetan religion, through Western mass media. The main emphasis here will be given to the question: Which role does Tibetan Buddhist nationalism play in the context for international support of the exile Tibetan struggle under the guidance of the CTA?

At present, more than 700 Tibetan Buddhist centers all over the world function as meeting places for members of the Tibetan Diaspora and the increasing number of so-called white convert Buddhists.[20] Additionally, the CTA hopes to involve exile Tibetans and Western Buddhists, but interestingly not Indian Buddhists,[21] in the Tibetan struggle through Buddhist philosophy and teachings—a concept that has failed because Tibetan monk teachers mostly do not focus on the political circumstances, despite the CTA's encouragement of Tibetan dignitaries in the West to stress political issues (interview with Mr Phuntsok Gonpo, Department of Religion and Culture, Dharamsala, April 2003).[22] Moreover, Amy Mountcastle (1997: 286) found that the majority of Western Buddhists have little or no interest in Tibetan political matters, people or culture, except for religion. Therefore, they have recently become a major focus of the 14th Dalai Lama, who is trying to unite Tibetan Buddhist religion with Tibet and the Tibetan nation. Such awareness also focuses on acquiring new predominantly monetary resources among the Tibetan Diaspora and Western Buddhists. Mary Gardner (1999: 135) found during her field study among exile Tibetans in Canada, an increasing participation and incorporation of Westerners in the Tibetan freedom movement, in the activities of the Tibetan administration and the mediating activities of the 14th Dalai Lama. This is due to the practice that exile Tibetan festivities and activities are increasingly performed in the Western world as cultural attractions, rather than as Tibetan activities in themselves. Consequently, Tibetan Buddhist centers have developed into cultural and religious institutions for the Tibetan Diaspora abroad and Western Buddhists (Ekvall 1967: 116).[23] There, exile Tibetans and non-Tibetans can communicate at the same level and share solidarity and a unifying theological superstructure. Axel Ström recognized in this context a similar position of the exile Tibetans and the Western followers of Tibetan Buddhism. Both groups can be considered to be refugees. While the Tibetans fled the threat to their way of life, which they want to retain, the Western followers break the spell of their own culture and want to create a new one. In this sense, the Tibetan and Western Buddhists meet on the same psychological level and cooperate and learn relatively easily from each other. Each group contributes something to this relation. The Tibetans provide examples for a religious way of life and prayers for the well-being of all creatures.[24] The 'white convert Buddhists' hand over financial and material resources that secure the daily survival of the exile Tibetans (Ström 1995: 10).

In this context, the Tibetan Buddhist centers in North America, Europe (*Tibetan Bulletin* 1984: 26; Baumann 1996: 355; Bishop 1993) and also Taiwan, with their thousands of members, have increasingly supported the financial situation of their spiritual teachers and therefore indirectly also the CTA (see Ch. 4). The economic power of these 'white convert Buddhists' is, in my opinion, most important and influences the CTA to encourage the founding of more Tibetan Buddhist centers. Their monetary support ranges from considerable donations to high exile Tibetan dignitaries, including the 14th Dalai Lama himself, and the sponsoring of simple monks in India and Nepal to the consumption of incense, meditation carpets, statues, texts and other articles to practice Tibetan Buddhism at home. Both direct and indirect monetary transfers support the material survival of all strata of the exile Tibetan community. Furthermore, self-made Western missionaries of Tibetan Buddhism take profit by the spread of Tibetan religion in the West. On the one hand, they act in the position as freerider but also emphasize the developments in spreading the Tibetan Buddhism in the West.[25]

According to Marie Dorsh DeVoe, the high economic dependency of the exile Tibetan community from the Western world, which is also illustrated in the CTA annual budget, is highly influenced by Western interests in a religious and cultural Tibet. The traditional priest–patron relationship (see Ch. 2) has been transformed. While the exile Tibetans act as clients through receiving generous aid, Westerners in return get the blessing of exile Tibetan dignitaries. DeVoe even argues that the survival of the exile Tibetans is a function of the existing donor networks of Westerners who are actively involved in the resettlement, and committed to Tibetans (DeVoe 1987: 55). This illustrates a high dependency of the exile Tibetan community on Western patronage and interest in Tibet. Moreover, it provides a reason for an absent economic sector in the exile Tibetan community (see Ch. 4). Large factions of the exile Tibetans, including the CTA structure itself, secure their survival through Western sponsorships and donations and therefore feel no need to develop economic niches. The whole process of the development of Tibetan patriotism has been reinforced by the 14th Dalai Lama's goal of preservation of culture and religion and flanked the cultural reconstruction in Tibetan exile. Tibetan patriotism moreover supports the role of the religious segment in the exile Tibetan society as a whole (McLagan 1996: 217).

In the process of a worldwide promotion of the exile Tibetan struggle, the transmission of an image of Tibet through mass media grew in importance. The image of Tibet as *tabula mystica* has been developed since the first contacts between Westerners and Tibetans in the early seventeenth century. It was shaped by the geographical and political isolation of Tibet until the early twentieth century. Only a few Western scholars and missionaries succeeded in crossing the Tibetan borders and managed to form their own opinion about the realities on the 'roof of the world' (Dodin and Räther 1997). This stereotypic mystical picture of Tibet has been recently reproduced by international journalism with its daily, weekly and monthly news that reaches all strata of the international community. In this regard, exile Tibetans have managed to create an impression of the Tibetan people as propagators of Tibetan

Buddhism, as a peaceful, friendly and never harming nation with a deep insight into religious practice. Facets of history, current political events, daily life in exile and fateful deeds of the Chinese are manipulatively portrayed from the exile Tibetan perspective.

In the 1980s, the 14th Dalai Lama's political status in the international sphere gained ground through his appeals in front of the US House of Representatives and the EU. His political role was finally highlighted by the awarding of the Nobel Peace Prize in 1989, when the Norwegian committee acknowledged both his religious and political position (CTA 1997: 65; Fossell and MacDougall 1989). Through the prize, the 14th Dalai Lama's position has been strengthened both within the Tibetan and the international community. But also the entire exile Tibetan community got wide access to the international media through the acknowledgement of his involvement in the exile struggle. During the 1990s Hollywood discovered the Tibetan issue for its media industry. According to Orville Schell, a complex marketing concept about the 14th Dalai Lama achieved dense public and media attention, the interest of celebrities, money and public relations (Schell 2000: 40). With the box-office hits *Kundun* and *Seven Years in Tibet*, almost everybody in the Western world could get some rudimentary knowledge about Tibet. During the production, the CTA political elite served as advisors. This direct interaction with the film-makers offered the CTA the chance to form the movies according to its political objectives and strategies. For instance, the 14th Dalai Lama edited the script of *Kundun* and '. . . was very concerned about the way some Tibetan characters and ceremonies might be presented, such as the Dalai Lama's court oracle' (*New York Times* 1997).

Consequently, the CTA was given the chance to influence the Hollywood productions that helped shape the so-called 'virtual' Tibet for the Western world (Schell 2000).[26] In this regard, the CTA and the exile Tibetan political elite in particular were able to draw attention to their political struggle in the name of the entire Tibetan nation. Moreover, for the media sector and its accompanying business structures, a popular figure like the 14th Dalai Lama as a front man of a marketing product 'Tibet', was most useful in selling the political Tibet issue.

Coming to Hollywood was a genuine opportunity for the CTA but for the 14th Dalai Lama in particular, to generate financial support through promoting the exile Tibetan struggle. He increasingly became an international symbol of wisdom and a protector of oppressed and dispossessed people. He successfully combined his divine status with his exile political struggle under a veil of non-violence, compassion and selflessness and opened a complete new book of hallmarks with celebrities who supported his philosophy, person and nation. Hollywood actors like Richard Gere, Pierce Brosnan, Sharon Stone, Meg Ryan and Brad Pitt and rock stars like Annie Lennox, Björk and the Beastie Boys became important for the exile Tibetan struggle as they, first, lobbied the film industry to put exile Tibetan concerns on screen, second, secured the media industry's profits through their celebrity status and, third, organized independently from the 14th Dalai Lama and the CTA concerts, readings and fund raising events for Tibet.[27] So the selling of a particular image of Tibet helps to motivate support from the international community but also to generate loyalty within the national community. The awareness-raising events are emphasized in the CTA press to show the exile Tibetans the success of the exile struggle in terms of mobilizing international celebrities to support the Tibetan freedom struggle (*Tibetan Review* 2001; Tashi 1996; Gere 1996; Brosnan 2000). Jamyang Norbu stated in this context that the international support is mostly exaggerated by the CTA (Norbu 1998: 22). But still, the press coverage fosters the legitimacy of the CTA to act in the name of the whole Tibetan nation and secures the loyalty of the Tibetans, both in exile and in the homeland. Furthermore, the Western-made movies also create a feeling of self-discovery among the young exile Tibetan generation and influence the adolescence's self-perspective. In this regard, the international mass media represents a second education medium for young exile Tibetans to learn about their own cultural background. The promoted nationalism in such movies through symbols and manipulated and simplified presentation of historic events create patriotic feelings: 'When the movies roll, the jeans-clad generation might find their forebears' period costumes absurd. But the message 'Tibet calls' will strike the same emotive chord in every exiled heart' (Tsering, Topden 1997c). In this regard, especially the young Tibetan generation in exile found through the lens of the Western media industry a source for self-discovery—Tibetan costumes and history—which are not part of their own experience. Through the media attention, the CTA is able to reach the young exile generation and mobilize them for the exile Tibetan struggle, which is, as seen before, only to a certain extent possible through the promotion of national symbols and traditional dress codes. In contrast, the Western media image of Tibet creates nationalistic feelings among large parts of the exile Tibetan youth and therefore contributes to the exile Tibetan struggle.

The media image becomes particularly obvious in the Tibetan settlements in India and Nepal, where tourism has been growing fast and, as seen before, created several income opportunities for the Tibetan and the local population. The aforementioned Tibetan cultural institutions play a crucial role in the promotion of the image of Tibet. They had been developed to cultural ambassadors according to Western expectations. So the initial institutions, set up to preserve Tibetan culture, became vehicles for the worldwide promotion of CTA politics and to entertain foreign patrons.

The media is also used as a tool for the exile Tibetans to struggle against the Chinese, as the Dharamsala press articles show how effective the Hollywood industry can be for the exile Tibetan struggle.[28] But the productions of the glitzy Hollywood machinery had not yet had a serious impact on the Chinese objectives in Tibet (Douglas 1997), which shows that the awareness of the international community is not always a guarantor for the success of the exile struggle to overthrow the home government. It is rather, as outlined earlier, determined by the international position and strength of the home government within the international political sphere.

The genuine opportunity for the CTA to promote its objectives among a wide public through mass media, wider than they ever reached before, was also a moment when the CTA lost control of the developments. The Tibetan image slowly became just another building stone of Western market-ing and of the construction of the Hollywood imperia, while the exile Tibetan struggle developed only as a side-effect. A black-and-white picture was cre-ated between Chinese and Tibetans: either you are a friend of Tibet or a friend of China; the latter implies that you are an enemy of Tibet. So Tibet-ans stand for everything that the Chinese are not (Mountcastle 1997: 293). This accelerating marketing process created well-founded fears within the exile Tibetan community, of becoming a victim of Hollywood's consuming image. This fear is communicated by Robert Barnett who points out that '. . . there is a risk that films of this kind will cast Tibetans as sweet, cuddly toys who we can make decisions for' (Robert Barnett, cited in Douglas 1997: 13). Tsering Shakya also stressed that access to the Tibetan cause through a religious lens may entail difficulties for the exile Tibetan struggle as a whole, because Tibetans are presented in a mystic light of compassionate and peace-ful people:

> The West has always reduced Tibet to its image of Tibet, and imposed its yearning of spirituality and solace from the material world onto Tibet. In the same process, the West has sought to define the Tibetan political struggle. Tibetans are seen merely as victims who are unable to speak for themselves ... After decades of being reduced to the status of mere recipients of charity and sympathy, the process of reduction of Tibetans to an endangered species of the human family is nearly complete. At one level, this has attracted sympathy, yet on another level, the Tibetan issue is treated as an inevitable question of 'backward people resisting the march of modernity'.
>
> (1992: 16)

So the stereotypic presentation of Tibet is a Western creation, but Tibetans gradually succumbed to the same idea of their home, while returning to Tibet becomes more of a distant and fantastic dream. The Western New Age movement has especially created a certain viewpoint on Tibet (Lopez 1994), which the CTA took up and pasted in as their own concept; as Jamyang Norbu said: 'The national struggle for an independent Tibet has been replaced by a squishy agenda of environmental, pacifist, spiritual, and "universal" concerns that has little or nothing to do with Tibet's real problems' (1998: 21). This explains that the CTA is in an internationally weak position and relies on the help of international supporters, regardless from which stratum. Because of this high dependency on international support, morally and financially, the CTA lost control of developments. The initial exile struggle has been transformed into a marketing product mainly shaped from the perceptions of the international patrons.

In summary, one can say to recreate and maintain a distinct Tibetan culture and religion, the CTA has been initiating and expanding a wide organizational network between exile Tibetans, Tibetans in the PRC and Tibetan and non-Tibetan members of the international community (Asp 1995: 3). In this regard, Tibetan Buddhist nationalism represents an important source for the CTA to cultivate national and international support.

First, the CTA emphasizes in its political course Tibetan nationalistic ideas to reach all Tibetan people independently from their place of living to motivate them to participate in the exile struggle. National symbols and a ceremonial calendar create a wide basis for loyalty to the CTA. Through the effective usage of such national symbolism, the CTA supports the development of a collective identity and the construction of a national consciousness, which fosters the CTA's political position within the Tibetan community. The CTA encounters difficulties among the young generation of exile Tibetans who are born in exile and whose knowledge about, and personal experiences with, the homeland are limited.

Second, the CTA has successfully promoted Tibetan Buddhist nationalism in the international sphere through the creation of an image of Tibet that is mainly based on Western perceptions. The CTA receives considerable moral and financial help that supports the position of the CTA because of its access to different international actors from all segments of Western society, including celebrities. The 14th Dalai Lama especially became, in the international sphere, a well-known activist for peace and freedom and a global celebrity supported by a wide media presence. Despite the fact that the CTA has not achieved official international recognition yet, his global role is still defined as a religious leader who calls himself 'a simple monk' (Mirsky 1987; Hammer 1991; Dalai Lama 1991: 11), chosen by his people to be a leading figure to promote their plight (Thinley 1996). Through the international mass media, the CTA is able to reach the new exile generations, which are reluctant to agree to the traditional symbolism.

From the theoretical point of view, it can be stated that an exile government's use of nationalistic ideas applies in the first instance to the mobilization of the national community. It supports the exile struggle in terms of emphasizing its meaning as a national cause. In the second instance, nationalism also provides an adequate instrument to reach and involve the international community into the exile struggle. This in turn helps an exile government to generate moral and operational support. Such results make Shain's examinations more explicit and provide a new look at nationalism in the context of exile governments.

Universal rights approach

This chapter answers the question: Why do the promotion of human, eco and women's rights in Tibet enjoy such a high priority in the CTA, while the main goal of the exile struggle is to regain the homeland? Looking from the theoretical perspective at the relationship between insiders and outsiders, one can say that a human rights-based approach may contribute to the limitation of potential conflicts between the two parties. Through the exiles' public articulation of the efforts that are made to improve the circumstances in the homeland, the compatriots at home are shown that they are not forgotten. Moreover, they are in the center of exile politics.

To inform the Tibetans in China in detail about the political happenings in exile, there are broadcasts by Radio Free Asia (RFA), Voice of Tibet (VOT) and Voice of America (VOA). They broadcast on frequencies that can be received all over Asia in different languages (also in Tibetan) and cover Asian issues, which include Tibet, India and China. While their headquarters are in the USA, they maintain bureaus with local reporters all over Asia and also in Dharamsala. According to Mr Ugyen Norbu, the RFA reporter in Dharamsala, the radio programs are viewed by the CTA primarily as important tools to provide the Tibetans inside the PRC with information that differs from the Chinese media. Nevertheless, he stated, all radio stations work independently from the CTA politics.[29]

To explain the importance of the promotion of human, eco and women's rights in the context of the exile struggle, one can look at the CTA's role in the international community. The exile government attempts to mobilize and enlarge its international support through the combination of Tibetan Buddhism and universal rights. Especially since the 1980s, when a new paradigm appeared in the exile Tibetan struggle that differed from the initial UN-orientated approach in the 1960s and 1970s, the CTA extensively focused on the international grassroots level (see Ch. 4). Since then the CTA has worked internationally with the 'universal rights strategy'—a term that combines Tibetan cultural protection and non-violence with the advocacy of human, environmental and women's rights as a vehicle to campaign for the exile Tibetan struggle (Pike 2001: 14). In this regard, one can say that the efforts to return home and to enlarge international support are indistinguishable from each other.

Each specific right representation provides a symbolical and ideological package that is utilized in the Western activists' discourse to categorize and promote the exile Tibetan claims of Chinese abuses in their homeland. Such categorization of the exile Tibetan struggle provides activists with a clear organizational framework, which makes a quick and efficient classification of any Tibet-related issue possible. Each key rightly demands its own audience and forum for articulation and therefore appeals to a wider range of potential supporters than the exile Tibetan political struggle would do alone. The promotion of universal rights can be regarded as 'purpositive incentive' that is invested by the CTA to mobilize international NGOs to participate in the exile struggle. While the 'universal rights strategy' gives the CTA an opportunity to expand international support, the NGOs profit from the satisfaction of having contributed something to the attainment of a worthwhile cause: the Tibetan freedom struggle. The success in communicating the exile Tibetan struggle in that specific way is the result of the existence of a market for universal rights in Western liberal societies. Upendra Baxi stated in that context:

> Human rights movements at all levels (global, national, and local) have tended to become capital-intensive. The praxis of protecting and promoting human rights entails entrepreneurship in raising material resources, including funding, from a whole variety of governmental, intergovernmental, international, and philanthropic sources. These sources are organized in terms of management imperatives, both of line management and upward accountability.
>
> (2002: 123)

In this regard, the promotion of human rights can also be interpreted as investment of material incentives that improve the international NGOs' position in the market situation of human rights. Through the promotion of human rights, the exile Tibetans are able to expand their own network of supporters and improve their organizational position (Bob 2002: 44). Such engagement in turn influences the political position of the CTA. Universal rights, including human, women's and environmental rights, have become political symbols that promote the notion of justice, which provides the CTA with a powerful instrument against China.

According to Baxi, this strategy may also lead to a situation of an overproduction of human rights in the international sphere (2002: 67–76). In this regard, the exile Tibetan struggle movement risks an over-employing of the issue, which may result that the Tibetan cause becomes just another human rights issue among others in the eyes of the international community. Furthermore, the communication of the exile Tibetan struggle in human and other rights-based discourses may:

> . . . fundamentally alter the sites in which the Tibet issue is heard, or even subsumed by a larger human rights rhetoric. In the long run then, the universal rights strategy as it is currently employed may be counterproductive to Tibetan nationalist interests.
>
> (Pike 2001: 74)

In this context, Pike called the international Tibet Support Groups (TSGs) opportunistic in making use of the various universal rights as soon as appropriate or possible (2001: 56–7). Frechette wrote in this context:

> What all of these groups [TSGs] have in common is a liberal humanist worldview that celebrates and supports the rights of individuals to maintain their own cultural heritage. They promote such values among the Tibetans as humanism, multiculturalism, environmentalism, and legal activism.
>
> (2004: 10)

The effects of 'universal rights strategy' can be summarized in two points: (1) it legitimizes the exile Tibetan struggle because it becomes concordant with international agreements on human and other rights; (2) it provides all international actors with an argument for expressing their dissatisfaction about the Tibet issue, despite the PRC's growing strength in international economics and politics.

During the last two decades, the exile Tibetan struggle has been transformed into a dynamic and multidimensional organizational movement, including a growing number of non-Tibetan supporters who are able to work on different fronts by using highly skilled methods of communication, such as reports and lobbying activities. In the year 1997, more than 350 TSGs placed morality, non-violence, truth and justice on the agenda of the international community (Tsering, Tempa 1997: 18–19). Of great potential are students, who are organized into a growing number of 'Student Support Groups' that campaign for a free Tibet. They follow a divestment and boycott strategy according to the exemplary success of the student protests in South Africa against the apartheid regime, when more than 200 companies gave way to public pressure and closed their branches. The students attack the PRC in the economic and intellectual sphere with boycotts, demonstrations, video shows, conferences and a wide range of Tibet-related cultural events (Sangay 1996; Hocevar 1996). Such involvement is widely discussed in the exile Tibetan media and the 14th Dalai Lama encourages young people during university visits. He is aware of the great number of Chinese students and intellectuals at foreign and particularly US universities, who are considered by the CTA as one of the most promising forces. The CTA statistics count approximately 80,000 Chinese students at US universities, which shows that the CTA indeed monitors them and shows how important they can be (Chang-Ching 1996; Wei 1996). They are addressed at international conferences and their traditional skepticism and criticism of the PRC is used to extend the CTA's struggle within the PRC. Therefore, '... Tibetan officials consider the frequent contacts between Tibetan exiles and pro-democracy Chinese important' (Samphel 1996: 16).

According to Pike, TSGs focus their work generally on the following activities: they try to raise awareness in the international arena through intellectual, financial and technical resources that are not available to the exile Tibetans. Additionally, they are actively engaged in the exile Tibetan struggle through lobbying of politicians and officials, while at the same time rallying the sympathetic public. Furthermore, TSGs create new and expanding links between the exile Tibetan struggle and other NGOs. And finally, they provide the exile Tibetans with models and methods of effective activism. The set of these skills fundamentally altered the whole exile Tibetan struggle in a way that the traditional concept of state has been widened to include transnational political action (2001: 35–44).

> If Tibetans abroad lacked diplomatic recognition, [official] embassies, or representation in important international organizations, they were

gaining crucial access to power, money, and the media through their newly forged partnership with these unofficial and ardent American groups and supportive celebrities. Thanks to the appeal of these organizations' cause, the compelling personality of the Dalai Lama, and the shrewdness of their tactical planning, they had managed to circumvent many of the conventional structures of intercourse between nation-states.

(Schell 2000: 38)

The CTA reacts ambivalently to the involvement of TSGs. Pike stated that the CTA regards the work of the international TSGs as important because these non-Tibetan activists are able to successfully lobby local and federal governments. They are by nature more skilled in navigating within the international community and more familiar with established communication mechanisms than most of the exile Tibetans. This enables the activists to communicate the exile struggle within a legal framework in the international arena (2001: 38). At the same time, the CTA also reacts with distance to the activism because the TSGs focus more on Tibetan independence, or Tibetan self-determination (Reynolds 2004: 448); the latter concept is rarely referred to by the 14th Dalai Lama (Sautman 2000: 63), except on the Dalai Lama's promotion of genuine autonomy as a '. . . basis for open support from some international organisations and certain governments' (Dalai Lama 1991: 11). The TSGs on their side criticize the CTA for not being dramatic enough in promoting the exile Tibetan struggle on an international level and of not providing the activists with adequate political directions, which creates confusion with the international public image of Tibet and weakens the exile Tibetan struggle as a whole (Pike 2001: 45–7). Consequently, the CTA refuses any responsibility for the action of the TSGs. Any kind of action, violent or non-violent, financial, ideological or any provision of any resources is seen officially with a relative indifference (Samdhong Rinpoche 2002: 8). Such reaction of the CTA shows the weak position of an exile administration with regard to international developments. The CTA successfully approached the international community at grassroots level but in turn, the supporters increasingly took up the exile Tibetan struggle and changed it according to their own objectives, which were not necessarily in line with the official CTA politics. The exile Tibetan struggle has been used by international activists for their own benefit and, moreover, developed independently from the CTA.

But the 'universal rights strategy' has not only Western advocates. It also attracts Tibetan supporters including the 14th Dalai Lama and the exile Tibetan NGOs that actively participate in the discourse. In their search for outside support, they have learned the language of the Western world and adopted Western ideas, skills and methods to navigate within the international political arena. For instance, the TWA promotes Tibetan women's rights, the DIIR's environmental desk emphasizes environmental issues in Tibet and the TCHRD communicates human rights abuses in the homeland.

In this regard, the Tibetans stress these issues in their Asian host countries, while the TSGs play a dominate role in the West. Consequently, Westerners and exile Tibetans fashion hand-in-hand new spaces in the global process, accompanied by a certain success in the implementation of the new skills, which in turn make these Western perceptions even more popular among the exile Tibetan elite. Especially important symbolic events and conferences are used to promote issues and to build networks '. . . even when their connection appears somewhat tangential to the Tibet issue' (Pike 2001: 85).

While the TSGs have been, so far, successful in legitimizing their work through increasing support around the world by following the 'universal rights strategy', many exile Tibetans remain confused about the initial goal of regaining the homeland (Pike 2001: 72). Some, especially the young exile generation, which are represented by the TYC, feel that the 'universal rights strategy' is ineffective and does not lead to any concrete step forward to free the homeland. It rather offers international agents a way to evade the exile Tibetan struggle in terms of lip service. But even these non-material acknowledgements of the exile Tibetan struggle can be a 'morale booster for Tibetan officials in India'.[30] Furthermore, the youngsters disagree that the universal rights-based discourse will affect the likelihood of the PRC to engage itself in a meaningful dialogue, neither with the Western activists nor with the Tibetans. Pike stated:

> While many Tibetan activists and young Tibetans increasingly question the efficacy of the Dalai Lama's moderate approach and opt to demand full independence, the universal rights strategy—crystallized in the campaigning of Tibet activists—is at odds with their radical goals. While the group of radical Tibetans is still a minority, there is allegedly growing function among Tibetan youths who are increasingly disposed toward adopting an independence approach. In addition, some TSGs are thinking of radicalising their demands for independence.
>
> (2001: 75)

This shows that the CTA's focus to promote the exile Tibetan struggle in the international sphere under the guise of universal rights is not uncompromisingly accepted by the exile Tibetan community. Furthermore, the international TSGs increasingly shape the whole debate, which puts the CTA on the verge. In this context, Pike pointed out that this new activist paradigm in combination with Tibetan nationalism has been predominantly articulated in the world arena by transnational TSGs, meaning by more non-national activists, in this case non-Tibetans, than any other nationalist movement (2001: 18–21). This in turn illustrates the high importance of the international supporters for the government-in-exile.

Such international involvement and the difficulties, which the CTA faces on the national front, are exemplarily portrayed in the following on the promotion of the exile Tibetan struggle under the guise of environmentalism. Since the mid-1980s the exile Tibetan struggle started to be partly presented in the context of eco rights and environmentalism, a so-called green Tibetan identity, became an integral part of the CTA policy. The idea to promote the environmental issue in the exile Tibetan context came up when Tibetans attended for the first time international conferences on ecology and religion in the USA, Great Britain, India and Italy. At these conferences, the CTA delegates came into contact with international NGOs, such as the World Wide Fund for Nature (WWF) and other Western environmental activists who advised them to take up the environmental issue to capitalize on the international issue (Mountcastle 1997: 303–4). They provided the exile Tibetans with examples of how they could link Buddhism and environmentalism and present this mixture to an international audience. A key moment in exile Tibetan environmentalism was the initiation of a research project, 'Buddhist Perception of Nature: A New Perspective for Conservation', of the CTA and international researchers[31] in 1985. The Asian project members conducted research on Buddhist philosophical literature to find links between religion and nature that could be used in Buddhist communities to conserve and protect nature. The Tibetan project was run by the Council for Religious and Cultural Affairs and the Information Office (later DIIR). The results displayed exile Tibetans' environmentalism, which '. . . also brought Dharamsala firmly within the orbit of the WWF, the world's largest private conservation organization' (Huber 1999: 110). From that moment on, the CTA was given space to work in the global environmental network to promote their Tibetan Buddhist point of view.

At present, the Tibetan ecological concept combines Buddhist ethics and Tibetan traditions, where the ecological equilibrium and philosophical harmony are interwoven with each other. This became a convincing argument in presenting Tibet in the worldwide media (Huber 1997: 103–6). Thus, the uniqueness of Tibetan environmentalism is given space by the linkage between an inherent eco-friendly Tibetan religion and the worldwide eco-friendly movement. Mountcastle stated, '[t]hus, Tibetans may promote environmentalism as Buddhism and Tibetans as inherently environmentalist' (1997: 301). The picture of eco-friendly Tibetans raises awareness within the international community because the Western ecological movement in particular responds to a green Tibetan nation. But the promotion also increasingly takes place on different agendas, as it appeals to a modern image of Buddhism and the exile situation of parts of Tibetan society. It links modern sciences with Buddhism, which in return became a fashionable idea and portrays the present validity of Buddhist philosophy despite its more than 2,500 years of existence. Evidence of the success of the new approach to communicate the exile Tibetan struggle was given by the awarding of the Nobel Peace Prize to the 14th Dalai Lama and his 'Five Point Peace Plan', where point four was especially dedicated to the Tibetan environment. Thus, environmentalism became a political focus that opened doors for the exile Tibetans in the international arena.

For marketing the environmental issue, the CTA specially set-up an Environmental and Development Desk in 1992,[32] which since then has been responsible for the promotion of Tibetan environmentalism through the publication and distribution of environmental material.[33] Following Toni Huber's research, no single publication or official statement stressed the topic of Tibetan environmentalism until 1986 (1997: 108). Before then, the CTA solely published material that showed exile Tibetans spraying pesticides and cutting trees to urbanize the allocated land in South India for resettling (Krull 1968). The present publications are used by the CTA to attack the PRC's detrimental politics, which is influenced by economic development, towards the environment and traditional Tibetan culture. Huber stated that most of the material is printed in English or other Western languages rather then in Tibetan, which clearly indicates the target group of exile Tibetan environmentalism. Furthermore, the high quality of the publications gives evidence of the importance of the subject compared with other exile Tibetan media (1997: 112).

Since the exile Tibetans entered the sphere of global environmentalism, they and their supporting eco-friendly activists have tried to participate in UN conferences on global ecological issues. But because of the status of the CTA as an internationally unrecognized government-in-exile, the Tibetan delegates have not been allowed to participate in the official proceedings. For instance, the 14th Dalai Lama and a delegation of activists were barred from the Earth Summit in Rio de Janeiro in 1992. Instead, they discuss Tibetan environmental concerns unofficially at the edge of these conferences, or appear at NGO-organized events. At the event of the Rio conference, the 14th Dalai Lama visited the Greenpeace flagship 'Rainbow Warrior' to promote the exile Tibetan non-violent and eco struggle (Ackerly 1992; Dalai Lama 1992b: 17).

But the internationally communicated environmentalism has only limited impact on the exile Tibetan's consciousness on that topic. There is still a wide gap between the promoted theory and the daily practice of the exile Tibetans. In Dharamsala, for instance, the CTA has set up a wide range of facilities, which point to an ecological awareness: There is a 'green shop' where all kinds of garbage is collected, water filtered and recycled stationery sold. Additionally, leaflets in Tibetan and English are displayed and handed out all over town, which instruct tourists and the local population to follow the '3 Rs' approach: to reduce consumption, re-use purchased goods and recycle or compost what is left over (CTA n.d. e). But despite such obvious environmental consciousness in the exile Tibetan headquarters, the exile Tibetans do not care more about environmental protection than their local counterparts. Looking at the Tibetans abroad regarding their habits in handling garbage, there are no differences to the host population. Moreover, many exile Tibetan settlements and monasteries in India and Nepal profit from investments by Western Tibet activists in ecological and sustainable energy production, like solar energy technology. But that was not the idea of the exile Tibetans themselves but rather of the international supporters.

In summary, the 'universal rights strategy' is carried out by the CTA to bridge the present and potential gaps between insiders and outsiders. The people at home are linked to the exile struggle and their hardship is promoted in the international sphere. Furthermore, this concept is applied to mobilize international NGOs to participate actively in the exile Tibetan struggle. In this regard, the CTA follows the promotion of universal rights with a two-fold strategy to secure both national and international support. Since the 1980s, the exile Tibetan struggle has been subdivided into different specific rights that are communicated in different international forums. The promotion of such specific rights provides the international activists with symbolic and ideological instruments that are utilized to categorize and support the exile Tibetans in their struggle to undermine Chinese abuses in their homeland. This in turn has positive effects on the position of the CTA because it legitimizes its political claims to act on behalf of the national cause, which is represented in the exile struggle. Furthermore, the 'universal rights strategy' has a beneficial impact on the organizational survival of the numerous NGOs.

The exile Tibetan environmental movement illustrates that this topic is especially brought up to mobilize international support, which indeed has worked successfully. The CTA approaches international activists through publications, conferences, but also Western tourists in India. In contrast, the exile Tibetans in Asia and abroad do not participate extraordinarily in the environmentalism, which illustrates that the CTA focuses on internationally promising topics in regard to promoting the exile Tibetan struggle, despite the fact that this has little or nothing to do with the daily practice within the exile Tibetan community. Shain did not specifically mention such universal rights approach in terms of how it can be used by an exile government to influence its status positively regarding national and international support. In this regard, the promotion of an exile struggle under the guise of universal rights represents a new focus in a theory of exile governments. Furthermore, the policies that are carried out to cultivate international support are indistinguishable from the efforts that are specifically designed to return home. The 'universal rights strategy' has become the exile struggle itself.

Exile Tibetan 'democracy'

The topic of the so-called exile Tibetan democracy has already been widely discussed by Tibetans and non-Tibetans. While the CTA in general stresses the improvements that have been achieved in the process of democratic transformation, Tibetan and Western intellectuals still criticize the reforms as insufficient and superficial. In the following examination, I go beyond these arguments and look also at the phenomenon of exile Tibetan democracy from a political science point of view, according to the previously outlined theory of governments-in-exile. First, I give an account of the external and internal problems of exile Tibetan democracy and the reasons out of which they derive. Second, I portray why the CTA keeps on implementing democracy, despite numerous upcoming obstacles. This will finally lead me to answer the question: Why are secular democratic ideas insufficiently applied within the exile Tibetan political structures?

Shain mentioned the topic of democratic elections in the context of an exile government's claim to be the lawfully elected representative of a nation. A government-in-exile draws its legitimate status to rule a nation, including people and territory, out of an electoral process. This legitimation is also given in the exile Tibetan context. The exile people's participation in the democratic process can be considered as 'purpositive incentive' because the CTA gives the members of the exile Tibetan community the opportunity to take an active part in the exile struggle. The people's benefits from such an incentive derive out of their individual satisfaction of having contributed to the attainment of a worthwhile cause, i.e. in the exile context, to regain the homeland. In this regard, the CTA encourages individual commitment to support the exile struggle through the election of members of the exile community as deputies and ministers who represent the will of the majority. The question that arises in this context is: How do the exile Tibetans react to such an incentive?

According to political theory, democratic systems have certain characteristics which make them distinguishable from non-democratic systems. These are: freedom of expression to join and form an organization, the right to vote in free and fair elections, the right of political opponents to compete for support, the eligibility for public office, and the access to alternative sources of information.[34] From a theoretical point of view, looking at the exile Tibetan 'democracy' one can see numerous obstacles, which can be categorized into internal and external problems. While the external problems of the CTA derive out of the nature of a government-in-exile of having a relatively weak political position in the international sphere, the internal problems are caused by the weak implementation of democratic ideas by the exile Tibetan political elite. I will first discuss the internal problems.

First, there are numerous critical aspects regarding the composition of the Tibetan legislature (see Ch. 4). The present number of exile Tibetan deputies does not reflect the composition of the exile Tibetan community regarding regional heritage and religious affinities. Instead, there is a fixed number of seats for regional and religious deputies. Furthermore, there are neither Tibetan members of the parliament who represent the exile Tibetans in Nepal, Bhutan or the Tibetan Muslim community, nor the Tibetans in the homeland (Asp 1995: 8–9; Hortsang 2003). Moreover, the TYC generally criticizes the concept of the differentiation along regional and religious lines because it intensifies regionalist and sectarian disputes, which consequently have a counter-effect on the CTA's ideal of harmony in exile. As indicated previously, the division of the exile Tibetan deputies into different provinces of Cholka Sum and religious sects fosters the CTA's claims to be the sole representative of all Tibetans. In fact, the CTA enlarged its representative claims despite historical facts regarding territorial and religious control.

Additionally, the ATPD composition gives evidence to an anticipated future power balance, where all Tibetans are going to be prepared to be ruled by one Tibetan government.

Second, there is unequal treatment of the monastic population compared with the exile laity. While monks and nuns have two votes (one for their regional heritage and one for their sectarian affiliation), ordinary exile Tibetans are only entitled to vote for their regional deputy. Such unequal treatment in the election procedure divides the exile Tibetan community rather than unifying it. It also discourages lay Tibetans, who are still the majority of the exile Tibetan population, from voting because they feel that their votes are only half as important as those of the monastic population (Dorjee 2000: 23). One exile Tibetan parliamentarian states that, while democracy means rule by the majority, the Tibetan community is ruled by a monastic minority, which hardly opposes any changes that would decrease its power (anonymous interview, 2006). Such voting practice, I believe, refers to the importance of the exile monastic institutions in the Tibetan political sphere and fosters the traditional structures of the CTA. In contrast, the present voting system, which is linked to the composition of the ATPD, represents the only way to preserve Tibetan culture, as every Tibetan identifies himself with a certain religious sect and birthplace. Thus, the voting system and composition of the exile Tibetan assembly foster, on the one hand, exile Tibetan unity and loyalty to the CTA, because every exile Tibetan can mirror their own identity. But on the other hand, they emphasize a general tendency of factionalism.

Third, the concept of an exile Tibetan 'democracy' is difficult to apply, both for exile Tibetans and Western supporters, because the 14th Dalai Lama is a traditionally installed rather than elected political leader. He acts theoretically as head of the CTA, a position that is neither questioned by the executive nor by the legislative powers. The 14th Dalai Lama is expected by the exile Tibetans to decide in the name of all Tibetans and consequently to take responsibility for the entire nation. He frequently stated that in a future Tibet, the position of the Dalai Lama will be exclusively a religious one. But the practice in Dharamsala shows that there is still a long way to go. With regard to the theoretical considerations, such superior political leadership is most desirable in an exile context because it improves the stability of any exile organization. Thus, the Dalai Lama's position can be less viewed as a power gap but more as a necessity to secure the exile Tibetan's survival. Nevertheless, in a 'democratic' context it is remarkable that he consults the state oracles for political decisions, confirms the authentic tulku rebirth system and gives religious initiations, teachings and blessings. The function of the state oracles, Nechung and Gadong, is especially critical in the exile 'democracy' because all major political decisions are confirmed by them. The Nechung oracle for instance, '. . . acts as a divine colleague in the conduct of His Holiness the Dalai Lama's spiritual and temporal responsibilities, and not as an advisor' (*Tibetan Bulletin* 1992b: 29). Moreover, the oracle is even granted the rank of a deputy minister in the CTA structures (*Tibetan Bulletin*

1992a: 18). At present, there is no solution to bridge the exile Tibetan people's wish to have the 14th Dalai Lama as leader, who is entitled complete authority, and a secular democratic system. Critics within the exile Tibetan community tend to question the CTA and its officials but not the 14th Dalai Lama himself (Grunfeld 1982: 19).

Fourth, the exile Tibetan 'democracy' lacks competition by different political actors for votes and support. There is no platform for any political party or opposition within the CTA structures, which was portrayed before by the example of the TYC (Asp 1995: 9; Norbu 1990: 14). Most important in this context is the position of the ATPD, which is officially entitled '... to play the role of opposition parties under the present circumstances because maintaining effective control of the Government [CTA] is not only a matter for the opposition, it is the responsibility of the Assembly as a whole' (TPPRC 1999: 34). This official statement about the ATPD's role as opposition is in sharp conflict with the position of the 14th Dalai Lama, who holds the ultimate legislative power. Additionally, the instrumental character of the annual voluntary contribution outlined earlier makes the oppositional role of the ATPD questionable, as it exclusively consists of and is voted by holders of the 'green book'.

Fifth, the CTA's claim to act as sole representative of the whole Tibetan nation is only 'democratically' legitimized by the exile community and not by the Tibetans in the homeland. So the opinion of the majority of Tibetans is nowhere represented within the political structures. Consequently, the present political structure in exile does not have the mandate of all Tibetans to operate on their behalf. Nevertheless, the CTA claims to represent all Tibetans even in the absence of a proper platform, and therefore, the whole political system appeals to the legitimate status of the CTA as the legal representative of the Tibetan nation (Tsering, Topden 1997b: 11; Ardley 2002: 178).

Sixth, another critical point describes the permanent employment of government officials that causes the danger that officials will nominate candidates of their liking for free vacancies. The practice of pleasing each other can be noticed between different departments and officials but also in the allocation of desirable posts by high government officials to their former supporters and friends. Expectation is very important in Tibetan society, which causes the exile Tibetan political system to refer to paternalistic hierarchical leadership, which describes the CTA structures and the settlement organization (Jongh 1995: 77; Norbu, D 1991a; Goldstein 1975b: 19). There are many rumors about 'scratching each other's back' circulating within the CTA structures, which make the democratic structures irrelevant for many exile Tibetans (Taksham 1993: 15–16; Norbu 1991a). Especially embarrassing affairs such as a 1994 press report on CTA officials who had been involved in intrigues and smuggling activities of shahtoosh rocked the exile community and did not promote the exile Tibetan's trust in officials in particular and politics overall (Bhattacharjea 1994: 20). The officials were called 'incompetent' and pulled into the 'quicksand of regionalism and sectarianism' (Dorjee 1992: 12).

Seventh, for a long period of time there was a lack of freedom of speech. According to Jamyang Norbu, during the 1980s the gap between factional lines in Tibetan exile became wider and the atmosphere became unpleasant. These years were overshadowed by some mysterious deaths—the leader of the aforementioned '13 Settlements' group and the husband of the 14th Dalai Lama's sister. Any statement against the 14th Dalai Lama often ended in physical attacks. Prime targets were intellectuals, both Tibetans and foreigners, who tried to give their own opinion about the exile Tibetan community.[35] Such action is, in Norbu's opinion, an outcome of excessive devotion to the 14th Dalai Lama, misplaced patriotism and religious fanaticism—actively promoted by the CTA. During that time, the CTA actively started to discourage freedom of speech through the censoring and banning of books, academic works on Tibetan history, newspapers and magazines to erase any idea not in line with official CTA politics (McLagan 1996: 238). Even officials who were interested in new ideas were transferred to remote places or shifted to undesirable posts. Nobody knows if this was done with or without the knowledge of the 14th Dalai Lama (Dixit 1991: 6). Despite the discouraging atmosphere in exile to express one's own opinion, there was an officially promoted freedom of speech and press. With the constitutional changes in the 1990s, new newspapers were founded and served as important forums for public discussions, but also as tools to fight Chinese propaganda and attract international support. At the end of the 1990s there was no exile Tibetan newspaper that gave alternative views on topics of the exile Tibetan struggle, other than the CTA controlled press (Norbu 1991a; Flynn 1998: 15–16). Today, exile Tibetans are more outspoken and express their dissatisfaction openly. Hot debates during the annual sessions of the ATPD are more and more on the agenda. But most critics are rather emotionally or personally motivated instead of content and development-orientated. In this regard, the situation changed only gradually because action-based criticism is absent in the exile political system.

These obstacles in turn highly influence the democratic culture among large parts of the exile Tibetan community. There is neither a real consciousness about the power of voting nor any interest in political matters at all. Despite a relative high participation in CTA elections, Tibetans are unwilling and/or unable to improve things by themselves and 'take responsibility for political action'. In this regard, people show 'no political commitment', do not stand for elections or even withhold their votes because of disinterest or as opposition to the CTA politics (anonymous interviews, 2006). For instance, this was the case in the 1995 referendum and the first direct election of the kalon tripa in 2001, which was opposed by exile Tibetans of a different regional heritage than the candidate. The total electoral turn-out had been relatively low, but there are no official numbers available (interview with Mr Phurpu Tsering, Election Commission, Dharamsala, June 2003).

In the context of a substantial political lack of interest, Tibetologists refer to Tibetan history where they found the following argument: Tibetans are generally seen as politically inactive people because of the traditional appointment of only members of the Tibetan aristocracy for government posts (Jongh 1995: 77). The majority of people could only apply for such jobs by entering a monastery and rising through the social strata (see Ch. 2). Consequently, most Tibetans were ruled but not encouraged to take any political responsibilities themselves—a tradition that was carried into exile (Asp 1995: 10–11).

Apart from Tibetan history, Jamyang Norbu stresses the influence of the international community, which has affected Tibetan political and secular self-perception. Western visitors of the exile Tibetan headquarters have always contributed to the political regression: 'Through their constant disdain of Western rationalism, democracy and science, Western travelers effectively discouraged Tibetans to revert to their old and fatal way of dealing with reality by burying their heads in sands of magic, ritual, and superstition' (1990: 15). Early Western travelers to Dharamsala in the 1960s and 1970s particularly refused democracy, business, self-interest, egoism and nuclear weapons, and rather looked for alternative ideas than the ones their own background provided. Even though there were only a small number of them in Dharamsala, they supported more the concepts of preservation of Tibetan traditions and the mystic ideas of Tibet rather than secular goals, which for exile Tibetans were essential in the struggle to regain the homeland. Today, tourists are predominantly religious seekers who, again, abandon in their discussions political and mundane topics. Despite the fact that they are raised in secular and democratic societies, they accept the traditional authoritarian Buddhist system where a religious patriarch stands above the disciple. Tibetans increasingly interact with tourists in restaurants, hotels or after Buddhist teachings and are interested in exchanging their viewpoints. In this regard, one can say that there is a considerable impact of the international community on the political self-perception of the exile Tibetans. In this context, the Tibetan Prime Minister, Samdhong Rinpoche, argues that the exile Tibetan's habit of dependency on any kind of Western aid is increasing and most hindering for the psychological development of the exile Tibetan community. Tibetans are mentally unsettled and incapable of being self-supporting in any way (interview with Mr Samdhong Rinpoche, Cabinet, Dharamsala, May 2006), which are preconditions for a functioning civil society and real democratic developments.

Another argument that explains the little interest in politics refers to the living conditions in exile. Wangchuk Dorjee remarked in the context of political participation: 'As living standard improves, many Tibetans tend to take less interest in our Tibetan community' (2000: 24). Most exile Tibetans are preoccupied with securing their daily livelihood, educating their children and securing their future on a material basis. They are busy with their material survival and show only limited commitment for politics (interview with Mr Kalsang Phuntsok, TYC, Dharamsala, May 2006). The will to sacrifice something of one's individual freedom and wealth for a broader political goal is absent (anonymous interview, 2006). Such correlation between living standard and participation in the exile struggle describes a new consideration according to the theoretical discourse on exiles. Based on Shain's theory, the exiles' activism is rather limited by a shortage of material wealth but not by a surplus above the subsistence level. Looking at the Tibetans, it is obvious that their involvement in the exile struggle becomes less with a growing base of material wealth. Consequently, it can be stated that the living standard of exile Tibetans influences their political involvement. Both ends of the income scale, i.e. too little income to live on (as in the initial years) and income above the basic needs (after decades in exile), describe a problematic situation for active participation in the exile struggle.

Rinzin Thargyal attributed the limited developments in the democratization process of the exile community to economic insecurity, traditional normative decorum and the before mentioned lack of education in exile. I interpret the economic insecurity as the lack of landholdings and a high dependency on international financial transfers. 'Polyvocality', meaning the expression of different opinions, which is indispensable for democratic processes, has become a trait of the exile intelligentsia but the majority of Tibetans is still constraint by ambivalent interfaces of their traditional, political indifference and the newly introduced democratic responsibilities. So one can state that the average exile Tibetan is still in a transitional period where traditional normative values and the anthropocentric individuation of each person are in conflict (Thargyal 1993: 34–5). Frechette found that Tibetans in Nepal view democracy in 'very interesting ways':

> When Tibetans in Nepal discuss democracy, they interpret it variously to mean the end of Tibet's hierarchical system of governance, equal access to government resources, equal rights to command respect, and equal opportunity. Some even discuss democracy as a ritual they should adopt because the Dalai Lama has asked it of them.
>
> (2004: 77)

Thus, one can see that there is still a general uncertainty about the meaning of democracy. Taking the previously examined political developments in exile into account (see Ch. 4), we can summarize that large parts of the exile Tibetan community are to a certain degree confused about exile politics in general and the goal and strategies of the exile struggle in particular. Nevertheless, there are still dissenting voices. For instance, Lobsang Sangay, pointed out that even in 1990, Tibetans in exile were ready for a democratization of their political system. Such general willingness for change would give reason for the 14th Dalai Lama to push forward the reforms (2003: 124–5).

In summary, it can be stated that the introduced democracy in the exile political system is not fully developed yet and, moreover, not accepted by large parts of the community. The CTA's investment of such 'purpositive incentive', i.e. the participation in the exile struggle through elections, is not responded to by all exile Tibetans. In this regard, the efforts of the CTA to mobilize the exile Tibetans have failed. But despite such resistance within the exile Tibetan community and the absence of any democratic tradition, the CTA continues to promote exile democracy. But why? To answer this question, it is reasonable to look at the motivation of the CTA to introduce democratic ideas according to external problems that derive from the political status of the CTA as government-in-exile in international politics.

An initial argument for the democratic transformation refers to the relationship between a government-in-exile and the host state. The CTA acts within the Indian system, the largest democracy in the world, which would probably not allow any autocratic administrative structure within its multicultural and religious system, even though Tibetans are more familiar with the communist system (always kept alive by the constant stream of new arrivals) and the traditional political system, '[t]here is no real choice for us, India is democratic' (anonymous interview, 2006). Additionally, the pluralistic structures in India had, especially in the early years, been beneficial to the exile Tibetans. As mentioned previously, the Indian society supported the Tibetans and forced Nehru to change his political standpoint. In this regard, the Tibetans initially had a good experience with democratic structures. Nevertheless, one can say that the CTA is not in the position to decide about the political system in exile. The enormous dependency of the CTA on the Indians can best be seen by the fact that, despite the 14th Dalai Lama's superior position of power within the CTA structures, all political decisions, executive, legislative or judicial, need to be approved by the GOI. This means that the exile Tibetan 'democracy' lacks political freedom and sovereignty (Norbu 1991a).

A second reason for the introduction of democracy in exile refers to the nature of the relationship between an exile government and the home country. The 14th Dalai Lama introduced democratic ideas on a top-down initiative as a necessary step towards a free Tibet. In the 14th Dalai Lama's future vision, Tibet will be a democracy where the institution of the Dalai Lama is limited to the religious sphere only. This future democratic system is intended to be set up according to the present experiences in exile (Dalai Lama 1992a). Upon coming into exile, the Tibetan leadership realized that the old institutions had failed and reforms were needed to face the new political circumstances (Norbu, J 1990: 14). In addition, the PRC has been constantly trying to legitimize the PLA invasion and the final take over by accusing the Tibetan traditional system of being autocratic and feudal. So in the exile context, the Tibetans work officially along the lines of Western democratic ideals, which make the Chinese arguments outdated (Bhattacharjea 1994: 10). The CTA rather portrays itself as the alternative to the existing communist system in China. In this regard, the Tibetans created an argument with which to judge the PRC and its invasion in Tibet, which was emphasized by the 1989 Tiananmen Square massacre.

A third argument that explains the introduction of democracy in exile Tibetan politics lies in the Tibetan efforts to promote their cause in the international sphere. Since the end of the Second World War, democratic ideas are given high importance in world politics, especially by the UN and European and North American countries. In this regard, international support and recognition is mostly granted to democracies or those countries that are in a democratic transformation process. Ann Frechette stated that US intergovernmental organizations in particular:

> maintain two interrelated narratives about the Tibetans. For them, the Tibetans are fellow anti-Communists as well as advocates for global democracy. U.S. intergovernmental organizations promote democratic governance among the Tibetans. Their goal is the development of a democratic system not just within the exile community but also in a future Tibet.
>
> (2004: 9)

The 14th Dalai Lama realized the importance of democratic ideas for the Western world (Asp 1995: 5–6; Ardley 2002: 86).

> If Tibet is to survive as an equal member of the modern international community, it should reflect the collective potential of all citizens, and not rely on one individual. This means the people must be actively involved in charting their own political and social destiny.
>
> (Dalai Lama cited in Thinley, P 1996: 13)

International NGOs are especially favorable to the democratic idea, such as the German Friedrich Naumann Foundation, which supports the exile Tibetan community with considerable monetary and material resources but also with diplomatic assistance, as was portrayed before in the case of TPPRC. Surprisingly, these international supporters of the CTA keep relatively quiet and seem to be satisfied with the Tibetan justification of the present political system in exile. To silence critical arguments about the incomplete implementation of Western democratic ideas, the CTA stresses cultural factors (Taksham 1993: 16). Tibetan 'democracy' is a special form of the Western secular concept because of the uniqueness of Tibetan culture and religion. Therefore, the exile Tibetan political system is also special, i.e. not comparable with Western democracies. Consequently, a distinct and cultural Tibetan heritage makes every action unique, whether politically, socially or religiously motivated (interview with Mr Pema Yungne, Dharamsala, 13th ATPD, April 2002). Even if the CTA structure lacks crucial characteristics of a Western democracy, it still enjoys considerable recognition among Western NGOs. But in the context of governmental support, Frechette cites a US consular officer in Kathmandu who said that the US support is only limited:

The main problem preventing the U.S. from fully supporting the Tibetan exiles is their lack of democracy. The U.S. is not fond of theocratic governments and especially of people who unquestioningly support any leader, even if he is the Dalai Lama.

(2004: 75)

Exile Tibetan officials promote democratic ideas as being compatible with central philosophical elements of Buddhist philosophy, such as individual responsibility and respect for diversity. The 14th Dalai Lama pointed out that '[d]emocracy also fits the Mahayana [Buddhist] concept, that progress comes from individual initiative' (1991: 12).

Finally, an argument that gives reason for the introduction of democracy in exile stresses the topic of Tibetan national unity in regard to the relationship between insiders and outsiders. The success of the outsiders' struggle is considerably influenced by the support of insiders because the overthrowing of the home government is regarded to be an impossible mission without help from within the home territory. The promotion of an exile 'democracy', in which all Tibetans are theoretically allowed to participate despite their religious affinities, social or regional heritage, is crucial for the survival of the exile Tibetan struggle under the leadership of the 14th Dalai Lama. Through such liberal political ideas, compared with the traditional Tibetan political concepts, all Tibetans are linked in the struggle to overthrow the Chinese occupational power, regardless of their place of living. In the official future vision of Tibet in particular, the 14th Dalai Lama views the Tibetan political system as democracy that is closely linked with Tibetan Buddhism, in which every Tibetan will have the chance to participate. That may awaken hopes and feelings that the CTA is struggling in the name of all Tibetans. The 14th Dalai Lama stated:

Generally, Tibetans inside Tibet welcome democracy, they are very pleased at the recent announcements. No doubt they also welcomed the 1963 draft constitution before. Tibetans inside and outside have the same feelings about democracy, even though those outside are a bit anxious right now.

(1991: 11)

In contrast, a member of the TYC even goes as far as to say that Tibetans in China 'don't care about democracy' at all. 'Democracy is just an exile experience' and the future Tibet will probably not be democratic but rather communist (anonymous interview, 2006). This shows that the opinions about the importance of democracy for insiders differ widely.

Nevertheless, in the context of the relationship between insiders and outsiders, it is also crucial to view the implementation of democracy in the exile Tibetan political system in the light of linking these two groups together. While outsiders are living mostly in democratic host countries and therefore are constantly influenced by political activism of the host population, insiders still live in the more restrictive political system that was introduced in Tibet after the theocratic pre-1959 system. In this regard, one can assume that most insiders still view Tibetan politics according to the traditions in the past and the communist present and not to the democratic changes that are made in exile. They have no experience and only limited knowledge of democracy. To represent both insiders and voters in exile, the CTA has, with the present implementation of democracy while also linking politics with religion, the chance to connect both groups. Insiders and outsiders may both see their viewpoint represented in the present exile system.

The most crucial point in the 14th Dalai Lama's future vision is that there will be no special posts reserved for the present CTA officials. Instead, the 14th Dalai Lama has assured that the present Tibetan political elite in the TAR would keep their positions of power at the return of the exiles. With such a gesture, the Tibetan leader appeals to the present Tibetan politicians at home to work together with the CTA, e.g. there is no need to fear their posts as they would work hand-in-hand with the CTA for the national cause—an idea that may be morally better, instead of serving Chinese political object-ives. In this context, the question comes up regarding the future of the present CTA officials; their work is mainly motivated out of a dedication for a free Tibet, a goal that if achieved, contains a high degree of uncertainty regarding their own careers. Thus, there is a paradox situation for the exile political elite: the present CTA officials work for a goal that in turn restricts their personal professional careers.

To sum up, the CTA relies highly on the international community, the host and the home country regarding the introduction of democracy in the polit-ical exile structures. This applies to Shain's argument of the importance of international support. So the CTA needs to serve the ideas and political objectives of the international patrons to mobilize their operational, moral and diplomatic support to secure its daily political survival. But according to Shain's theory, the CTA also depends on the loyalty of Tibetans who are scattered all over the world. As seen before, many exile Tibetans withhold their participation and do not respond to the incentive to play an active role in exile politics and therefore in the exile struggle. The exile Tibetans' support of the CTA is rather determined by their loyalty towards the institu-tion of the Dalai Lama and therefore according to Tibetan non-democratic traditions.

This analysis explains why secular democratic ideas are insufficiently applied within the exile Tibetan political structures. The CTA needs to com-ply with the interests of the international agents and the Tibetan people, which is highly difficult because of the strong ties between religion and polit-ics. The CTA is not in a position to decide voluntarily when and how it will develop into a secular democracy. It rather needs to limit upcoming conflicts within the national community and focus on the continuation of inter-national support. Such a situation arises out of the special political position of a government-in-exile, which is widely illustrated in Shain's theory. But the dilemma of a government-in-exile, in terms of mobilizing international and national supporters to take an active part in the exile struggle, has not yet been considered. Only through tactical efforts and the skilful investment of incentives can a government-in-exile foster its position as sole representative of a nation.

6   Summary and conclusions

This book has analyzed the Tibetan government-in-exile from a political science point of view. The Central Tibetan Administration of His Holiness the Dalai Lama (CTA) was founded right after the young Tibetan leader arrived in India in 1959. Since the early 1950s, there has been a constant flow of Tibetans who left their homes and poured into the Indian subcontinent. Especially with the departure of the 14th Dalai Lama, the number of exile Tibetans in India, Nepal and Bhutan rose significantly. Since then, the Tibetan community has grown to more than 122,000. In the early 1960s, whole families followed the example of the Dalai Lama and left their homeland for an uncertain period of time because of fear of the Chinese invasion. Since the 1980s, many individual Tibetans have searched for temporary refuge in Asian countries, being motivated by religious, economic and educational aspects.

Since its founding, the Tibetan government-in-exile has claimed to be the sole and legal representative administration of the whole Tibetan nation. This political status is not recognized internationally. The same claims are declared by the present government in Beijing, which enjoys effective power over the Tibetan people and territory. Due to this conflicting situation I have focused on the following questions:

1   How did the CTA foster its claim to be the sole representative of all Tibetans over the years in exile?
2   Which policies have been carried out to regain the homeland and how can they be explained and characterized?

Yossi Shain's theoretical approach on exile organizations provided a fundamental basis for such an analysis. In his book *The Frontier of Loyalty: Political Exiles in the Age of the Nation-State* he characterizes the nature of exile organizations and describes their main focus, regardless of their history, political and representative claims, the origin of their members and the degree of outside support, on the struggle from a base abroad to overthrow and/or replace the present political system in the homeland. Shain stated that the central difficulties of such an exile struggle lie in an organization's ability to cultivate national loyalty and international recognition. But how can an exile organization create and/or even expand national loyalty and international support? And which political strategies need to be carried out to achieve the desired national and international acknowledgement of the exile struggle?

As Shain did not look at a specific case study but rather provided a preliminary theoretical framework, I took James Wilson's organization theory to identify the available instruments of an exile organization which could motivate its members to take an active part in the structure and goals. Wilson looked at formal organizations with voluntary membership, a specification that is applicable for the case of a government-in-exile. He categorizes four different incentives, which can be invested to mobilize present and potential organizational members. There are material or so-called tangible rewards, readily priced in monetary terms. Furthermore, there are three groups of intangible incentives, which are not exchangeable on regular economic markets and have little or no resale value, these are: specific solidarity incentives that arise when associating with an organization; collective solidarity incentives, which are awarded to all members of an organization and are comparable with economic public goods; and 'purposive incentives' that derive from a sense of individual satisfaction of having contributed to a worthwhile cause. In the next step of my attempt to form a suitable theoretical framework for the analysis of the Tibetan government-in-exile, I combined Shain's and Wilson's research findings and created a model to explain and analyze an exile government's efforts of struggle from a base abroad to gain national loyalty and international recognition.

With the help of my empirical data, this model leads me to the following four hypotheses:

H₁: The representative claims of the CTA are to a large extent based on Tibetan history and on international support, which has been granted to the exile Tibetan community since 1959.

The pre-1959 period provides the CTA with numerous political concepts that secure its administrative structure but also the exile community's social and economical survival. In short, the CTA was set up along the lines of the pre-exile political traditions of the former Ganden Phodrang government. In this regard, the political course of the exile Tibetan administration refers to the political practice of the pre-exile period; the combination of politics and religion. In 1960, the 14th Dalai Lama officially proclaimed that the CTA would function according to the Western secular concept of democracy and Tibetan Buddhist religion, a synthesis of modern political ideas with Tibetan traditions. Furthermore, the posts in the newly founded Tibetan administration in India were offered to officials who had already served in the former central Tibetan government in Lhasa. These officials and a few young aristocrats were able to maneuver within the new environment due to their level of education and language skills and their experiences and approved loyalty to the 14th Dalai Lama, which provided them with an indispensable advantage in gaining political power, compared with the poorly educated majority. This succession of traditional leadership, which was implemented both on the governmental but also settlement level, was widely agreed by the Tibetans and played a crucial role in the successful adaptation process of the Tibetans to their exile life right from the beginning. These developments exemplarily illustrate the importance of the pre-exile context in the situation of exile, which has also been stressed by Shain.

While the initial situation in exile demanded emergency help, over the years, a long-term rehabilitation and resettlement program for the exile Tibetans was implemented. This was only successful because of the tremendous help of the Government of India (GOI) and numerous international governmental organizations and NGOs. Right from the beginning, the CTA was empowered to interact with the Indian authorities and international aid organizations in the position of legal representative of all exile Tibetans and they could decide which projects were to be implemented and which not. Such delegation of authority by the international supporters of the exile Tibetan community emphasized the representational claims of the CTA. Consequently, the CTA had the upper hand from the start and fostered its political position right from the beginning through its access to foreign donor agencies. This position has not changed. In particular, the promotion of universal rights and the 'export' of Tibetan Buddhism motivate Western NGOs, transnational organizations, governments and individuals to support the exile Tibetan community. The CTA still acts as an interface between the international sphere and ordinary exile Tibetans who live scattered around the world. In this position, the Tibetan government-in-exile has the authority to decide for whom and where the available financial resources in particular are invested. In this regard, the CTA has been in a powerful position to allocate the granted support since the early years in exile—a situation that portrays the importance of outside support. One result is that the increasing international financial aid in particular hinders the CTA's goal to develop a self-supporting economy and, moreover, maneuvers all strata of exile Tibetan community into a high dependency on international grants. Additionally, the increasing wealth negatively influences the Tibetans' will to participate actively in the exile Tibetan struggle.

H$_2$:   The functioning and political legitimation of the CTA as Tibetan government-in-exile is determined by the institution of the Dalai Lama.

The institution of the Dalai Lama is at present the central unifying element of Tibetan politics and religion. A Dalai Lama is considered by all Tibetans as the ancestor of the Tibetan race; as the Buddha of compassion. Since the seventeenth century, the Dalai Lamas have held superior religious and political power in Tibet. This dominant position is still in existence in the present exile context. Despite the introduction of democratic ideas in the exile Tibetan political system the 14th Dalai Lama is vested with superior power over legislative, executive and judicial matters, inasmuch as they are not controlled by the Indian hosts. Moreover, he considerably expanded his traditional political authority by controlling the work of the so-called constitutional bodies that are intended to work independently from the CTA through direct installation of the heads of the election, audit and public service commissions. From a theoretical point of view, such a power structure is necessary to secure a certain degree of organizational stability in exile. Moreover, a legitimized leadership in exile considerably contributes to the success of any exile struggle.

The 14th Dalai Lama's superior position within the Tibetan community has positive effects for the CTA because he emphasizes the political credibility and stability of its organizational structure. In the position as charismatic political and religious leader, he enjoys the loyalty of all Tibetans. He is able to link all Tibetans despite their place of living and therefore creates, as a unifying force, the national loyalty for the CTA. In this regard, the example of the 14th Dalai Lama widens Shain's insider–outsider dilemma to a certain extent. The theory can be extended inasmuch as a charismatic and traditionally legitimated political leader may be in the position to overcome the upcoming gaps between an exile community and the national compatriots who still live in the homeland. In the international sphere, the 14th Dalai Lama increasingly acts as global celebrity, a role that was highlighted with his being awarded the Nobel Peace Prize in 1989. At present, he is in an extraordinarily favorable position from which to generate international financial and moral support, which provides the CTA with international support and acknowledgement. Through a wide network of international Tibet Support Groups (TSGs) and the CTA, he contributes considerably to the economic survival of the exile Tibetans in Asia and the CTA. Yet, his superiority hinders a secular democratic transformation of the exile Tibetan political system as a whole. The 14th Dalai Lama holds, theoretically, the ultimate power in the CTA, which indicates that the rest of the CTA structure functions merely symbolically. So, for instance, the 'democratically' elected assembly is downgraded to nothing more than a 'debating circle'.

The 14th Dalai Lama is able to mobilize both the national and international communities to support the CTA. In this regard, his authority is most useful for the organizational survival and political position of the CTA within the Tibetan community. But in this context, interesting questions arise regarding his succession: What will happen upon the death of the 14th Dalai Lama? Is the exile Tibetan political system in a position to handle his death in terms of keeping things stable and controllable?

These questions are not easy to answer, but they can be addressed as follows. The institution of the Dalai Lama is based on the traditional concept of succession of leadership, the tulku-concept of reincarnation, which since the seventeenth century has provided a framework to ensure relative stability in the Tibetan political sphere. Only when such a leader was missing did the

Tibetan political system tend to instability. Such unsteadiness is most likely at the death of the 14th Dalai Lama because of a *de-facto* existing factionalism along regional, religious and political lines in Tibetan exile. To prevent a collapse of the exile Tibetan community and, at worst, the end of the exile struggle, the 14th Dalai Lama has tried, at several events, to prepare and remind his national compatriots that there is a need for an adequate concept to ensure succession.

The *Charter of the Tibetans-in-Exile* of 1991 provides a solution in Articles 31–35, where the traditional concept of regency is discussed. Three Regents, who will serve for a three-year term, will be elected by the exile Tibetan assembly and cabinet; a chief Regent will hold ultimate executive power. The whole council of regency will exist until a new Dalai Lama is found and able to handle the political affairs of the CTA. This concept clearly applies to the will of large parts of the Tibetan community, which favors the traditional concept of reincarnation rather than a democratic election, the alternative to ensure succession of leadership. In regard to the people's preference, the 14th Dalai Lama has already stated that his successor will not be found within the present Chinese borders. Recently, he declared that he believes that a successor from the exile community would be '. . . in a better position to "fulfill the objective" of getting their homeland back for the Tibetans'.[1] This clearly shows that the installation of a new Dalai Lama by the Chinese in Beijing, following the example of the 11th Panchen Lama, will be impossible. If they do so, the new incarnation would be seen as no less than a puppet of Chinese political objectives. The Chinese leadership reacted promptly on the proclamation of the 14th Dalai Lama in pointing out that, nonetheless, the 15th Dalai Lama will be born within the borders of the PRC and chosen with traditional methods. Another option for succession may be the present 17th Karmapa, a high ranking tulku of the Tibetan Kagüpa sect. He fled the PRC in January 2000 at the age of 14 and since then has lived under tight Indian security in a monastery near Dharamsala. His spectacular escape, similar to that of the 14th Dalai Lama in 1959, attracted a wide media presence (*Berliner Morgenpost* 2000; *Newsweek* 2000; Brown 2004). Furthermore, he will be of an age able to handle the political affairs of the CTA and, more-over, enjoy wide loyalty within the exile Tibetan community but also among Western supporters. The most important question is whether he has the exceptional personal qualities, the expertise, and the charisma comparable with those of the 14th Dalai Lama, which allow him to handle political affairs until a new Dalai Lama can succeed. In short, he needs to be suitable and capable to fill the power vacuum. However, the solution will be in the future; the CTA needs to ensure that the exile Tibetan community does not collapse and that the exile Tibetan struggle will continue. In my opinion, the death of the 14th Dalai Lama will reveal the real strength of the CTA to act as an exile government on behalf of the entire Tibetan nation.

H₃: The structure and policies of the CTA can be explained with Yossi

Shain's political theory of exile organizations. According to this theory, the political survival of any exile organization depends to a large extent on the degree of granted national loyalty and international support and recognition.

The CTA's institutional structure has developed over time into an elaborate network of departments, institutions and exile Tibetan NGOs in order to address, as much as possible, members of the national and international communities to take an active part in the exile struggle. The organizational structure of the CTA emphasizes its claims of struggle as the sole representative for the Tibetan national cause and to induce unity among Tibetans and non-Tibetans. Today there are abundant Tibetan and non-Tibetan activists engaged in supporting the CTA's policies and goals.

In the initial decades in exile, the CTA's attempt to induce international support and recognition by lobbying the UN failed. Since the 1980s, the focus was changed towards a grassroots orientated approach involving international NGOs. This alteration was flanked in the 1980s by a shifted goal of the exile struggle from an independent to an autonomous homeland. The decisions were made by the 14th Dalai Lama with regard to international and Chinese politics, which shows, on the one hand, the vulnerability of the CTA to international developments and, on the other hand, the political strength of the present leadership in the homeland. According to Shain's theory, such political adjustments are natural. Moreover, the changes were indispensable for the CTA's organizational survival. The changed politics were backed up in 1995 by a referendum of the exile Tibetan community. It is not evident how many Tibetans really took part in the voting but it can be judged that the majority were not satisfied with the final outcome of this concession to international politics. They rather retain their perception of a future independent homeland—an idea that creates tension and fear within the exile community because it is not compatible with the now official course of the exile struggle. To bridge the gap between wishes and *realpolitik*, the CTA uses different languages to communicate its political goals. While the Tibetan community is addressed in Tibetan using the term 'rangzen' (independence), the CTA talks with international supporters in English about 'autonomy'. Such clever use of language to minimize fears at the national level and at the same time make concessions to the international community has not yet been covered by Shain. Nevertheless, such developments show that the CTA is not in a position to exercise sovereign politics but rather relies on the will of the outside world, while putting aside the wishes and doubts of the national community. This ignorance of the will of the national community is only possible through the superior position of the Dalai Lama who, as previously mentioned, is able to unify the divergent opinions of his countrymen.

Another example of the politically shaky position of the Tibetan exile government is the relationship between the CTA and the host country, India. Since the arrival of the 14th Dalai Lama in 1959, there has been a deep involvement of Indian politics in exile Tibetan affairs. The CTA depends, in any legislative, executive, judicative matter, on Indian goodwill. For instance, the GOI prohibited any political activities of the CTA, mainly because of India's position in Asia and the security threat at the northern borders. Consequently, the CTA was never allowed to struggle officially for a free Tibetan homeland. This restriction forced the exile Tibetans to focus predominantly on the preservation of their culture and religion. In this regard, the initial political ideas and energies of the Tibetans in India, to free their homeland, were immediately directed to a topic that moreover referred to human rights violations in the homeland and supported the idea of a Tibetan traditional setting in exile, where politics and religion are combined. In this regard, the traditional succession of leadership, the use of state oracles for political decisions and the increasing power of the exile ecclesiastic stratum, was put in a new light in exile Tibetan politics.

Since the 1980s, the preservation of Tibetan culture and religion increasingly became a vehicle with which to approach the international community to emphasize the exile Tibetan freedom struggle in a wider context. Thus, the Indian restrictions have turned out to work in favor of the exile Tibetan political elite, and moreover, the idea of preserving Tibetan culture and religion has significantly contributed to the scope and scale of the monetary transfers from the West to the Tibetans. At present, the GOI and CTA cooperate in partnership, where each administration has its responsibilities. The Indians have vested the Tibetan political elite with powers such as organizing daily life in the settlements and deciding on allocations of international aid. However, Indian authorities still remain in a position to prohibit and restrict the CTA's room for maneuver.

H_4: Both foci of a government-in-exile, to gain national loyalty and international support, are interdependent. The striving for national loyalty and international acknowledgement leads to policy effects that support each other but also create discrepancies. Consequently, the amended theory of governments-in-exile provides a model to categorize CTA policies and to explain discrepancies caused by the struggle for national and international support.

In my research, I looked exemplarily at different exile policies that are implemented by the CTA to mobilize national loyalty and/or international recognition and support. A useful model to analyze the CTA's political position provided the amended theoretical approach on governments-in-exile, which combines Shain's and Wilson's research. It opened the possibility of looking at the incentives invested by the CTA to motivate present and potential members of the exile Tibetan struggle and, in turn, reveal their reactions on such investments. In general, the CTA's access to material resources is limited. In contrast, the investment of symbolic and religious means plays an important role in the process of inducing support. The CTA increasingly use non-material or so-called soft resources to cultivate loyalty and recognition, or more drastically stated: Tibet has been created and used as a resource itself to promote its own cause.

First, I looked at the investments that are made by the CTA to create unity within the exile Tibetan community. The CTA invented three different 'books' that prove membership of the exile Tibetan community for exile Tibetans, exile Tibetan institutions and non-Tibetans. While the exile Tibetan institutions and non-Tibetans benefit from 'purpositive incentives', the exile Tibetans who live in the Indian subcontinent draw tangible (e.g. scholarships, job opportunities) and intangible advantages (e.g. participation in elections) from their 'green book'. With such investment, the CTA counteracts the general problem of denaturalization in exile and instead provides the exile Tibetans with a source of identity and membership in the exile Tibetan community. Because of the material shortages in Asia, the so-called voluntary payments to the CTA have a tax character. Many exile Tibetans are not in an economic position to decide if they want to pay the requested amount of money; rather, they rely on the allocation of international aid, which is bound to the ownership of a 'green book'. The payments secure the exile Tibetans' loyalty to the CTA and therefore foster its political position and claims. (This concept of an 'exile citizenship' has not been considered by Shain yet.) The process of creating national loyalty is flanked by the CTA by pointing out Tibetan patriotic ideas and initiating legal hurdles in India in particular (supported by the GOI) to discourage exile Tibetans from taking new citizenship. In this regard, the efforts of the CTA to create unity among the exile Tibetans—which in turn generates national loyalty—and involve non-Tibetan actors in the exile struggle, has been carried out successfully with the help of material and non-material investments.

Second, I investigated why the CTA established exile Tibetan schools instead of enrolling the Tibetan children in the already existing Indian, Nepali and Bhutanese schools, and what role the educational sector has played in exile politics. I found that investment in education is a key factor in securing national loyalty; investments that have been not stressed by Shain, and therefore extend the focus in the theoretical discourse on exile governments. In this regard, investments in the educational sector contribute to the exile struggle as it is used by the CTA to foster its superior political position within the exile Tibetan community. Tibetan culture and religion are major parts of the educational course in the exile Tibetan schools and contribute significantly to the creation of a Tibetan identity abroad from the homeland. Crucial are the scholarship and sponsorship programs of the CTA, which foster its political position through the monopoly on financial resources and exclusive access to international universities. In this regard, only those who are bright, politically active in supporting the official CTA policy and hold a 'green book' benefit from grants. Furthermore, the educational system encourages many Tibetan parents who live within the Chinese borders to send their children to an exile Tibetan school. Many of these temporary exiles are encouraged by the CTA to return home after finishing their educational course. Once they return, they contribute to the exile Tibetan struggle through their knowledge of CTA politics, which they pass on to their parents and friends. In this regard, they link the exile Tibetan community with Tibetans in the homeland, which, according to Shain's theory, is most helpful in minimizing present and future discrepancies between insiders and outsiders. This, in turn, supports the claimed position of the CTA as representative of all Tibetans. Additionally, the exile Tibetan schools provide a source to interact with the host population, which also uses the educational opportunities. Thus, the CTA can promote its political ideas among the local population, which in turn affects domestic politics in the host countries, as outlined in the examples of India and Switzerland. Here the mass popularity of the exile Tibetans influenced the political course of the host governments and in the end created favorable circumstances for them.

Third, as material incentives like scholarships and benefits in schooling in India are not sufficient for the most well-off members of the Tibetan Diaspora in the West, the CTA invests a wide range of non-material resources, like the image of a non-violent, eco-friendly and religious Tibetan nation, or traditional symbolism to remind them about their heritage and the Tibetan struggle. The most important source is the promotion of nationalistic ideas linked to Tibetan Buddhist religion. Symbolism and religion play an important role in the creation of nationalistic feelings among the compatriots at home and abroad. This in turn mobilizes them to take an active part in the exile Tibetan struggle under the guidance of the CTA. Through well-considered usage of such traditional symbolism and the creation of a ceremonial calendar in exile, the CTA recreates a Tibetan identity in the new environment and emphasizes the development of a national consciousness. Only among the exile Tibetan youth does the CTA encounter certain difficulties, since the traditional symbols do not motivate the youngsters to participate in the exile struggle and moreover stand in contrast to their preferred living standards. The CTA has been able to approach international NGOs in its 'snowball' course (see previous text) and was able to set-up religious institutions worldwide to successfully promote Tibetan Buddhist nationalist ideas. The 14th Dalai Lama acts increasingly as ambassador for Tibet in the international sphere, supported by a wide media presence that opens doors to celebrities and all strata of Western society. Thus, the exile Tibetans are able to mobilize enormous moral and financial international support for the Tibetan struggle. As an important side-effect, the new exile generations also accept the internationally promoted image of Tibet, while at the same time refusing the traditional symbolism. So Tibetan Buddhist nationalism represents an important source for the CTA to generate national and international support. Furthermore, this strategy emphasizes the official course of the CTA to preserve a distinct Tibetan culture and religion.

Fourth, since the 1980s, the CTA has stressed the topic of universal rights in order to mobilize international NGOs to participate actively in the exile

Tibetan struggle. This struggle has been subdivided into different specific rights: human, eco and women's rights, which are all communicated in different international forums. The promotion of these specific rights provides the activists with symbolic and ideological instruments that are utilized to categorize and support the exile Tibetan struggle. Moreover, the 'universal rights strategy' also creates beneficial effects for the organizational survival of numerous NGOs, who are able to maintain and even expand their international network and/or numbers of members. The CTA profits from the 'universal rights strategy' as the increasing international support legitimizes its political claims to act on behalf of the national cause, which is represented in the exile struggle. The promotion of an exile struggle under the guise of universal rights represents a new focus in a theory of exile governments and has not been mentioned by Shain. Furthermore, the promotion of universal rights shows exemplarily that the efforts that are designed to reach the final goal of an exile struggle—the return home—are indistinguishable from the striving for outside support. On the national front, the 'universal rights strategy' contributes to a fruitful relationship between insiders and outsiders, as it demonstrates to Tibetans in the homeland that the exiles care about their plight. In this regard, the CTA follows the communication of universal rights with a two-fold strategy to secure both national and international support. In contrast, the exile Tibetans in Asia and abroad do not participate extraordinarily in the 'universal rights strategy', which illustrates that the CTA gives attention to internationally promising topics. One could say that the strategy is controversially adopted: while the international community reacts favorably to the promotion of human, eco and women's rights, the exile Tibetans widely ignore these international values and rather rely on their traditions.

Fifth, an important move towards international support was the introduction of democratic reforms in exile. The CTA clearly applied to the ideas and political objectives of the international patrons to mobilize operational, moral and diplomatic support, despite a general affinity with communism and Tibetan traditional law and order. The exile Tibetan leadership has been exceptionally successful in internationally promoting their Tibetan 'democracy', which motivated numerous NGOs and also governments and transnational organizations to support the exile political system, despite considerable shortcomings according to the Western understanding of democracy. Thus, the official introduction of democratic ideas in the exile Tibetan political system portrays the importance of the international sphere for a government-in-exile. At the same time, the CTA faces problems with the democratic concepts to secure national loyalty within the exile Tibetan community. Many Tibetans withhold their active participation in the democratic transformation and in this regard, also in the exile struggle. Their support for the CTA is more determined by loyalty towards the institution of the Dalai Lama and therefore by the non-democratic Tibetan traditions. The CTA is thus in a problematic situation, trying to serve the differing international and national interests. This contradiction explains why secular democratic ideas are insufficiently applied within the exile Tibetan political structures. The same problems face the CTA in its emphasized political course of non-violence. While the international community responds favorably to a peaceful struggle, acknowledged by the Nobel Peace Prize in 1989, large parts of the exile Tibetan community do not agree with it, especially the new generation in exile which favors more violent means to achieve the goals of the exile struggle and calls the non-violent strategy a 'non-action strategy' (anonymous interview, 2003). The CTA thus needs to serve different interests at the same time; the ones of the international agents and the Tibetan people. This is very difficult because of the strong ties between religion and politics.

In conclusion, the CTA is in no position to decide voluntarily which political strategies it will implement. Instead, it needs to maneuver within a complex political situation to cultivate national and international support. Such a situation arises out of the special position of a government-in-exile, which is illustrated in Shain's theory. While the promotion of Tibetan Buddhist nationalist ideas is successfully responded to by both Tibetans and Western supporters, the examples of democracy and non-violence in particular show that the implementation of certain policies creates considerable problems at national level, while the international community reacts favorably.

In general, it can be stated that the CTA successfully promoted its cause in the international sphere. The Tibetans navigate internationally in a favorable climate mainly because of the promotion of universal rights combined with Buddhist philosophy and the 14th Dalai Lama as the front man. In contrast, national loyalty is highly determined by the institution of the Dalai Lama. In this regard, the CTA needs to focus in the future on a limitation of conflict within the national community in particular. A turning point, in time to come, will be the death of the 14th Dalai Lama. This event will challenge the CTA to show strength. It needs to handle new circumstances and open up the way ahead. Only through tactical effort and clever and prudent investments of the available resources will the CTA be able to foster its position as sole representative of the whole Tibetan nation.

Appendices

Appendix 1: Transliteration of Tibetan terms

Amdo	a mdo	Ganden Phodrang	bod gzhung dgan
Bö	bod		lden pho drang
Bö Cholka Sum	bod chol ka gsum	Garpön	sgar dpon
Böpa	bod pa	Gartok	sgar thok
Bön	bon	Gelugpa	dge lugs pa
Cham	'cham	Gerpa	sger pa
Chamdo	chab mdo	Gu-Chu-Sum	dgu bcu gsum
Chenrezig	spyan ras gzigs	Gyantse	rgyal rtse
Chikyab Khenpo	spyi skyabs	Gyami	rgya mi
	mkhan po	Gyelsab	rgyal tshab
Chö yön	mchod yon	Hor	hor
Chörten	mtchod rten	Kadampa	bka' gdams pa
Chösi Nyiden	chos srid	Kagüpa	bka' brgyud pa
	gnyis ldan	Kalon	bka' blon
Chupa	chu pa	Kalon Tripa	bka' blon khri pa
Dalai Lama	tā la'i bla ma	Kashag	bka' shag
Denpay Utsug	bden pa'i u gtsugs	Kham	khams
Depön	sde dpon	Labrang	bla brang
Dorje Shugden	rdo rje shugs ldan	Lama	bla ma
Drepung	'bras spungs	Lam Uma	lam dbu ma
Drogpa	'brog pa	Lhasa	lha sa
Drungdrag	drung drag	Lho	lho
Drungdring	drung 'bring	Lönchen	blon chen
Drungkhor	drung khor	Losar	lo gsar
Drungkyü	drung dkyus	Miser	mi ser
Drungyik Chemo	drung yig chen mo	Mönlam Chenmo	smon lam
Düchung	dud chung		chen mo
Dzongpön	rdzong pon	Nagchu	nag chu
Gadong	dgar gdong	Nangpa	nang pa
Ganden	dga' ldan	Nangzen	nang gzan

Nechung	gnas chung	Theji	tha'i ji
Ngari	mnga' ris	Trälpa	khral pa
Nyingmapa	rnying ma pa	Tsang	gtsang
Öpame	'od dpag med	Tsekhor	rtse khor
Panchen Lama	pan chen bla ma	Tsongdu	tshong du
Rangzen	rang btsan	Tsongkhapa	tsong kha pa
Rangzen Lakhdeb	rang btsan lag deb	Tsongpa	tsong pa
Reting	rwa sgreng	Tulku	trul ku
Sakyapa	sa skya pa	Ü	dbus
Sera	se ra	Yabshi	yab gzhis
Shigatse	gzhis ka rtse	Yak	yag
Songtsen Gampo	srong rtsen	Yatung	ya grong
Taktra	stag brag	Yigtsang	yig tshang

Appendix 2: The Foreigners Registration Act: Regulation for Tibetans in India

NOTIFICATION REGULATING ENTRY OF TIBETAN NATIONALS INTO INDIA

1 In exercise of the powers conferred by section 3 of the Foreigners Act, 1946 (31 of 1946) and section 3 of the Registration of Foreigners Act, 1939 (16 of 1939), the Central Government is pleased to direct that any foreigner of Tibetan nationality, who enters India hereafter, shall—

(a) at the time of his entry into India obtain from the Officer-in-Charge of the Police post at the Indo–Tibetan frontier, a permit in the from specified in the annexed schedule;

(b) comply with such instructions as may be prescribed in the said permit; and

(c) get himself registered as a foreigner and obtain a certificate of registration.

SCHEDULE

PERMIT

Serial No. ....

  Mr. ...., son of ...., a foreigner of Tibetan nationality whose description is given below having arrived in India from Tibet via ....is hereby permitted to stay in India for a period of ......months from the date hereof and to travel to the places mentioned below. If he/she does not leave India before ... he/she will, unless he/she has obtained the permission of the Central Government to remain for a longer period, be liable to prosecution for a contravention of the provisions of the Foreigners Act, 1946, punishable with imprisonment for a period of five years and with fine and will also be liable to expulsion from India. Application for an extension of this permit should be made at least fifteen days before ....and must be addressed to the Central Government through the State Government.

2   This permit must be produced on demand of any Registration Officer, Magistrate or Police Officer not below the rank of head constable.
3   This permit must be surrendered to the Officer-in-Charge of the Police post at the place of departure from India.
4   The contents of this permit have been explained to the holder thereof.

[Seal]   Signature of the Issuing Authority

Description of holder:

(a)   Age
(b)   Sex
(c)   Height
(d)   Colour of eyes
(e)   Occupation

Please permit to visit.   _____

Appendix 3: Sample of stamps for the 'Green Book' issued by the CTA

Notes

1 Introduction

1 The terms 'Western', 'Western world' and 'West' are used in this book to describe the countries of Europe and North America, Australia, New Zealand and Japan.
2 For detailed information on the 11th Panchen Lama, see Hoppe 1995, 1997: 113–36 and Hilton 2003.
3 See among others, CTA 1969, 1981, 1992b, 1994a, 2000f, 2001.
4 This may be because many Tibetologists are more interested in the past and present life in Tibet and therefore conduct field research in China rather than in exile.

2 Modern Tibet: A historical account

1 For detailed information on that time and the founding of Lhasa, see Larsen and Sinding-Larsen 2001 and Yeshe De Project 1986.
2 Ethnography is the scientific description of the customs and individual peoples and cultures, which has nothing to do with the here used form to define the area of Tibet. The here so-called ethnographic definition is rather a fourteenth-century political description of the Tibetan plateau employed by the Chinese imperium under the Mongol Yuan Dynasty.
3 On the one hand, there are still Tibetans who live in or come from regions which were not under the direct control of the Lhasa government but still view themselves as Tibetans. On the other hand, bringing up the subject of a unified nation under the rule of a Dalai Lama, as practiced in the present exile context, inherits many emotions and difficulties (anonymous interview, 2003).
4 For detailed information, see Schmitz 1998 and Hoppe 1997: 36.
5 For a detailed list of sources that estimated different population figures, see Grunfeld 1987: 218–22.
6 In the following, I use the term monk only to describe the monastic population, as nuns had a subordinate position in terms of numbers.
7 This approximate number matches with the 9.8 per cent that have been mentioned by Tandzin 2004: 54.
8 For more information on the history of Tibetan Buddhism, see Bell 1931; Snellgrove and Richardson 1995.
9 Sir Charles Bell became a close friend of the 13th Dalai Lama after his visit to Lhasa in 1920–1, acting as Political Officer of Sikkim under the British Empire. Bell mentions for the year 1917 that the annual revenues of the army were GB£150,000, the Lhasa government revenues amounted to GB£720,000, while the monastic revenues came to GB£1,000,000 (Bell 1987: 184–90).

10 For detailed information, see Goldstein 1986: 50, 72–4; Goldstein 1993: 3; Wiley 1986: 9–10; Michael 1986: 75; CTA 1981: 76; Fjeld 2005: 26–8.
11 In Tibet, a family belongs to the aristocracy under the premise that at least one family member during the entire genealogy had been serving in the government and that it holds landed property rights (Goldstein 1993: 6).
12 For the discourse, see Goldstein 1968: 79–87; Michael 1986: 70–8; Dargyay 1978: 65–83; Grunfeld 1987: 7; Redwood French 2002: 120, Fjeld 2005: 32–4; Coleman 1998.
13 Goldstein mentions 400–500 officials in the period 1913–51 and refers to Israel Epstein, who cites a figure of 616 (333 monks and 283 lay officials) (1993: 5–6).
14 For detailed information on the choice of the Regents, see Dhondup 1993: 12; Burman 1979: 47; Goldstein 1993: 11–12.
15 The composition of the cabinet members changed over time: four laymen (1728–51, 1804–78) or three laymen, one monk (1751–1804, 1878–1959) (Petech 1973: 235; Rahul 1969: 142).
16 Those were the districts of Kham, Ngari, Lho, Dromo, Hor, Changtang and Tsang (Tethong 2000: 37).
17 For information about the search for the 14th Dalai Lama, see Goldstein 1993: 314–30.
18 The term 'Great Game' is attributed to Arthur Connolly, who worked for the British East India Company, and it became popularized by the British author and poet Rudyard Kipling (1865–1936). The Great Game describes the time between 1813 and 1917 when the British and the Tsarist Russian empires struggled for supremacy in Central Asia. See: http://en.wikipedia.org/wiki/The_Great_Game (accessed November 2004).
19 For detailed information on Russian–Tibetan relations, see Shaumian 2000; Burman 1979: 13–18; Richardson 1984: 78–82.
20 For more information on the Younghusband military expedition, see Sood 2004.
21 The representatives for Britain were Sir Henry McMahon and Sir Charles Bell, for China Mr Ivan Chen and for Tibet Mr Lönchen Shatra, the Tibetan Prime Minister at that time (Richardson 1984: 107).
22 For detailed information of Bell's perception of the 13th Dalai Lama, see Bell 1987.
23 There are two different numbering systems of the Panchen Lama lineage. The mentioned 9th incumbent is according to the Lhasa governmental system the 7th Panchen Lama. I will refer in this context to the Tashilhunpo system because this system has been in use since 1952. For more information, see Shakya 1996: 24–9; Huber 1999: 112.
24 The Buddha of wisdom is the counterpart of the Buddha of compassion in the sphere of meditation. The Buddha of compassion is its projection in the worldly sphere and incarnated in the Dalai Lama. Both compassion and wisdom are necessary in the Tibetan religion for enlightenment and complete each other in the religious and mundane spheres (Richardson 1984: 54–6; Snellgrove and Richardson 1995: 219–20).
25 The time between the death of the 5th Dalai Lama, 1682, and the empowerment of the 13th Dalai Lama, 1895, was characterized by a relatively weak institution of the Dalai Lama. Many incarnations died early or had only little impact on Tibetan politics. Instead, Regents were entrusted to lead the country, who in many cases were motivated by their personal interests only.
26 For more information on the political relationship between the Dalai Lama and the Panchen Lama, see Mehra 2004.
27 There are different versions of the status of the area and the amount of money that needed to be paid by the Lhasa government (Goldstein 1993: 316–22; Richardson 1984: 154).

28 At that time, the explorer, scholar, author and American ambassador in China, William W. Rockhill, met with the 13th Dalai Lama.

29 For detailed information on the CIA involvement, see Knaus 1999.

3 An approach towards a theory of governments-in-exile

1 From a political science point of view, three relevant theoretical foci classify migrants: first, on the basis of social and psychological experiences that had taken place before people left their home; second, on motivations and attitudes that led to the departure; and third, on the ability of adjustment and assimilation in the host country. See Shain 1989: 8; Tabori 1972: 24–6; Nuscheler 1994: 8–10; Peterson 1958: 261; Coser 1984.

2 For detailed information on the different definitions of Diaspora, see Appadurai 1996 and Brah 1996: 181–6.

3 In this book, ideology is defined as the normative philosophical concept of a society that forms social standards and the political process.

4 Tibetans in exile: A portrait of the CTA

1 Sikkim was semi-independent when the first exile Tibetans came and was annexed by India in 1975. Tibetans had already lived and studied in this Himalayan Kingdom for centuries. Because of its location, Sikkim was an ideal place for the migrating Tibetans to settle in the 1950s, considering both its climatic and cultural conditions.

2 According to the *Charter of the Tibetans-in-Exile*, a Tibetan is any person who was born within the boundaries of Greater Tibet or any person whose biological father or mother is of Tibetan descent (CTA 1991: Article 8).

3 It has to be noted that Tibetan Muslims and Tibetan soldiers fighting in the Indian army are excluded from this survey; reason unknown (interview with Mr Masood Butt, DIIR, Dharamsala, June 2003).

4 Grunfeld examines the number of exile Tibetans only until the 1980s. In contrast to that analysis are the numbers of exile Tibetans in the CTA statistics between 1994 (125,777 exile Tibetans) and 1998 (122,078), which show a decrease in the numbers of Tibetans who are already in exile, while the CTA reports about a constantly growing Tibetan exile community (CTA 1994b: 5; 2000f: 7).

5 Despite increasing shortages of resources to handle the steady flow of refugees in a proper way, India has neither ratified the 1951 UNHCR Convention on Refugees nor taken any initiative to create an administrative infrastructure that eases the control of the refugee problem (Roy 2001b: 56).

6 Woodcock states that there were approximately 7,000 Tibetan recruits (1970: 411).

7 See: www.bharat-rakshak.com/LAND-FORCES/Special-Forces/SFF.html (accessed October 2003).

8 The present CTA changed its name several times: Government of Tibet-in-Exile or Tibetan Administration in Exile (CTA 1969: i; 1981).

9 The following information about the set-up can also be found at the CTA presentation, available online at: www.tibet.net. The area of Gangchen Kyishong was purchased by the CTA in 1967 from a leading Indian lawyer of Dharamsala (Samphel 1998: 15; CTA 1999).

10 For instance, in Tibet the people used to drink water from rivers and dry meat in the air. Such habits led India to diseases and health risks.

11 But the increasing employment also created conflicts between the Tibetan settlers and the locals. The latter saw themselves suddenly in a disadvantageous situation because now they needed to compete with the new settlers over cheap workers,

who mostly belonged to the caste of the 'untouchables'. Similar competitive situations also appeared in the questions of the allocation and use of the available land resources (Subramanya 2006).

12 For more information, see Goldstein 1975a: 182; 1975b: 17; Palakshappa 1978; Methfessel 1995; Shekhawat 1995: 14–17; Roemer 2001.

13 The Tibetan Muslim community traces its origins back to areas in Nepal, China and Kashmir. The exclusion of the Tibetan Muslims in official CTA reports is an outcome of the White Paper Convention between India and China in 1952, when Kashmiri Muslims became Indian citizens. Ten years later, large parts of the Muslim community of Lhasa left the town as a consequence of the withdrawal of the Indian representative there. They migrated with most of their belongings to the lands of their ancestors. The present Tibetan Muslim population in Srinagar has Indian citizenship but is also financially supported by the CTA. Because of their citizenship, they are not recognized by the exile Tibetan Buddhists as part of the exile Tibetan community, despite several visits from the 14th Dalai Lama to the settlement (Gray 1997; Butt 1994: 8–9, 16; Butt and Choephel 1988: 12–13; Griebenov 1936: 127–9; interviews with Mr Masood Butt, DIIR, Dharamsala, March and June 2003).

14 As Bhutan did not ratify the 1951 Geneva Convention on Refugees, the Tibetans in Bhutan enjoy only limited rights.

15 Various articles on the Tibetans in Bhutan can be found in the *Tibetan Review* 1974–9. For further information, see CTA 1979.

16 The CTA in 1994, counted about 15,000 Tibetans in Nepal (CTA 1994a: 79). The Tibetan Planning Council talked of about 13,720 Tibetans in Nepal in 1998 (CTA 2000f: 7). The Tibet office in Kathmandu mentioned in 2003 a number between 25,000–30,000 Tibetans in Nepal (interview with Mr Jigme Wangdu, CTA Office of Tibet, Kathmandu, May 2003).

17 For detailed information on Tibetans in Switzerland, see Lindegger 2000; Olschak 1976: 187–94; Ekvall 1967: 113–17.

18 See: www.tibet.net (accessed November 2004).

19 For an overview of the development of the exile Tibetan school system, see John 1999: 298.

20 See: www.tibet.net (accessed November 2003).

21 CTA, n.d. f: 3. See also: www.tibet.net/edu/eng/ (accessed November 2003).

22 For further information on this issue, see Sautman 2000: 31–91; TPPRC 2005.

23 For detailed information on the 'Middle-Way' position, see Ardley 2002: 106–10; CTA 2005.

24 See: www.tibetinfonet.net (accessed August 28, 2006).

25 To diminish the practice of ranking in 1965, the highest governmental titles of the government in Lhasa, such as the teiji, were annulled by their holders in accordance with democratic principles and the changed circumstances.

26 For one example of the nepotism within the family of the 14th Dalai Lama, see Backman 2004: 209–11.

27 Wangpo Tethong himself is a scion of the aristocratic elite of Tibet. His forefathers held high posts in the Lhasa administration and his present relatives are still serving in high posts in the CTA.

28 Interviews with Mr Tashi Norbu, Public Service Commission, Dharamsala, April 2003 and Mr Thupten Samphel, DIIR, Dharamsala, April 2003; Gupta 2005: 224–5, 231.

29 For detailed information on the Bön Community in exile, see Karmay 1993.

30 For detailed information on the deity, see Nebesky-Wojkowitz 1995: Ch. 8; Dryfus 1999.

31 See: www.tibetinfonet.net (accessed May 25, 2007)

32 See: www.tibetinfonet.net (accessed March 29, 2006).

33 The Dalai Lama's appeal was in turn opposed by the Chinese authorities who subsequently promoted the wearing of wildlife fur. See: www.tibetinfonet.net (December 30, 2006). For photographs of the occasion, see: http://www.tibetinfonet.net/content/list_images/4 (accessed August 19, 2007).

34 There are no deputies of the small exile Tibetan Muslim community or exile Tibetans in Nepal and Bhutan.

35 In the 2006 election, the Dalai Lama for the first time did not appoint three members of the exile Tibetan parliament and rather renounced his right.

36 It consists of 12 members: two from each Tibetan region, one from each religious sect and one direct nominee of the 14th Dalai Lama.

37 In 2001, the election rules of the ATPD and the cabinet were changed on the initiative of the 14th Dalai Lama. From a direct installment by the Dalai Lama, the appointment of the kalons was shifted to the public, who have been able to decide on the ministers ever since. This change prompted many concerns among the exile Tibetans because this practice undermined and limited the power of the Dalai Lama.

38 The present Prime Minister, Mr Samdhong Rinpoche, is a high religious dignitary of the Tibetan Gelugpa sect.

39 There is no special rotation system within the CTA but, from time to time, the kashag decides on a change of responsibilities.

40 For detailed information, see: www.tibet.net/en/diir/intr.html (accessed June 2006).

41 The founding dates are in accordance with interviews with officials of the CTA, with Tibetan scholars and visits to numerous offices. In contrast, the CTA shows in the following cases, different founding years: New Delhi (1959), Kathmandu (1962), London (1982), Budapest (1992), Moscow (1992) (CTA 1994a: 212).

42 See: www.tibetanyouthcongress.org (accessed October 2003); Tibetan Youth Congress. Brochure (Dharamsala: Tibetan Youth Congress, n.d.).

43 For detailed information, see Schwartz 1996.

44 Two examples that emphasize the claims of TYC regarding Tibet's independence are the letters of the Tiger–Dragon Youth Association of Tibet, which were translated and reprinted in the *Tibetan Review* 1982 and 1983.

45 For detailed information on the revival of the TWA in 1984, see Butler 2003: 45–50.

46 The international network also generated support for the TWA. For instance in 1995, the TWA set up the project 'Stitches of Tibet' with the help of a Danish NGO. 'Stitches of Tibet' is still a successfully run enterprise in India that employs and educates Tibetan women.

47 See also: www.tibetanwomen.org (accessed October 2003).

48 See also: www.tchrd.org (accessed October 2003).

49 Gu-Chu-Sum derives its name from the months September, October, and March when in 1987, 1988 and 1989, three major demonstrations took place at the main bazaar in Lhasa, where predominantly monks and nuns participated (Gu-Chu-Sum. Brochure n.d.) See: www.guchusum.org (accessed October 2003).

50 See, for instance Mehrotra 1996; TPPRC 1996a, 1996b.

51 The 14th Dalai Lama had brought parts of the gold deposit to the small Himalayan kingdom on his journey to the celebrations of Buddha's birth. At that time, the young Tibetan leader had already anticipated that the continuing threat of the Chinese would lead to changes in the future. This farsightedness became fundamental for the survival in the first years of exile.

52 To make the amount of money comparable over the entire period of time, I exchanged the data of the CTA finance department from Indian Rs. to US$. For the exchange rates from Indian Rs. to US$ between the 1960s and 2002, see: http://fx.sander.ubc.ca/etc/USDpages.pdf (accessed November 2004).

53 The fiscal year of the CTA runs from 1 April to 31 March of the following calendar year.

54 In Tibetan tradition it is common that part of the belongings of a dead person are donated to a high religious dignitary. The same happens in cases of childbirth and illness. Because of that tradition, the 14th Dalai Lama inherits considerable numbers of material belongings from Tibetans in exile and in the homeland. Even relatives of a dead Tibetan in the PRC send, partly at risk of their own life, the belongings to Dharamsala (interview with Mr Ugyen Chaksam, Department of Finance, Dharamsala, April 2003; Sangay 1984).

55 The system of a voluntary contribution was not introduced right away in all host countries. For instance, in Germany the annual contribution to the CTA was only introduced in 1986.

56 In 2001, the newly elected cabinet decided to sell all CTA business units (in total 24) by the year 2003. This was decided because, first, business does not go in line with the CTA principle of non-violence (killing and selling meat dishes, competition with other business), second, due to the high risks regarding profits and, third, there were rumors about corruption (interview with Mr Dawa Dorje, Department of Finance, Dharamsala, April 2003; *Tibet Times* (2001); *Paljor Bulletin*, 2005d).

57 Before the different CTA departments took care of all projects that fell within their duties. Since 2001, the Tibetan cabinet controls, with the help of the SARD section, all project funds.

58 For an example of the Dorji School, see Frechette 2004: 159–63.

5 Theoretical characterization of CTA policies

1 In 1998, only 8,694 exile Tibetans lived in Dharamsala, out of which 2,297 were pupils in a residential TCV school and 647 belonged to the monastic population of the 13 monasteries and nunneries (CTA 2000f: 87).

2 During my fieldwork in spring 2003 in India, the cabinet introduced a new tax for private businessmen. The basis of valuation is an annual income or profit of more than 21,000 Indian Rs. In that case, 0.5 per cent of the income should be contributed to the CTA (interview with Mr Ugyen Chaksam, Department of Finance, Dharamsala, April 2003).

3 For instance, in Germany the Association of Tibetans in Germany (Verein der Tibeter in Deutschland) is responsible for collecting the annual contribution.

4 The amount in US$ is representative of the currency of the country the exile Tibetans live in. For instance, a Tibetan in Germany pays the same amount in Euros instead of US$.

5 A sample of different stamps is provided in Appendix 3.

6 This fact was confirmed by numerous interview partners in India and Nepal who want to remain anonymous.

7 Especially in the beginning, leading monks proved to be an indispensable resource in reorganizing the Tibetan government-in-exile (Tandzin 2004: 47).

8 For more information on the disagreements between the Dorji School and the CTA, see Frechette 2004: 159–63.

9 See also McGraham 2001.

10 See also Smith 1992: 436–56.

11 The preferred country is the USA with 273 students, followed by Japan (17 students), the UK (16), Taiwan (12), Italy and Thailand (6 each), Poland and France (4 each), Germany, Hungary and Norway (3 each) and Israel (2). See: www.tibet.net/education/english/scholarships/ (accessed February 2004).

12 See: www.tibet.com (accessed November 2003).

13 Such a sponsorship program has existed since 1975.

14 Until 1986, English was the medium for teaching. Slowly, the TCV schools started using Tibetan instead of English as the medium of teaching, which was followed by all other schools. By 1995, all schools in exile had been changed to Tibetan (interview with Mr Tashi Rika, Department of Education, Dharamsala, April 2002).

15 For monthly and annual rites of the lingshed ritual calendar, see Mills 2003: 348–52.

16 According to Klieger, the militant lyrics of the uprising song are patriotic but stand in contrast to the non-violent lyrics of the anthem (Klieger 1992: 62–3).

17 For all English language (translated March 10) speeches by the 14th Dalai Lama between 1961 and 1998, see Shiromany 1998: 349–462.

18 The Tibetan national flag, which was officially introduced by the 13th Dalai Lama in 1912, shows a design that is based on the Tibetan royal lineage. Designed and modified out of numerous Tibetan military flags, the present national flag '. . . in its symbolism, gives a clear indication of all aspects of Tibet such as the geographic features of the religious, snowy land of Tibet, the customs and traditions of Tibetan society, the political administration of the Tibetan government and so forth' (CTA 2000a: 14). For detailed information on the national flag, see Albers and Fuchs 1993: 16.

19 In the 2003 commemoration, the CTA Tibetan prime minister urged the exile Tibetans for a silent and peaceful demonstration because of promising contacts with the Chinese leadership regarding the status of Tibet.

20 For detailed information on numbers and motivations, see Baumann 1993, 1997; Prebish 1995.

21 Such involvement of Indian Buddhists would provide the exile Tibetans with an enormous resource for their political struggle both in terms of financial and moral support.

22 The topic of political awareness raising among Western Buddhists during philosophy classes is also mentioned in Powers 2004: x; Baumann 1993: 97.

23 One example describes the Tibetan Monastic Institute in Rikon-Zürich; see: www.tibet-institut.ch (accessed February 2004).

24 One interesting example described the special prayer for the victims of the terrorist attacks in the USA in 2001 that had been organized and led by the 14th Dalai Lama (*Tibetan Bulletin* 2001: 15).

25 An example represents the Danish couple 'Lama' Ole and Hannah Nydhal who founded by February 2004, 425 Tibetan Buddhist centers and retreat sites in 43 nations, mainly in Europe. For more information, see Nydhal 2003: 248, 1994: 433. See also: www.diamond-buddhism.org (accessed February 2004).

26 A detailed list on all film and video productions is available online at: www.tibet.com/films.html (accessed February 2004).

27 One example is described by McLagan 1997.

28 For instance, see *Tibetan Review* 1996b, 1998; Tsering, Topden 1997c.

29 Interview with Mr Ugyen Norbu, RFA, Dharamsala, April 2002. See also: www.rfa.org and www.voa.gov (accessed October 2003).

30 See: www.tibetinfonet.net (accessed July 2007).

31 The international researchers came from the WWF in the USA, from Hong Kong and from the New York Zoological Society.

32 Between 1992 and 1994, it was solely called the Environment Desk.

33 For examples, see CTA 1992a, 1998, 2000b, 2000c.

34 For more information on the wide discourse on democracy, see Arthur 1992; Dahl 1998.

35 Jamyang Norbu mentioned a Japanese man who criticized one of the 14th Dalai Lama's books. He received death threats and his university in Japan was urged by

exile Tibetans to expel him. Norbu himself was also attacked, both physically and with the rhetoric of the Chinese Cultural Revolution, by a Dharamsala mob led by the TWA (1990: 16).

6 Summary and conclusions

1   See: www.tibetinfonet.net (accessed August 2006).

Bibliography

Ackerly, John (1992) 'Tibet at the Earth Summit: A Review', *Tibetan Review* 27(9): 11–13.

Alam, Jayanti (2000) *Tibetan Society in Exile*, Delhi: Raj.

Albers, Hans and Fuchs, J. (eds) (1993) *Vom Dach der Welt: Tibeter in der Schweiz*, Zürich.

Aleman, Ulrich von; Kissler, Leo and Simonis, Georg (eds) (1995) *Grundwissen Politik No. 1*, Opladen: Leske + Budrich.

Almond, Gabriel A. and Powell, Bingham G. (1966) 'Comparative politics: A Developmental Approach', *The Little, Brown Series in Comparative Politics*. Boston: Little, Brown.

Anand, Dibyesh (2000) '(Re) Imagining nationalism: identity and representation in the Tibetan diaspora of South Asia', *Contemporary South Asia* 9(3): 271–88.

Andrugtsang, Gompo T. (1973) *Four Rivers, Six Ranges. A True Account of Khampa Resistance to Chinese in Tibet*, Dharamsala: Information and Publicity Office of His Holiness the Dalai Lama.

Appadurai, Arjun (1996) *Modernity at Large: Cultural Dimensions of Globalization*, Minneapolis: University of Minnesota Press.

Arakeri, A.V. (1998) *Tibetans in India: The Uprooted People and Their Cultural Transplantation*, New Delhi: Reliance.

Ardley, Jane C. (1998) 'The Art of Dying? Gandhian Principles and Tibetan Protest', *Tibetan Review*, 33 (12): 14–17.

Ardley, Jane C. (2001) 'One man's democracy? The modernisation of the Tibetan government in exile', unpublished draft paper.

Ardley, Jane C. (2002) *The Tibetan Independence Movement: Political, Religious, and Gandhian Perspectives*, London: RoutledgeCurzon.

Ardley, Jane C. (2003) 'Learning the art of democracy? Continuity and change in the Tibetan government-in-exile', *Contemporary South Asia* 12(3): 349–63.

Arpi, Claude (2004) *Born in Sin: The Panchsheel Agreement. The Sacrifice of Tibet*, New Delhi: Mittal.

Arthur, John (ed.) (1992) *Democracy: Theory and Practice*, Belmont: Wadsworth.

Asp, Søren (1995) 'Democratization, Electoral Systems and the Tibetan Exile-Community', Belmont: Aarhus.

Aukatsang, Kelsang D. (1991) 'The myth of Tibetan youth militancy', *Tibetan Review* 26(8):19–20.

Avedon, John F. (1997) *In Exile from the Land of Snows: The Definitive Account of the Dalai Lama and Tibet since the Chinese Conquest*, New Delhi: Viking (first published in 1984, New York: Alfred A. Knopf).

Aziz, Barbara N. (1978) *Tibetan Frontier Families. Reflections of Three Generations from D'ing-ri*, Durham, North Carolina: North Carolina Academic Press.

Backman, Michael (2004) *The Asian Insider. Unconventional Wisdom for Asian Business*, New York: Palgrave Macmillan.

Balekjian, W. H. (1970) *Die Effektivität und die Stellung nichtanerkannter Staaten im Völkerrecht*, The Hague: Martinus Nijhoff.

Banerjee, Brojendra N. (1982) 'India's assistance to the Tibetan Refugees since 1959', *Tibetan Bulletin* 13(2): 15–17.

Bangsbo, Ellen (2004) 'The Tibetan monastic tradition in exile: Secular and monastic schooling of Buddhist monks and nuns in Nepal', *The Tibet Journal* 29(2): 71–82.

Barbalet, J. M. (1988) *Citizenship: Rights, Struggle and Class Inequality*, Minneapolis: University of Minnesota Press.

Bataille, Par G. (1992) 'Lamaism, the Unarmed Society', *Lungta* 6: 33–40.

Baumann, Martin (1993) *Deutsche Buddhisten. Geschichte und Gemeinschaften*, Marburg: Diagonal.

Baumann, Martin (1996) 'Buddhism in the West. Phrases, orders and the creation of an integrative Buddhism', *Internationales Asienforum* 27(3–4): 345–62.

Baumann, Martin (1997) 'The Dharma has come West: A survey of recent studies and sources', *Journal of Buddhist Ethics* 4: 195–211. Online. Available: http:// jbe.gold.ac.uk/4/baum2.html (accessed February 2006).

Baxi, Upendra (2002) *The Future of Human Rights*, Oxford, New Delhi: Oxford University Press.

Bhattacharjea, Ajit (1994) *Tibetans in Exile. The Democratic Vision*, New Delhi: TPPRC.

Bhattacharjea, Ajit (1995) 'The exile identity and democratic vision', *Liberal* 37(2): 8–11.

Bell, Sir Charles (1928) *The People of Tibet*, Oxford: Clarendon.

Bell, Sir Charles (1931) *The Religion of Tibet*, Oxford: Clarendon.

Bell, Sir Charles (1987) *Portrait of a Dalai Lama. The Life and Times of the Great Thirteenth*, London: Wisdom (first published in 1946, London: Collins).

Berger, Peter L. (1980) *Der Zwang zur Häresie. Religion in der pluralistischen Gesell-schaft*, Frankfurt/Main: S. Fischer (first published in 1979: *The Heretical Impera-tive; Contemporary Possibilities of Religious Affirmation*, New York: Anchor).

Berliner Morgenpost (2000) 'Lebender Buddha' lief China davon', 8 January.

Bernstorff, Dagmar Gräfin and Welck, Hubertus von (eds) (2002) *Tibet im Exil*, Baden-Baden: Nomos.

Bernstorff, Dagmar Gräfin and Welck, Hubertus von (eds) (2004) *Exile as Challenge. The Tibetan Diaspora*, New Delhi: Orient Longman.

Bishop, Peter (1993) *Dreams of Power. Tibetan Buddhism and the Western Imagination*, London: Athlone.

Bob, Clifford (2001) 'Marketing rebellion: Insurgent groups, international media, and NGO support', *International Politics* 38(3): 311–33.

Bob, Clifford (2002) 'Merchants of morality', *Foreign Policy* 129: 36–45.

Bose, Tapan K. and Manchanda, Rita (eds) (1997) *States, Citizens and Outsiders. The Uprooted Peoples of South Asia*, Kathmandu: South Asia Forum for Human Rights.

Boyd, Helen R. (1999) 'The political modernization of a people in exile: The Tibetans in Northern India', PhD dissertation, St. John's University, New York.

Brah, Avtar (1996) *Cartographies of Diaspora. Contesting Identities*, London: Routledge.

Brauen, Martin (eds) (2005) *Die Dalai Lamas. Tibets Reinkarnationen des Bodhisattva Avalokiteśvara*, Völkerkundemuseum der Universität Zürich: Arnoldsche.

Bronger, Dirk (2001) *Lhasa. Vom Zentrum des Tibetischen Buddhismus zu einem Chinesischen Regionalzentrum. Historische, strukturelle und funktionale Entwicklung 633–1998 n. Chr.*, Bochumer Geographische Arbeiten no. 67. Bochum: Geographisches Institut der Ruhr-Universität.

Brosnan, Pierce (2000) 'It's all in the heart', *Tibetan Review* 35(10): 17–18.

Brown, Mick (2004) *The Dance of 17 Lives: The Incredible True Story of Tibet's 17th Karmapa*, New York: Bloomsbury.

Brück, Michael von (1999) *Religion und Politik im Tibetischen Buddhismus*, München: Kösel.

Burman, Bina R. (1979) *Religion and Politics in Tibet*, New Delhi: Vikas.

Butler, Alex (2003) *Feminism, Nationalism and Exiled Tibetan Women*, New Delhi: Kali for Women.

Butt, Masood (1994) 'Muslims of Tibet', *Tibetan Bulletin* 25(1): 8–9, 16.

Butt, Masood and Choephel, Ngawang (1988) 'The Tibetan Muslims', *Tibetan Bulletin* 19(5): 12–13.

Carr, Edward H. (1981) *The Romantic Exiles. A Nineteenth-Century Portrait Gallery*, Cambridge, MA: MIT Press.

Carrasco, Pedro (1959) *Land and Polity in Tibet*, Seattle: University of Washington Press.

Chang-Ching, Cao (1996) 'Independence: The Right of the Tibetan People', *Tibetan Bulletin* 27(5): 19–20.

Chashar, Tenzin Pembar (2006) 'Budget: The Tibetan Growth Story', *Tibetan World* 2(10): 16–17.

Chaturvedi, Gyaneshwar (2004) 'Indian visions', in D. Bernstorff and H. von Welck (eds) *Exile as Challenge. The Tibetan Diaspora*, New Delhi: Orient Longman, p. 72–86.

Central Tibetan Administration (CTA) (1963) *Constitution of Tibet: Promulgated by His Holiness the Dalai Lama March 10, 1963*, Dharamsala: Bureau of His Holiness the Dalai Lama.

Central Tibetan Administration (CTA) (1969) *Tibetans in Exile 1959–1969. A Report on the Years of Rehabilitation in India*, compl. Office of His Holiness the Dalai Lama. Dharamsala: Bureau of His Holiness the Dalai Lama.

Central Tibetan Administration (CTA) (1979) *Reports on the Tibetan Refugees' Problem in Bhutan*, New York: The Office of Tibet.

Central Tibetan Administration (CTA) (1981) *Tibetans in Exile 1959–1980. A Report on the Years of Rehabilitation in India*, Dharamsala: Information Office of His Holiness the Dalai Lama.

Central Tibetan Administration (CTA) (1985) *Tibetan Education. 25 Years in Exile*, Dharamsala: Council for Tibetan Education.

Central Tibetan Administration (CTA) (1991) *Charter of the Tibetans in-Exile*, Draft Unofficial Translation of the Charter, Dharamsala.

Central Tibetan Administration (CTA) (1992a) *Environment and Development Issues*, Dharamsala: Department of Information and International Relations.

Central Tibetan Administration (CTA) (1992b) *Tibetan Refugee Community. Integrated Development Plan 1992–1997*, Dharamsala: Planning Council.

Central Tibetan Administration (CTA) (1994a) *Tibetan Refugee Community. Integrated Development Plan-II. 1995–2000*, Dharamsala: Planning Council.

Central Tibetan Administration (CTA) (1994b) *Medical and Social Survey of Tibetans in Dharamsala*, Dharamsala: Delek Hospital.

Central Tibetan Administration (CTA) (1995) *His Holiness the Dalai Lama: Speeches, Statements, Articles, Interviews 1987 to June 1995*, Dharamsala: Department of Information and International Relations.

Central Tibetan Administration (CTA) (1997) *International Resolutions and Recognitions on Tibet (1959–1997)*, Dharamsala: Department of Information and International Relations.

Central Tibetan Administration (CTA) (1998) *Tibet's Environment: A Crucial Issue*, Dharamsala: Department of Information and International Relations, CTA, 1998.

Central Tibetan Administration (CTA) (1999) *Dharamsala. A Guide to Little Lhasa in India*, Dharamsala: Department of Information and International Relations.

Central Tibetan Administration (CTA) (2000a) *Tibetan National Flag and Anthem*, Dharamsala: Library of Tibetan Works and Archives.

Central Tibetan Administration (CTA) (2000b) *Tibet 2000. Environment and Development Issues*, Dharamsala: Department of Information and International Relations.

Central Tibetan Administration (CTA) (2000c) *Demilitarisation of the Tibetan Plateau. An Environmental Necessity*, Dharamsala: Department of Information and International Relations.

Central Tibetan Administration (CTA) (2000d) *His Holiness the 14th Dalai Lama of Tibet. Dedicated to His Holiness the 14th Dalai Lama on the Occasion of the 60th Anniversary of His Enthronment* [sic] *and the 50th Anniversary of His Assuming Political Power of Tibet*, Dharamsala: Department of Information and International Relations.

Central Tibetan Administration (CTA) (2000e) *The Social and Resource Development Fund (SARD). Annual Report 1998/1999*, Dharamsala: SARD.

Central Tibetan Administration (CTA) (2000f) *Tibetan Demographic Survey 1998*, Dharamsala: Planning Council.

Central Tibetan Administration (CTA) (2001) *Introduction to the Central Tibetan Administration*, Dharamsala: Department of Information and International Relations.

Central Tibetan Administration (CTA) (2003) *Tibetan Community in Exile. Integrated Development Plan-III. Investment & Implementation Guidelines 2003–2006*, Dharamsala: Planning Commission.

Central Tibetan Administration (CTA) (2004) *Tibetan Community in Exile. Demographic and Socio-Economic Issues 1998–2001*, Dharamsala: Planning Commission.

Central Tibetan Administration (CTA) (2005) *Introduction to the Middle-Way Policy and Its History*, Dharamsala: Department of Information and International Relations.

Central Tibetan Administration (CTA) (n.d. a) *Tibetan Library & Archives*, Dharamsala: Council of Cultural and Religious Affairs.

Central Tibetan Administration (CTA) (n.d. b) *Library of Tibetan Works & Archives. Brochure*, Dharamsala: Library of Tibetan Works and Archives.

Central Tibetan Administration (CTA) (n.d. c) *The Worship of Shugden. Documents*

Related to a Tibetan Controversy Resolution, Dharamsala: Department of Religion and Culture.

Central Tibetan Administration (CTA) (n.d. d) *State of Tibetan Refugees in Nepal. Brochure*, Kathmandu: Office of His Holiness the Dalai Lama in Nepal.

Central Tibetan Administration (CTA) (n.d. e) *A Practical Guide to Keep McLeod Alive*, Dharamsala: Tibetan Welfare Officer.

Central Tibetan Administration (CTA) (n.d. f) *Education in Exile: Building Our Future through Education. An Informative Guide*, Dharamshala: Department of Education.

Central Tibetan Administration (CTA) (n.d. g) *His Holiness the Dalai Lama's Charitable Trust 1964–1989. Silver Jubilee Year Souvenir*, New Delhi: His Holiness the Dalai Lama's Charitable Trust Silver Jubilee Sub-Committee.

Clarke, John (1997) *Tibet. Caught in Time*, Reading: Garnet.

Cohen, Robin (1997) *Global Diasporas. An Introduction*, London: UCL Press.

Coleman, William M. (1998) 'Writing Tibetan history: The discourse of feudalism and serfdom in Chinese and Western historiography', MA dissertation, University of Hawaii.

Correia, Alexandra (1998) 'Tibetan Education, the Way Ahead', *Tibetan Review* 33(9): 15–16.

Coser, Lewis A. (1984) *Refugee Scholars in America. Their Impact and Their Experiences*, New Haven: Yale University Press.

Dahl, Robert A. (1961) *Who Governs? Democracy and Power in an American City*, New Haven: Yale University Press.

Dahl, Robert A. (1998) *On Democracy*, New Haven: Yale University Press.

Dalai Lama (1991) ' "Democracy, Very Nice Word . . ." ', *Himal* 4(2): 11–12.

Dalai Lama (1992a) 'Guidelines for future Tibet's polity and the basic features of its constitution', *Tibetan Review* 27(10): 10–14.

Dalai Lama (1992b) 'Universal responsibility and our global environment', *Rangzen: Documentation*, Summer: 17–18.

Dalai Lama (1996) *Freedom in Exile. The Autobiography of the Dalai Lama of Tibet*, London: Abacus.

Dalai Lama (1999) *My Land and My People. The Memoirs of His Holiness, The Dalai Lama*, New Delhi: Srishti (first published in 1962: *My Land and My People: The Original Autobiography of His Holiness the Dalai Lama*. New York: Warner).

Dale, Ernest (1969) 'Tibetan immigration into the United States', *The Tibet Society Bulletin* 3: 42–5.

Dargyay, Eva (1978) 'Grundherr und Abhängiger Bauer in Tibet. Eine Analyse der Machtverhältnisse', in L. Ligeti (ed.) *Proceedings of the Csoma the Körös Memorial Symposium*, Budapest: Akademiai Kiado, p. 65–83.

Despares, Leo A. (ed.) (1975) *Ethnicity and Resource Competition in Plural Societies*, The Hague: Mouton.

DeVoe, Dorsh Marie (1981) 'The refugee problem and Tibetan refugees', *The Tibet Journal* 6(3): 22–42.

DeVoe, Dorsh Marie (1983) 'Survival of a refugee culture: The long term gift exchange between Tibetan refugees and Western donors', PhD dissertation, Berkeley University of California.

DeVoe, Dorsh Marie (1987) 'Keeping refugee status: A Tibetan perspective', in Scott M. Morgan and Elizabeth Colson (eds) *People in Upheaval*, New York: Center for Migration Studies, 54–64.

Dharlo, Rinchen (1994) 'A brief of Tibetans in North America', *Tibetan Review* 29(10): 12–17.

Dhondup, K. (1977) 'Tibet's influence in Ladakh and Bhutan', *The Tibet Journal* 2(2): 69–73.

Dhondup, K. (1993) 'The Regents Reting and Tagdra', *Lungta* 7: 11–20.

Dixit, Kanak M. (1991) 'Discovering Dharamsala', *Himal* 4(2): 5–10.

Dodin, T. and Räther, H; Kunst- und Ausstellungshalle der Bundesrepublik Deutschland (eds) (1997) *Mythos Tibet*: Wahrnehmungen, Projektionen, Phantasien. Bonn: Dumont.

Dolkar, Yangchen (1995) 'The role of youth in the struggle for Tibetan independence', *Liberal* 37(2): 17–18.

Dorjee, Nawang (1992) 'An assessment of the exile situation', *Tibetan Review* 27(2): 11–14.

Dorjee, Nawang (1993) 'Problems and possibilities', *Tibetan Review* 28(6): 15–18.

Dorjee, Nawang (1996) 'Tibetan education in exile: have we reached a plateau?', *Tibetan Bulletin* 27(4): 17–19.

Dorjee, Wangchuk (2000) 'For a full, secular democracy', *Tibetan Review* 35(12): 23–4.

Dörner, Andreas (1995) *Politischer Mythos und symbolische Politik. Sinnstiftung durch symbolische Formen am Beispiel des Hermannsmythos*, Essen: Westdeutscher Verlag.

Douglas, Ed (1997) 'Tibet's tryst with Hollywood', *Tibetan Bulletin* 1(5): 12–13.

Downs, Anthony (1957) *An Economic Theory of Democracy*, New York: Harper & Row.

Dryfus, Georges (1998) 'The Shuk-den Affair: History and Nature of a Quarrel', *Journal of the International Association of Buddhist Studies* 21(2): 227–70.

Dryfus, Georges (1999) *The Shuk-den Affair. Origins of a Controversy*, Dharamsala: Narthang.

Easton, David (1965) *A Systems Analysis of Political Life*, New York: Wiley & Sons.

Edelman, Murray (1964) *The Symbolic Uses of Politics*, University of Illinois Press.

Edin, Maria (1992) *Transition to Democracy in Exile. A Study of the Tibetan Government's Strategy for Self-Determination*, Minor Field Study No. 16, Uppsala: University of Uppsala.

Ekvall, Robert B. (1960) 'The Tibetan Self-Image', *Pacific Affairs* 33(4): 375–82.

Ekvall, Robert B. (1967) 'Tibetans in Switzerland', *The Tibet Society Newsletter* 1(2): 113–17.

Epstein, Israel (1983) *Tibet Transformed*, Beijing: New World Press.

Fiedler, Wilfried (1988) 'Das Staatsoberhaupt im Exil', in H.-J. Schlochauer, I. von Münch, O. Kimminich and W. Rudolf (eds) *Archiv des Völkerrechts* 26(2), Tübingen: Mohr, 181–202.

Fjeld, Heidi (2005) *Commoners and Nobles. Hereditary Divisions in Tibet*, Copenhagen: NIAS.

Flynn, Sean (1998) 'The ethics of journalism in the Tibetan exile community', *Tibetan Review* 33(7): 15–16.

Forbes, Ann A. (1989) *Settlements of Hope: An Account of Tibetan Refugees in Nepal*, Cambridge, MA: Cultural Survival.

Fossell, Karen and MacDougall, Colina (1989) 'Dalai Lama chosen for Nobel Peace Prize', *Financial Times* 10 June, 20.

Frechette, Ann (2004) *Tibetans in Nepal: The Dynamics of International Assistance among a Community in Exile*, Studies in Forced Migration vol. 11, New York: Berghahn Books.

French, Patrick (2003) *Tibet, Tibet. A Personal History of a Lost Land*, New Delhi: Harper Collins.

Fürer-Haimendorf, Christoph von (1989) *The Renaissance of Tibetan Civilization*, Oxford: Oxford University Press.

Gardner, Mary J. (1999) 'Exile, transnational connections, and the construction of identity: Tibetan immigrants in Montreal', MA dissertation, Concordia University Montreal, Quebec.

Garratt, Kevin (1997) 'Tibetan Refugees, Asylum Seekers, Returnees and the Refugees Convention—Predicaments, Problems and Prospects', *The Tibet Journal* 22(3): 18–56.

Garratt, Kevin (2003) 'Dalai Lama speeches: a source for modern Tibetan History', draft paper presented at the Tenth Seminar of the IATS, Oxford.

Gere, Richard (1996) 'Create the Causes of Happiness', *Tibetan Review* 31(5): 19–20.

Ghosh, Partha S. (1997) 'Destination India. A political study of international migrations', in Tapan K. Bose and Rita Manchanda (eds) *States, Citizens and Outsiders. The Uprooted Peoples of South Asia*, Kathmandu: SAFHR, 153–89.

Goldner, Colin (1999) *Dalai Lama—Fall eines Gottkönigs*, Aschaffenburg: Alibri.

Goldstein, Melvyn C. (1968) 'An anthropological study of the Tibetan political system', PhD dissertation, University of Washington.

Goldstein, Melvyn C. (1971) 'The balance between centralization and decentralization in the traditional Tibetan political system: an essay on the nature of Tibetan political macro-structure', *Central Asiatic Journal* 15: 170–82.

Goldstein, Melvyn C. (1975a) 'Ethnogenesis and resource competition among Tibetan refugees in South India', in Leo A. Despares (ed.) *Ethnicity and Resource Competition in Plural Societies*, The Hague: Mouton, 159–86.

Goldstein, Melvyn C. (1975b) 'Tibetan refugees in South India: A new face to the Indo–Tibetan interface', *The Tibet Society Bulletin* 9: 12–29.

Goldstein, Melvyn C. (1986) 'Re-examining choice, dependency and the command in the Tibetan social system: Tax appendages and other landless serfs', *The Tibet Journal* 11(4): 79–112.

Goldstein, Melvyn C. (1993) *A History of Modern Tibet 1913–1951. The Demise of the Lamaist State*, New Delhi: Munshiram Manoharlal.

Goldstein, Melvyn C. (1997) *The Snow Lion and the Dragon. China, Tibet and the Dalai Lama*, Berkeley: University of California Press.

Goldstein, Melvyn C. (1998) 'The revival of monastic life in Drepung Monastery', in Melvyn C. Goldstein and Matthew T. Kapstein (eds) *Buddhism in Contemporary Tibet. Religious Revival and Cultural Identity*, Berkeley: University of California Press, 15–52.

Goldstein, Melvyn C. (with Shelling, T. N. and Surkhang, J. T.) (2001) *The New Tibetan–English Dictionary of Modern Tibetan*, Berkeley: University of California Press.

Goldstein-Kyaga, Katrin (1993) *The Tibetans: School for Survival or Submission: An Investigation of Ethnicity and Education*, Stockholm: HLS.

Goldstein-Kyaga, Katrin (2003) 'The Tibetan culture of non-violence—its transmission and the role of education', in Birgitta Qvarsell and Christoph Wulf (eds) *Culture and Education*, European Studies in Education, 16. München, Berlin: Waxmann, 89–102.

Gombo, Ugen (1985) 'Tibetan refugees in the Kathmandu Valley. A study in socio-cultural change and continuity and the adaptation of a population in exile', PhD dissertation, State University of New York at Stony Brook.

Gray, Henry (ed.) (1997) *Islam in Tibet and the Illustrated Narrative: Tibetan Caravans*, Louisville, KY: Fons Vitae.

Griebenov, M. G. (1936) 'Islam in Tibet', *The Moslem World* 26(2): 127–9.

Grodzins, Morton (1956) *The Loyal and the Disloyal. Social Boundaries of Patriotism and Treason*, Chicago: University of Chicago Press.

Grunfeld, A. Tom (1982) 'Some thoughts on the current state of Sino–Tibetan historiography', *Tibetan Review* 17(2): 18–22.

Grunfeld, A. Tom (1987) *The Making of Modern Tibet*, Bombay: Oxford University Press.

Grunfeld, A. Tom (1999) 'The Question of Tibet', *Current History* 98(629): 291–5.

Gruschke, Andreas (1998) 'The Dorje Shugden issue: A changing society's clash with stereotyped perceptions', *Tibetan Review* 33(10): 15–19.

Gu-Chu-Sum (n.d.) *Gu-Chu-Sum. Brochure*, Dharamsala.

Gupta, Monu Rani (2005) *Social Mobility and Change among Tibetan Refugees*, New Delhi: Raj.

Gyaltag, Gyaltsen (2002) 'Exiltibeter in Europa und Nordamerika', in Gräfin Dagmar Bernstorff and Hubertus von Welck (eds) *Tibet im Exil*, Baden-Baden: Nomos, 193–213.

Gyatso, Sherab (2004) 'Of monks and monasteries', in Dagmar Bernstorff and Hubertus von Welck (eds) *Exile as Challenge. The Tibetan Diaspora*, New Delhi: Orient Longman, 213–43.

Hammer, Christiane (1991) 'Gott–König ohne Land', *Neue Zürcher Zeitung*, 7 April, 11.

Heberer, Thomas (1995) 'Die Tibet-Frage als problem der internationalen politik', *Aussenpolitik* 46(3): 299–309.

Hilton, Isabel (2003) *Die Suche nach dem Panchen Lama. Auf den Spuren eines verschwundenen Kindes*, München: Piper.

Hocevar, John (1996) 'Students for free Tibet chapters mushroom in America', *Tibetan Bulletin* 27(3): 25.

Hodges, Tony (2001) *Angola: From Afro-Stalinism to Petro-Diamond Capitalism*, Bloomington: Indiana University Press.

Holborn, Louise W. (1975) 'Refugees in the Asian subcontinent: Tibetan refugees in India', in UNHCR *Refugees: A Problem of Our Time. The Work of The United Nations High Commissioner for Refugees 1951–1972* vol. 1. Metuchen, NJ: Scarecrow, 715–93.

Hoppe, Thomas (1995) 'Theatrum mundi, Widersprüche rund um die Wahl der 11. Reinkarnation des Panchen Lama. Die Situation im November–Dezember 1995', *China aktuell* 24(12): 1115–26.

Hoppe, Thomas (1997) *Tibet heute. Aspekte einer komplexen Situation*, Mitteilungen des Instituts für Asienkunde Hamburg 281.

Hortsang, Jigme (2003) 'Growth of democracy in the Tibetan exile community', draft paper presented at the Tenth Seminar of the IATS, Oxford.

Huber, Toni (1997) 'Green Tibetans: a brief social history', in Frank J. Korom (ed.) *Tibetan Culture in the Diaspora*, papers presented at a panel of the Seventh Seminar of the IATS in Graz. Wien: Verlag der Österreichischen Akademie der Wissenschaften, 103–19.

Huber, Toni (1999) Book review of *The Snow Lion and the Dragon. China, Tibet and the Dalai Lama* by Melvyn C. Goldstein, Berkeley: University of California Press, 1997, in: *Journal of Buddhist Ethics* 6: 110–13. Online. Available: http://jbe. gold.ac.uk/6/huber991.html (accessed February 2006)

Huitzi (1993) 'The institution of the Dalai Lamas in question', *Lungta* 7: 24–31.

Huntington, Samuel P. (1968) *Political Order in Changing Societies*, New Haven: Yale University Press.

Huntington, Samuel P. (1984) 'Will more countries become Democratic?' *Political Science Quarterly* 99(2): 193–218.

Huntington, Samuel P. (1996) *The Clash of Civilizations and the Remarking of the World Order*, New York: Simon & Schuster.

Hvattum, Mari (1991) *Tibetans in Exile. Case Study of Settlements in North India*, Trondheim: Norwegian Institute of Technology.

Ilchman, Warren F. and Uphoff, Norman T. (1997) *The Political Economy of Change*, New Brunswick, London: Transaction.

International Campaign for Tibet (2002) *Gefährliche Flucht. Bedingungen tibetischer Flüchtlinge*, Berlin.

International Commission of Jurists (1959) *The Question of Tibet and the Rule of Law*, Geneva: ICJ.

International Commission of Jurists (1960) *Tibet and the Chinese People's Republic. A Report to the International Commission of Jurists by its Legal Inquiry Committee on Tibet*, Geneva: ICJ

International Commission of Jurists (1997) *Tibet—Human Rights and the Rule of Law. Executive Summary*, Geneva: ICJ

International Studies (1969) *Special Issue on Tibet* 10(4).

Iwańska, Alicja (1981) *Exiled Governments: Spanish and Polish*, Cambridge, MA: Schenkman.

Jha, Hari Bansh (1992) *Tibetans in Nepal*, Delhi: Book Faith India.

John, Gudrun (1999) *Tibetische Erziehung im Wandel. Eine Studie zur Erforschung des familiären und schulischen Erziehungswesens von den Anfängen in Tibet bis zur Gegenwart im Exil*, PhD dissertation, University of Tübingen: published privately.

Jongh, Richard de (1995) 'Democracy, the only road to Democracy. A survey of the Tibetan struggle for Democracy in-exile', MA dissertation, University of Amsterdam.

Junius, Andreas (1989) *Der United Nations Council for Namibia*, Europäische Hoch-schulschriften Reihe 2, 817. Franfurt/M: Peter Lang.

Kamenetz, Rodger (1994) *The Jew in the Lotus. A Poet's Rediscovery of Jewish Identity in Buddhist India*, San Francisco: Harper.

Kamenetz, Rodger (2000) 'Partners in exile. Tibetans and Jews compare survival strategies in diaspora', *Tibetan Bulletin* 4(1): 31–2.

Karmay, Samten (1993) 'The exiled government and the Bonpo community in India', *Lungta* 7: 21–3.

Karthak, Peter J. (1991) 'A personal look at the Tibetan exiles. Part I: Nostalgia', *Tibetan Review* 26(8): 15–20.

Katz, Daniel and Kahn, Robert L. (1978) *The Social Psychology of Organizations*, New York: Wiley & Sons.

Kelly, Petra, Bastian, Gert and Aiello, Pat (eds) (1990) *The Anguish of Tibet*, Berkeley: Parallax.

Kimminich, Otto and Hobbe, Stephan (2000) *Einführung in das Völkerrecht*, Tübingen, Basel: Francke (first published in 1975).

Klieger, P. Christiaan (1989) 'Accomplishing Tibetan identity: the constitution of a national consciousness', PhD dissertation, University of Hawaii.

Klieger, P. Christiaan (1992) *Tibetan Nationalism. The Role of Patronage in the Accomplishment of a National Identity*, Meerut: Archana.

Klieger, P. Christiaan (ed.) (2002) *Tibet, Self, and the Tibetan Diaspora. Voices of Difference*, PIATS 2000 Tibetan Studies: Proceedings of the Ninth Seminar of the IATS in Leiden. Leiden: Brill.

Kloos, Stephan (2006) 'The ethico-politics of the Dharamsala Men-Tse-Khang (India)', draft paper presented at the Eleventh Seminar of the IATS in Königswinter, Germany.

Knaus, John K. (1999) *Orphans of the Cold War. America and the Tibetan Struggle for Survival*, New York: Public Affairs.

Kolås, Åshild N. (1994) 'The struggle for an independent Tibet', PhD dissertation, University of Oslo.

Kolås, Åshild N. (1996) 'Tibetan nationalism: the politics of religion', *Journal of Peace Research* 33(1): 51–66.

Kolmas, Josef (1993) 'Was Tibet of 1913–1914 Fully *sui juris* to enter into treaty relations with another state?' *Tibetan Review* 28(2): 12–16.

Korom, Frank J. (ed.) (1997) *Constructing Tibetan Culture. Contemporary Perspectives*, Quebec: World Heritage Press.

Korom, Frank J. (ed.) (1997) *Tibetan Culture in the Diaspora*, papers presented at a panel of the Seventh Seminar of the IATS in Graz 1995. Wien: Verlag der Österreichischen Akademie der Wissenschaften.

Koslowski, Kristin (n.d.) 'Die tibetische 'Exilregierung: Spannungsverhältnis zwischen normativen Anspruch und Funktionsfähigkeit', MA dissertation, university unknown.

Krull, Germaine (1968) *Tibetans in India*, Bombay: Allied.

Larsen, Knud and Sinding-Larsen, Amund (2001) *The Lhasa Atlas. Traditional Tibetan Architecture and Townscape*, Boston: Shambhala.

Lazar, Edward (ed.) (1998) *Tibet. The Issue Is Independence. Tibetans-in-Exile Address the Key Tibetan Issue the World Avoids*, Delhi: Full Circle.

Ligeti, Louis (ed.) (1978) *Proceedings of the Csoma the Körös Memorial Symposium*. Budapest: Akademiai Kiado.

Lindegger, Peter (2000) *40 Jahre Tibeter in der Schweiz. Versuch einer Bestandsaufnahme für die Jahre zwischen 1960 und 2000*, Kleine Arbeiten aus dem Tibet-Institut Rikon 29. Zürich: Opuscula Tibetana.

Lopez, Donald S. (1994) 'New Age orientalism: The case of Tibet', *Tricycle* 3(3): 37–43.

Lopez, Donald S. (1998) *Prisoners of Shangri-La: Tibetan Buddhism and the West*, Chicago: University of Chicago Press.

Lourie, Samuel A. and Meyer, Max (1943) 'Governments-in-exile and the effect of their expropriatory decrees', *The University of Chicago Law Review* 11: 26–48.

Ludwar, Gudrun (1975) *Die Sozialisation Tibetischer Kinder im Soziokulturellen Wandel, dargestellt am Beispiel der Exiltibetersiedlung Dhor Patan (West Nepal)*, Beiträge zur Südasien-Forschung vol. 13. Südasien-Institut Universität Heidelberg. Wiesbaden: Franz Steiner.

Magnusson, Jan (2002) 'A myth of Tibet: Reverse orientalism and soft power', in

P. Christiaan Klieger (ed.) *PIATS 2000: Tibet, Self, and the Tibetan Diaspora. Voices of Difference*, Tibetan Studies: Proceedings of the Ninth Seminar of the IATS in Leiden. Leiden: Brill, 195–212.

Mattern, Karl-Heinz (1953) *Die Exilregierung. Eine historische Betrachtung der internationalen Praxis seit dem Beginn des Ersten Weltkrieges und deren völkerrechtliche Wertung*, Tübingen: Mohr.

McGraham, Carole (2001) 'Arrested histories: between empire and exile in 20th century Tibet', PhD dissertation, University of Michigan.

McGuckin, Eric A. (1997) 'Postcards from Shangri-La: tourism, Tibetan refugees, and the politics of cultural production', PhD dissertation, University of New York.

McKay, Alex (1997) *Tibet and the British Raj. The Frontier Cadre 1904–1947*, London: Curzon.

McLagan, Margret J. (1996) 'Mobilizing for Tibet: Transnational politics and diaspora culture in the post-cold war era', PhD dissertation, University of New York.

McLagan, Margret J. (1997) 'Mystical visions in manhattan: deploying culture in the year of Tibet', in Frank J. Korom (ed.) *Tibetan Culture in the Diaspora*, papers presented at a panel of the Seventh Seminar of the IATS in Graz 1995. Wien: Verlag der Österreichischen Akademie der Wissenschaften.

Mehra, Parshotam (2004) *From Conflict to Conciliation: Tibetan Policy Revisited. A Brief Historical Conspectus of the Dalai Lama–Panchen Lama Standoff, ca. 1904–1989*, Wiesbaden: Harrassowitz.

Mehrotra, Lakhan L. (1996) *India's Tibet Policy*, New Delhi: TPPRC.

Melander, Göran (1981) 'Refugee and international cooperation', *International Migration Review* 15(1–2): 35–41.

Messerschmidt, Donald A. (1976) 'Innovation in adaptation: Tibetan immigrants in the United States', *The Tibet Society Bulletin* 10: 48–70.

Methfessel, Thomas (1995) *35 Jahre Tibeter im Exil. Eine Analyse der sozio-ökonomischen Anpassungsprozesse in Indien und Nepal*, Marburg/Lahn: published privately.

Meyer, Max and Torczyner, Harry (1943) 'Corporations in exile', *Columbia Law Review* 43: 364–75.

Michael, Franz (1982) *Rule by Incarnation. Tibetan Buddhism and Its Role in Society and State*, Boulder: Westview.

Michael, Franz (1986) 'Traditional Tibetan polity and its potential for modernization', *The Tibet Journal* 11(4): 70–8.

Mills, Martin A. (2003) *Identity, Ritual and State in Tibetan Buddhism. The Foundations of Authority in Gelukpa Monasticism*, London: RoutledgeCurzon.

Mirsky, Jonathan (1987) 'Sadness and hope of the God King', *The Observer* 12 October.

Misra, R. C. (1982) 'Tibetans in Bhutan: problem of repatriation', *China Report* 18(5): 25–32.

Monnier, Michel A. (1993) 'Talks with Lhasang Tsering', *Lungta* 7: 32–7.

Morgan, Scott M. and Colson, Elizabeth (eds) (1987) *People in Upheaval*, New York: Centre for Migration Studies.

Morris, Katrina K and Scoble, Andrew M. (1990) 'Tibet and the United Nations', in Petra Kelly, Gert Bastian and Pat Aiello (eds) *The Anguish of Tibet*, Berkeley: Parallax. 174–95.

Mountcastle, Amy (1997) 'Tibetans in exile: the construction of global identities', PhD dissertation, New Brunswick University, NJ.

Moynihan, Maura (2004) 'Tibetan refugees in Nepal', in Dagmar Bernstorff and Hubertus von Welck (eds) *Exile as challenge. The Tibetan diaspora*, New Delhi: Orient Longman, 312–21.

National Democratic Party of Tibet (NDPT) (2000) *National Democratic Party of Tibet. Brochure*. Dharamsala.

Nauer, Josef (1980) *Mazzini und Garibaldi: Revolutionäre Aktivität und Anhängerschaft (1848–1953)*, PhD dissertation, University Zürich: published privately.

Nebesky-Wojkowitz, Réne de (1995) *Oracles and Demons of Tibet. The Cult and Iconography of the Tibetan Protective Deities*, Taipei: SMC.

New York Times, 9 July 1997.

News Letter (1965) 'Rehabilitation of Tibetan Refugees', 5(2): 4.

News Letter (1967) 'Oversea-Tibetans', 3(2): 7–9.

Newsweek (2000) 'Turmoil over Tibet', 3 June.

Norbu, Dawa (1974) *Red Star Over Tibet*, London: Collins.

Norbu, Dawa (1978) 'Tibetan refugees and Tibetan culture', *Tibetan Review* 13(4): 15–16.

Norbu, Dawa (1982) 'The 1959 Tibetan rebellion: an interpretation', *Tibetan Review* 17(2–3): 7–17.

Norbu, Dawa (1991a) 'The limits of Tibetan Democracy. Viewpoint', *Himal* 4(2): 13.

Norbu, Dawa (1991b) 'Karmic ethos in Lamaist society', in Tanka B. Subba and Karubaki Datta (eds) *Religion and Society in the Himalayas*, New Delhi: Gian, 9–31.

Norbu, Dawa (1996) 'Tibet in Sino–Indian relations and politics of "card" playing', *Tibetan Bulletin* 27(1): 27.

Norbu, Dawa (2001a) 'Refugees from Tibet: structural causes of successful settlements', in Sanjay K. Roy (ed.) *Refugees and Human Rights: Social and Political Dynamics of Refugee Problem in Eastern and North-Eastern India*, Jaipur, New Delhi: Rawat, 199–235.

Norbu, Dawa (2001b) *China's Tibet Policy*, Richmond: Curzon.

Norbu, Jamyang (1990) 'Opening of the political eye. Tibet's long search for democracy', *Tibetan Review* 25(11): 13–17.

Norbu, Jamyang (1993) 'Broken images. Cultural questions facing Tibetans today, Part I', *Tibetan Review* 28(12): 15–19.

Norbu, Jamyang (1994) 'Broken images. Cultural questions facing Tibetans today, Part II', *Tibetan Review* 29(1): 11–12.

Norbu, Jamyang (1997) 'Non-violence or non-action. Some Gandhian truth about the Tibetan peace movement', *Tibetan Review* 32(9): 18–21.

Norbu, Jamyang (1998) 'Dances with yaks: Tibet in film, fiction and fantasy of the West', *Tibetan Review* 33(1): 18–23.

Norbu, Jamyang (1999) *Rangzen Charter. The Case for Tibetan Independence*, revised edn. Dharamsala: TYC.

Norbu, Jamyang (2004) *Shadow Tibet. Selected Writings 1989 to 2004*, New Delhi: Bluejay.

Nowak, Margaret (1984) *Tibetan Refugees. Youth and the New Generation of Meaning*, New Brunswick: Rutgers University Press.

Nuscheler, Franz (1994) *Internationale Migration. Ein Hauptproblem für Global Governance*, INEF Report No. 9, Duisburg: Gerhard Mercator Universität Gesamthochschule.

Nuscheler, Franz (1995) 'Internationale Migration. Flucht und Asyl', in Ulrich von

Aleman, Leo Kissler and Georg Simonis (eds) *Grundwissen Politik No. 14*, Opladen: Leske + Budrich.

Nydhal, Lama Ole (1994) *Über alle Grenzen*, Sulzberg: Joy.

Nydhal, Lama Ole (2003) *Die Buddhas vom Dach der Welt*, Bielefeld: Aurum.

Olschak, B. C. (1976) 'Tibetans in migration', *International Migration* 5(3–4): 187–94.

Oppenheimer, Franz E. (1942) 'Governments and authorities in exile', *American Journal of International Law* 36: 568–95.

Palakshappa, T. C. (1978) *Tibetans in India. A Case Study of Mundgod Tibetans*, New Delhi: Sterling.

Paljor Bulletin (2005a) 'CTA's Budget at a Glance', 1: 8.

Paljor Bulletin (2005b) 'Future Economic Policy Will Depend on the Degree of Autonomy', 1: 13–15.

Paljor Bulletin (2005c) 'Economic Activities of Tibetans in India: Issues and Challenges', 1: 20–1.

Paljor Bulletin (2005d) 'Privatisation was Necessary for CTA's Financial Stability', 1: 22–3.

Paljor Bulletin (2005e) 'Why Entrepreneurial Culture is Grim amongst Exile Tibetans?', 2: 34–5.

Pardesi, Ghanshyam (1975) 'Some observations on the draft constitution of Tibet', *The Tibet Journal* 1(1): 63–71.

Pathak, Nupur (2004a) 'Ethnic and cultural components in responses to cultural bereavement of immigrant Tibetans in India', *The Tibet Journal* 28(3): 53–60.

Pathak, Nupur (2004b) 'Revitalisation movement gripping the exile Tibetan diaspora: a model of non-violent struggle for peace', *The Tibet Journal* 29(1): 85–90.

Peissel, Michel (1972) *Cavaliers of Kham: The Secret War in Tibet*, London: Heinemann.

Petech, Luciano (1973) *Aristocracy and Government in Tibet, 1728–1959*, Roma: Instituto Italiano per il Medio ed Estremo Oriente.

Peterson, William (1958) 'A general typology of migration', *American Sociological Review* 23(3): 256–66.

Pichler, Michaela (2000) 'Change and continuity within the Tibetan community in exile in India: social reform and the nuns of Gaden Choeling', MA dissertation, California Institute of Integral Studies.

Pike, Robert A. D. (2001) 'Campaigning for a free Tibet: transnational activism and the "universal rights strategy" ', BA dissertation, Harvard College.

Powers, John (2004) *History as Propaganda: Tibetan Exiles Versus the People's Republic of China*, Oxford: Oxford University Press.

Prebish, Charles S. (1995) 'Ethics and integration in American Buddhism', *Journal of Buddhist Ethics* 2: 125–39. Online. Available: http://jbe.gold.ac.uk/2/prebish.txt (accessed February 2006).

Qvarsell, Birgitta and Wulf, Christoph (eds) *Culture and Education*, European Studies in Education No. 16, München: Waxmann.

Rahul, Ram (1969) *The Government and Politics of Tibet*, New Delhi: Vikas.

Rahul, Ram (1992) *Modern Tibet*, New Delhi: Munshiram Manoharlal.

Rahul, Ram (1995) *The Dalai Lama. The Institution*, New Delhi: Vikas.

Ran, Cheng (1991) *Herkunft und Wesen der sogenannten—'Unabhängigkeit Tibets'*, Beijing: Verlag Neuer Stern.

Redwood French, Rebecca (2002) *The Golden Yoke. The Legal Cosmology of Buddhist Tibet*, London: Cornell University Press.

Reynolds, Alison (2004) 'Support for Tibet worldwide', in Dagmar Bernstorff and Hubertus von Welck (eds) *Exile as Challenge. The Tibetan Diaspora*, New Delhi: Orient Longman, 447–53.

Rhodes, Nicholas and Deki (2006) *A Man of the Frontier: S.W. Laden La (1876–1936). His Life and Times in Darjeeling and Tibet*, Kolkata: Mira Bose.

Richardson, Hugh E. (1976) 'Political role of the four sects in Tibetan history', *Tibetan Review* 11(9): 18–23.

Richardson, Hugh E. (1984) *Tibet and Its History*, Boulder: Shambhala (first published in 1962, London: Oxford University Press).

Richardson, Hugh E. (with Skorupski, Tadeusz) (1986) *Adventures of a Tibetan Fighting Monk*, Bangkok: Tamarind Press.

Roemer, Stephanie (2001) *Tibetische Flüchtlingsökonomie in Indien. Eine Fallstudie der gewerblichen Siedlung Bir*. Diskussionspapiere der Freien Universität Berlin, 81. Berlin: Das Arabische Buch.

Roemer, Stephanie (2004) *Tibetan democracy in exile: The CTA in conflict between securing loyalty and international support*, paper presented at the International Symposium on Exile Tibet Issues: Freedom, Human Rights and Democratic Transition of Exile Tibetan, 28 Nov, Taipei: MTAC, 68–88.

Roy, Sanjay K. (ed.) (2001a) *Refugees and Human Rights: Social and Political Dynamics of Refugee Problem in Eastern and North-Eastern India*, Jaipur: Rawat.

Roy, Sanjay K. (2001b) 'Refugees and human rights: the case of refugees in eastern and north-eastern states of India', in Sanjay K. Roy (ed.) *Refugees and Human Rights: Social and Political Dynamics of Refugee Problem in Eastern and North-Eastern India*, Jaipur, New Delhi: Rawat, 17–60.

Rubin, Barnett R. (1991) 'Afghanistan: political exiles in search of a state', in Yossi Shain (ed.) *Governments-in-Exile in Contemporary World Politics*, New York: Routledge, 69–91.

Said, Edward W. (1978) *Orientalism*, New York: Pantheon.

Said, Edward W. (1980) *The Question of Palestine*, London, Henley: Routledge & Kegan Paul.

Said, Edward W. (1984) 'The mind of winter: reflections on life in exile', *Harper's* 9: 49–56.

Saklani, G. (1984) *The Uprooted Tibetans in India: A Sociological Study of Continuity and Change*, New Delhi.

Samdhong Rinpoche (2002) *Concluding Speech at the First Asian Tibet Support Group Conference*, Delhi: unpublished.

Samphel, Thubten (1996) 'Bringing down the great wall. Contacts between Tibetan exiles and pro-democracy Chinese', *Tibetan Bulletin* 27(5): 15–16.

Samphel, Thubten (1998) 'Dharamsala's Tibetan bureaucracy: the early years', *Tibetan Bulletin* 2(1): 12–15.

Samuel, Geoffrey (1993) *Civilized Shamans. Buddhism in Tibetan Societies*, Washington: Smithsonian.

Sangay, Lobsang (1996) 'How U.S. students are building a grassroots campaign for Tibet', *Tibetan Bulletin* 27(2): 24–5.

Sangay, Lobsang (2003) 'Tibet: exiles' journey', *Journal of Democracy* 14(3): 119–30.

Sangay, Thupten (1984) 'Tibetans ritual for the dead by Thupten Sangay', trans. Gavin Kilty, *Tibetan Medicine* 7: 30–40.

Sautman, Barry (1999) 'The Tibet issue in post-summit Sino–American relations', *Pacific Affairs* 72(1): 7–21.

Sautman, Barry (2000) 'Association, Federation and "Genuine" Autonomy, The Dalai Lama's Proposals and Tibet Independence', *China Information* 14(2): 31–91.

Sautman, Barry (2006) (with Teufel Dreyer, June) (eds) *Contemporary Tibet: Politics, Development, and Society in a Disputed Region*, New York: M.E. Sharpe.

Scheidegger-Bächler, Theres (2001) 'Strukturen und Strategien sozialer Sicherheit der tibetischen Exilgemeinschaft in Indien', PhD dissertation, Zürich.

Schell, Orville (2000) *Virtual Tibet: Searching for Shangri-La from the Himalayas to Hollywood*, New York: Metropolitan.

Schlochauer, H.-J., von Münch, I., Kimminich, O. and Rudolf, W. (eds) (1988) *Archiv des Völkerrecht* 26(2), Tübingen: Mohr.

Schmitz, Gerald (1998) *Tibet und das Selbstbestimmungsrecht der Völker*, Berlin, New York: De Gruyter.

Schwartz, Ronald D. (1996) *Circle of protest. Political ritual in the Tibetan uprising*, Delhi: Motilal Banarsidass.

Schweizer Tibethilfe Solothurn (ed.) (1961). *Die Leiden eines Volkes: Die Tragödie Tibets und der tibetischen Flüchtlinge*, Solothurn: Veritas.

Shain, Yossi (1989) *The Frontier of Loyalty: Political Exiles in the Age of the Nation-State*, Middletown: Wesleyan University Press.

Shain, Yossi (ed.) (1991) *Governments-in-Exile in Contemporary World Politics*, New York: Routledge.

Shakabpa, Tsepon W. D. (1967) *Tibet. A Political History*, New Haven: Yale University Press.

Shakya, Tsering W. (1982) 'The Tibetanization of Ladakh', *Tibetan Review* 17(11): 16–19.

Shakya, Tsering W. (1992) 'Tibet and the occident. The myth of Shangri-la', *Tibetan Review* 27(1): 13–16.

Shakya, Tsering W. (1993) 'Whither the Tsampa eaters', *Himal* 6(5): 8–11.

Shakya, Tsering W. (1996) 'The man who wasn't allowed to tell the truth: the 7th Panchen Lama', *Lungta* 10: 24–9.

Shakya, Tsering W. (1999) *The Dragon in the Land of Snows. A History of Modern Tibet since 1947*, London: Pimlico.

Shastri, Tephun Tenzin (2006) '47 years of Tibetan struggle', *Tibetan World* 2(10): 18–23.

Shaumian, Tatiana (2000) *Tibet. The Great Game and Tsarist Russia*, New Delhi: Oxford University Press.

Sheffer, Gabriel (2003) *Diaspora Politics: At Home and Abroad*, Cambridge: Cambridge University Press.

Shekhawat, Prahlad Singh (1995) 'McLeod Ganj: A Cross-Cultural Town in India', *Tibetan Review* 30(9): 14–17.

Shiromany, A. (ed.) (1998) *The Political Philosophy of His Holiness the XIV Dalai Lama. Selected Speeches and Writings*, New Delhi: TPPRC.

Sinha, Nirmal (1987) 'The Simla Convention 1914: A Chinese Puzzle', *Bulletin of Tibetology*, 22(2): 5–12.

Smith, Anthony D. (1992) 'Chosen peoples: why ethnic groups survive', *Ethnic and Racial Studies* 15(3): 436–56.

Smith, Anthony D. (2001) *Nationalism. Theory, Ideology, History*, Cambridge: Polity.

Smith, Warren W. (1996) *Tibetan Nation. History of Tibetan Nationalism and Sino–Tibetan Relations*, Boulder: Westview.

Snellgrove, David and Richardson, Hugh (1995) *A Cultural History of Tibet*, Boston: Shambhala.

Sondhi, M. (2003) *India, Tibet and China*, New Delhi: Institute for Asia–Pacific Security.

Sood, Shubhi (2004) *Younghusband. Troubled Campaign*, New Delhi: India Research Press.

Sparham, Gareth (1996) 'Why the Dalai Lama rejects Shugden', *Tibetan Review* 31(6): 11–13.

Ström, Axel K. (1995) *The Quest for Grace. Identification and Cultural Continuity in the Tibetan Diaspora*, occasional papers in social anthropology 24, Oslo.

Subba, Tanka B. (1990) *Flight and Adaptation. Tibetan Refugees in the Darjeeling–Sikkim Himalaya*, Dharamsala: LTWA.

Subramanya, Nagarajarao (2006) 'South Indian Tibetans. Preliminary Results from a Study of Life Patterns and Development Dynamics in the Tibetan Refugee Settlement Lugsum Samdupling, Bylakuppe', unpublished draft paper presented at the Eleventh Seminar of the IATS in Königswinter, Germany.

Tabori, Paul (1972) *The Anatomy of Exile: A Semantic and Historical Study*, London: Harrap.

Taksham, Lobsang S. (1993) 'Implementation of the Tibetan democratic constitution', *Tibetan Review* 28(7): 15–16.

Talmon, Stefan (1998) *Recognition of Governments in International Law: With Particular Reference to Governments in Exile*, Oxford: Clarendon.

Tandzin, Eeling Wong (2004) 'Ecclesiastical rule—relinquishment in exile?', *The Tibet Journal* 29(4): 43–74.

Tashi, Tsering (1996) 'Richard Gere: "My job is to tell the truth" ', *Tibetan Bulletin* 27(3): 26.

Tethong, Wangpo (2000) *Der Wandel in der politischen Elite der Tibeter im Exil. Integrations & Desintegartionsprozesse in der politischen Führungsschicht 1950–1979*, Tibet-Institut Rikon No. 30, Zürich: Opuscula Tibetana.

Thargyal, Rinzin (1993) 'Forming the nation: the process of polyarchic laterality among the Tibetan diaspora', in Per Kværne and Rinzin Thargyal (eds) *Bon, Buddhism and Democracy: The Building of a Tibetan National Identity*, Copenhagen: NIAS Report 12, 29–51.

The Indian Express (2002) Interview with Mr Penpa Tsering, TPPRC, New Delhi, February.

Thinley, Karma, compl. (1998) 'Chronology of events surrounding the hunger strike', *Tibetan Bulletin* 2(2): 22.

Thinley, Pema (1990) 'A judicial dimension to Tibetan democracy', *Tibetan Review* 25(11): 9–11.

Thinley, Pema (1996) 'Democracy is an integral part of the Tibetan freedom struggle', *Tibetan Bulletin* 27(3): 11–13.

Tibet Times (2001) (bod kyi dus bab) 10 September, 3.

Tibetan Bulletin (1984) 'Tibetan Buddhism fastest growing in Europe', 15(6–7): 26.

Tibetan Bulletin (1991) 'His Holiness visits Mongolia, Baltics, Bulgaria', 22(6): 23–4.

Tibetan Bulletin (1992a) 'Nechung—the state oracle of Tibet', 23(4): 18–19.

Tibetan Bulletin (1992b) 'To become Nechung's medium is not an ordinary duty', 23(4): 25–9.

Tibetan Bulletin (1995) 'Exile Tibetan community honoured', 26(4): 4.

Tibetan Bulletin (1997a) 'Radio free Asia begins Tibetan Programme', 1(1): 23.

Tibetan Bulletin (1997b) 'Review of Dharamsala–Beijing relations', 1(4): 25–8.

Tibetan Bulletin (2001) 'His Holiness the Dalai Lama leads special prayer for US tragedy', 5(4): 15.

Tibetan Parliamentary and Policy Research Centre (TPPRC) (1996a) *Tibetan People's Right of Self-Determination*, New Delhi.

Tibetan Parliamentary and Policy Research Centre (TPPRC) (1996b) *World Press on Panchen Lama-Selections from Press Report*, New Delhi.

Tibetan Parliamentary and Policy Research Centre (TPPRC) (1999) *Tibet's Parliament in Exile*, New Delhi.

Tibetan Parliamentary and Policy Research Centre (TPPRC) (2003) *Tibet's Parliament in Exile*, New Delhi.

Tibetan Parliamentary and Policy Research Centre (TPPRC) (2005) *Autonomy and the Tibetan Perspective*, New Delhi.

Tibetan Parliamentary and Policy Research Centre (TPPRC) (n.d.) *Tibetan Parliamentary and Policy Research Centre. Brochure*, New Delhi.

Tibetan Review (1978) 'The murder of Gungthang Tsultrim', 13(7): 9–10.

Tibetan Review (1982) 'A letter from secret organizations in Tibet', 17(10): 4–5.

Tibetan Review (1983) 'A message to youths in exile', 18(10): 5–6.

Tibetan Review (1995) 'Preparing Tibetan youth for leadership', 30(7): 17–21.

Tibetan Review (1996a), 'Chinese agents caught in Dharamsala', 31(1): 7–8.

Tibetan Review (1996b) 'Film Flimflam', 31(5): 1.

Tibetan Review (1997) 'Gruesome murders shock exile Tibetan community', 32(3): 10.

Tibetan Review (1998) 'Hollywood factor puts Tibet on political map', 33(7): 24.

Tibetan Review (2000) 'Exile government refutes Shugden Aalegations', 35(12): 11.

Tibetan Review (2001) 'Hollywood Star for Buddhism', 36(11):13.

Tibetan Women's Association (TWA) (1996) *Tibetan Women's Delegation Report on the United Nations Fourth World Conference on Women, Beijing 1995*, Dharamsala.

Tibetan Women's Association (TWA) (2005) *Tibetan Women. The Status of Exiled Tibetan Women in India*, Dharamsala

Tibetan Youth Congress (TYC) (2005) *Tibet: The Gap Between Fact and Fabrication. Tibetan Response to China's White Papers*, Dharamsala.

Tibetan Youth Congress (TYC) (no date) *Tibetan Youth Congress. Brochure*, Dharamsala.

Tsarong, Dundul N. (2000) *In the Service of His Country: The Biography of Dasang Damdul Tsarong Commander General of Tibet*, Ithaca: Snow Lion.

Tsering, Bhuchung K. (1997) 'Challenges Before Radio Free Asia', *Tibetan Review* 32(1): 17–18.

Tsering, Tempa (1997) 'Culturecide? Tibetocide? De-Shangrialised?' *Tibetan Bulletin* 1(1): 18–20.

Tsering, Thondup (1990) 'Should Tibetan students in India become Indian citizens?' *Tibetan Review* 25(2): 12–14.

Tsering, Thondup (1996) 'Priorities in Higher Education of Tibetan Children in Exile', *Tibetan Bulletin*, 27 (4): 23–5.

Tsering, Topden (1997a) 'Peace march ushers in: "do and die" spirit in mass activism', *Tibetan Bulletin* 1(3): 11–16.

Tsering, Topden (1997b) 'Tibetan referendum: from here to where?' *Tibetan Bulletin* 1(4): 11–13.

Tsering, Topden (1997c) 'Tibet revisited on celluloid', *Tibetan Bulletin* 1(5): 14.

Universal Law Publishing (2003) *The Foreigners Act, 1946*, New Delhi: ULP.

van Walt van Praag, Michael C. (1987) *The Status of Tibet: History, Rights and Prospects in International Law*, London: Wisdom.

Verdross, Alfred and Simma, Bruno (1984) *Universelles Völkerrecht. Theorie und Praxis*, Berlin: Duncker & Humblot (first published in 1976).

Wangdi, Tashi (1997) 'Self-determination and the Tibetan issue', *Tibetan Bulletin* 1(4): 20–2.

Wangyal, Tsering (1976) 'The long road to Utopia', *Tibetan Review* 12(3–4): 8.

Wangyal, Tsering (2000) 'Why more scholarships for CTA staff', *Tibetan Review* 35(2): 21–2.

Weber, Max (1976) *Wirtschaft und Gesellschaft. Grundriss der verstehenden Soziologie*, Vol. 1, Tübingen: Mohr.

Wei, Jing (1989) *100 questions about Tibet*, Beijing: Review.

Wei, Xue (1996) 'Tibet and China: brothers or neighbours', *Tibetan Bulletin* 27(5): 17–18.

Wersto, Thomas J. (1979) 'Self-determination and the future of Tibet', *Tibetan Review* 14(3): 14–21.

Wheeler, Mark C. (1980) *Britain and the War for Yugoslavia, 1940–1943*, East European Monographs No. 64. New York: Columbia University Press.

Wiley, Thomas W. (1986) 'Macro exchanges: Tibetan economics and the roles of politics and religion', *The Tibet Journal* 11(1): 3–20.

Wilson, James Q. (1973) *Political Organizations*, New York: Basic Books.

Woodcock, George (1970) 'Tibetan refugees in a decade of exile', *Pacific Affairs* 43(3): 410–20.

Wulf, Christoph, Althans Birgit, Audehm, Kathrin et al. (2001) *Das Soziale als Ritual. Zur performativen Bildung von Gemeinschaften*, Opladen: Leske + Budrich.

Wylie, Turell V. (1959) 'A standard system of Tibetan transcription', *Harvard Journal of Asiatic Studies* 22: 261–76.

Wylie, Turell V. (1978) 'Reincarnation: A political innovation in Tibetan Buddhism', in Louis Ligeti (ed.) *Proceedings of the Csoma the Körös Memorial Symposium*, Budapest: Akademiai Kiado: 579–86.

Xu, Guangqiu (1997) 'The United States and the Tibet Issue', *Asian Survey* 37(11): 1062–77.

Yeshe De Project (1986) Ancient Tibet. Research materials from the Yeshe De Project, Berkeley: Dharma Publishing.

Index

For Product Safety Concerns and Information please contact our EU
representative GPSR@taylorandfrancis.com
Taylor & Francis Verlag GmbH, Kaufingerstraße 24, 80331 München, Germany